O9-AIC-876

Touching All Bases

Touching All Bases

The Collected Ray Fitzgerald 1970–1982

Edited by Kevin and Michael Fitzgerald
Foreword by Leigh Montville

The Stephen Greene Press
Brattleboro, Vermont Lexington, Massachusetts

To Dad

Arthur G. Miller, *Consulting Editor*

First Edition

This book is manufactured in the United States of America. It is designed by Dixie Clark, typeset by Neil W. Kelley and published by The Stephen Greene Press, Fessenden Road, Brattleboro, Vermont 05301.

Library of Congress Cataloging in Publication data

Fitzgerald, Ray, 1926–1982
Touching all bases.

1. Fitzgerald, Ray, 1926–1982—Collected works.
2. Sportswriters—United States—Collected works.
I. Fitzgerald, Kevin, 1952– . II. Fitzgerald,
Michael, 1955– . III. Title.
GV742.42.F57A2 1983 070.4′49796′0924 83–17191
ISBN 0–8289–0507–X

Contents

Foreword

He was buried in his hometown of Westfield, Mass., down the street from a Howard Johnson's restaurant, which was a real laugh because Ray Fitzgerald always hated Howard Johnson's. The franchising of America was one of his favorite peeves.

"They call these fried things clams?" he would ask when thrust by fate or circumstance under an orange roof for dinner. "Where do they find clams that all grow to the same, uniform size? What ocean did these clams ever visit?"

There was a good-sized crowd at the grave site, a hell of a crowd, really, and when the service was finished everyone was invited to his mother's house. Fold-out chairs had been spread around the backyard. Sandwiches and beer were served from a long table.

"Is this where Ray grew up?" I asked his brother, Jack.

"In a way," Jack Fitzgerald said. "Our house was on the next block. We built this one, smaller, for my mother after we all were grown. But before the house was built, this was a vacant lot. A field. This was where we came every day. This was where we played baseball."

He pointed toward the spots where home and first and second and third had been. See that tree? He pointed where the good hits had gone, the second decks in the Yankee Stadium of the imagination. See? Not much had changed.

"Have you ever been to Westfield before?" Jack Fitzgerald asked.

The day was middle-of-the-summer perfect. The men had removed their suitcoats and sports jackets and many of the women were carrying their high heels. The talk was anything but solemn as everyone stood in the sun and breathed the small-town air while yesterday's ground-rule doubles rolled forever.

"No," I lied, "I've never been to Westfield."

I'd been here many times. I'd read Ray.

* * *

He worked for sixteen years as a sportswriter for the Boston Globe, most of them as a sports columnist, most of them at a desk next to mine. He was a good-sized guy with a flattened nose that would have looked great on a middleweight contender and a heart that had been captured long ago by baseballs covered with black electrical tape and cracked bats that were held together by little hardware brads. He was a last champion for innocence.

The best description of his approach to sports is that he was the exact opposite of that breathless buffoon on the 11 o'clock news who reports the results of this night's Armageddon at Fenway Park and the potential of tomorrow night's parting of the Red Sea at Boston Garden. Ray Fitzgerald was always calm about it all. Measured. Loving? Pretty much. Loving. Caring . . . but only in the right way.

Sports were played in italic letters, not five-inch headlines. The curls and the whirls, the charm of the games, were what were important. The fun, not the money or the machinations to sign this guy for a five-year contract or to send that event into so many Neilsen homes. Fun. Laughs. Crocodile tears. Fun. The standard for games was those long Westfield days. That was how sports should be played.

"Little League," he would say with disgust at the taste of the term in his mouth. "Kids standing around in big-time uniforms, holding $40 gloves while some adult tells them what to do. Let 'em just go out and play. Choose up sides . . ."

"Went to a high school game last night," he would say. "Didn't have anything to do. Just went. Coach is screaming on the sidelines. Kids are running through play after play like robots, afraid to shoot. Nobody's smiling. Not the winners. Not the losers. Not anyone . . ."

"George Steinbrenner," he would say. "Howard Cosell . . . Marvin Miller . . . TV timeouts. . . ."

The idea that he was doing something important, writing about sports, was just as amusing to him as the idea he wasn't doing something important. He would be amazed when some six-figure executive would say, "You go to all the games, talk to all the players, do that for a job?" Ridiculous. He would be equally amazed when some cosmic wit from another part of the newspaper would dismiss sportswriting as pure games and entertainment, removed from the happenings of real people.

"Why is life supposed to be more real at a four-alarm fire or at a Combat Zone strip joint or in some lawyer's office than it is at the ballpark?" he would ask. "There are real people at all these places. Interesting people."

The reader of his column always knew the point of view to expect every morning on the lefthand side of the page, but never could be sure how it would be served. Fact or fiction, sense or nonsense, the reader never knew because Ray Fitzgerald never knew. He would take the predominant event of the day, hold it to the light, stand it on its head, smile and begin typing about what he saw. Somehow it usually was better than what the rest of us saw.

His best efforts sometimes came from his worst days, the days when there wasn't an easy and fast topic available. He would smoke his pipe, type a few words, then throw the paper in the wastebasket. Type again. Throw again. Take a walk. Buy a cup of coffee. Start typing.

"What'd you do in the end?" someone would ask as he was leaving the office.

"Oh, terrible," he would grumble. "I wrote a poem."

A poem?

You'd go into a Dorchester coffee shop the next morning and some guy who hadn't read a poem since a seventh-grade teacher had hit him with a mallet would be laughing and smiling. A poem. Sure. A terrific poem. About the Red Sox. Patriots. About baseball, the way it should be.

There were characters, too, who stumbled onto the stage between the real-life Derek Sandersons and Carl Yastrzemskis, a collection of bumbling innocents who somehow hadn't heard the latest news. They were named Clancy and Forbush and The Last Baseball Fan In America, pleasant souls who always needed explanations of the controversies and skullduggery that suddenly had surfaced. Ray always gave it to them. Preposterous as the news may sound.

"What's that strange noise?" old Forbush would ask.

"An aluminum bat hitting a baseball covered with cowhide," Ray would reply.

"Aluminum?" Forbush would ask. "Cowhide?"

One thing that made Ray different from most sportswriters was that he was a pretty good athlete. Cut the average sportswriter open and you will find a kid who was a collector of baseball cards, a chronicler of averages, a late-night reader of magazines with foldouts of Pete Rose in the middle. Ray was all of that, but he also was a player of all the games. He was a football end, a basketball guard, a left-handed pitcher, and a first baseman talented enough at Westfield High to attend Notre Dame on a baseball scholarship.

He played minor-league baseball for two years. He shot left-handed golf in the high 70's, low 80's. He was the anchor man in all conflicts with the dreaded Massachusetts candlepin. Set up a wastebasket and have five people firing balled-up wire service reports at it and he would hit it first. Probably banked, off the nearest desk.

He had an assortment of jobs before he landed at the Globe. He wrote press releases at the General Electric plant in Schenectady in the same office where Kurt Vonnegut later worked. He wrote sports at the Springfield Union at the same time Tom Wolfe was covering fires of suspicious origin. He even owned his own newspaper, the Westfield Advertiser.

"That's always your dream, owning your own paper, isn't it?" he once said. "Another guy and I bought the paper and we figured we'd make this the greatest, best-written small-town paper in America. After about two weeks, I found myself at my 14th consecutive hearing on sewer variances and couldn't wait to figure a way to get out of there."

The way was the Globe. He arrived on April Fool's Day of 1966 and turned out to be a better, more-enduring local gift than even Yaz and Lonborg and the Impossible Dream team that captured the headlines next to his name. He was Boston's unique sports voice. Literate. Funny. Moral.

"I'd been elected the Massachusetts Sportswriter of the Year a few times," columnist Tim Horgan of the Boston Herald said. "Then Ray came along. He won the thing eleven straight times. I never asked for a recount."

He was a constant. It didn't matter if he were in the press box at the Kentucky Derby, at ringside near Ali, or walking the 18th fairway at Franklin Park's pitted municipal golf course. His eyes were open, seeing the things that everybody sees, but seeing them better. Finding the perspective. Telling the story. Better.

In the last year of his life, he selected most of the columns in this book. He had to work with his wife, Barbara, because one of the quirky dysfunctions from the operation for a brain tumor was that he had trouble reading. He could talk and think and laugh as well as ever, but somehow he had trouble reading. A therapist was trying to help.

"When will I make some progress?" he asked one day, grumpy at the slow steps he was taking. "What about it? When'll I be able to read better?"

"Now-now, Mr. Fitzgerald," the therapist replied. "This is complicated. These things take time."

"Complicated?" Ray Fitzgerald said. "I'm not looking to read 'War and Peace,' you know. I only want to read the sports page."

He had to laugh about that. Only the sports page? Sit on a porch in Westfield. Fold out the Sunday stats. Check the numbers in the box scores. Supply the adjectives yourself. See the men running around the bases. Listen to the noise behind the big plays. Imagine.

Enjoy.

Leigh Montville
Boston Globe Feature Writer

Introduction

"Picking the best of anything is a presumptuous, subjective and arbitrary endeavor."

Ray Fitzgerald

With this in mind, Dad began to select his best articles to compile in a book. Unfortunately, he did not finish before his untimely death at the age of 55 in August of 1982. We decided to finish the book as a tribute to a man we loved, and so that you, his readers, could again enjoy the columns that greeted you each morning for the past 15 years.

With our mother's assistance, Dad had already selected some 200 articles from the years 1966–1976 and we then selected another 150 articles from the remaining years. Then came the hard part as we had to reduce these 300 to 400 articles down to a manageable number. To do this, we had to cut out many very good articles, some of which we are sure were favorites of yours. The result is 99 columns which we think are representative of fifteen years of Dad's writing.

The columns are arranged in chronological order so that you get a sense of the passing of time. Although the columns cover a wide spectrum of the sporting world, there are more articles about baseball than any other sport, but this is not surprising. Baseball was by far Dad's favorite sport to play, watch and write about. To him, baseball had a unique character and just the right mix of action, strategy and anticipation.

If you could have asked Dad what his most memorable sports event was, he probably would have replied, "My 25 foot birdie putt on the 18th at Marshfield last Thursday." He then would have gotten serious and told you that nothing affected him quite like his visit to Puerto Rico following the death of Roberto Clemente. As his column which appears in Chapter 2 demonstrates, Dad was deeply touched by the reverence of the people of Puerto Rico toward Clemente.

As for excitement, he felt nothing could match the drama of the 6th game of the 1975 World Series or the 1980 USA–USSR Olympic hockey game. We have included Dad's columns on both these games because they are excellent writing, and are an indication of Ray Fitzgerald the fan. Former Massachusetts Senator Ed Brooke thought so much of Dad's column on the 1975 World Series that he had it read into the CONGRESSIONAL RECORD.

Included in the book are a number of articles about ex-Patriot coach Rommie Loudd and his battle for justice form the Florida courts. Loudd's long fight to be cleared of very questionable drug charges angered Dad like few other events in sports. He felt that Loudd had been singled out because he was the first Black to try to run a professional football team. When Loudd was ultimately released from prison, Dad felt a sense of personal satisfaction unmatched by anything else he had done as a sports journalist.

Dad's most treasured column was his poem "The Ballad of Baseball Past" which appears in Chapter 5. This was his effort to capture the essence of what made baseball the national pastime. He was especially proud of this column because he received a note from novelist Roger Kahn praising it and passing along the praise of John Updike.

The one article in the book which has nothing to do with sports is "A Little Girl is Now a Doctor" (Chapter 7). Family was the most important part of Dad's life, and the day his daughter graduated from medical school was one of his proudest moments. Because of this and the large number of complimentary letters it brought, we felt the article belonged in the book.

The final article appeared in the *Globe* on September 13, 1981, and thus is a bit out of sequence. However, we felt it was a fitting end to the book, because it demonstrates Dad's ability to look at sports and sportswriting with tongue-in-cheek.

We hope you enjoy reading this collection of some of our father's best articles. We also hope you keep this book around so that years from now, you, your children and your grandchildren can again enjoy the timeless writing of Ray Fitzgerald.

Kevin and Mike Fitzgerald

1

1970–1971

That old glove had lots of life

July 26, 1970—The old glove is dead.

The Richie Ashburn model for lefthanders, veteran of 10,000 baseballs, has expired at the age of 23.

Present when death came were its owner, who writes this column, and his two sons, who were mainly responsible for the glove's demise.

Services tomorrow will be private and burial will be early next week at the Scituate dump.

Ah, there was a glove. The kids in the neighborhood made fun of it, with its four stubby fingers, funny-looking thumb and inadequate webbing.

"How can ya catch anything with that hunk of leather?" they'd say, waving their super-trap, $40, hand-tooled Reggie Smith models in the air.

What do the kids know? They weren't around that spring day in 1947, when the man in the South Bend, Indiana, department store handed the glove over, for $18 cash.

Brand new the mitt was then, with the leather oiled and shiny, the button that held the wrist strap pure gold.

"Richie Ashburn" was written strong and clear across the heel of the glove, and though a fleeting thought at the time was that Richie Ashburn wasn't much of a fielder, the thought was immediately dismissed.

The glove had major league potential, but its owner didn't. It went through college, grabbing a line drive here and a pop fly there, but the glove couldn't hit the ball for the guy who owned it.

There were some big moments—an over-the-head catch in a summer league in Glens Falls, New York, a diving back-hander in another summer league in Brattleboro.

But little by little, the glove began spending more time on the front closet shelf under a shoe box and a lady's umbrella.

Once it came out of retirement when the owner, who by this time was writing about baseball for a living, took it on a road trip. He thought it would be fun to work out with the team.

But the players laughed at the glove. They giggled and threw the ball hard, to see what would happen. The owner caught the ball casually, as though the glove made catching baseballs easy,but that wasn't so.

His right palm ached for a week, and he put the glove back on the shelf.

In recent years, the Richie Ashburn model has been in disrepute. The leather is dryer than a starlet's bathing suit and a rip inside the thumb has become larger, spewing large quantities of stuffing.

The glove has had to stoop to the indignity of family outings, Class reunions, pickup softball games and backyard games of catch.

A year ago, the leather thongs that held the webbing together snapped. Having worked overtime for 22 years and having been ignored all that time, they were entitled.

Since then the webbing has been secured with shoestring tied in a square knot. It's been a makeshift arrangement and yesterday the end came.

One of the few surviving members of the Society for the Preservation of Richie Ashburn models has urged a transplant.

"Bring it over to Fitizie in the Red Sox Clubhouse," he said, "he'll sew it up for you."

But that would only prolong the agony. The webbing would be OK, but the thumb would go. This way, a nice clean death, is better.

A man gets attached to certain things in his life—a dog, a favorite putter, an old wallet.

That's the way it was with the Richie Ashburn glove. It was a link with the past when a man felt that with a little break here and there, he could be anything he wanted to be.

Now he has to face the fact. That dream about standing on the mound at Yankee Stadium with the bases full and striking everybody out is just not going to come true.

The glove is gone and its owner feels a lot older than he did yesterday.

Mr. Rank and Mr. File tell how they scored golf win

August 30, 1970—The best-ball golf tournament—created to keep grown men off the streets on weekends—has been a popular country club event for years.

In covering one of these safaris, the tendency is to concentrate on the first division.

Thus, you'll read about Wallie Wedge rolling in tricky 20-footers and Freddie Flagstick reaching the green in two on a 540-yard hole.

Nobody reads much about those competitors in the ninth and 10th divisions. These people pay just as much for the privilege of beating up a golf ball. They battle hard and the best they get in the papers is a fouled-up line of agate type something like this:

> Rank and File defeated Hill and Dale, 2 and 1, six-run inning, etaein shrdluxxxxx pick up . . .

Rank and File deserve better than this. They deserve the in-depth interview, which might go something like this:

—Excuse me. I'm from the Morning Dispatch-Tribune and Star and I'd like some information on your match. Are you Mr. Rank?

—No, I'm File. That's Rank over there fishing for the olive.

—I see. Well, Mr. File, congratulations. How would you say you hit the ball today?

—Often. We hit the ball often. Ha, ha, ha. That's a little joke, get it?

—Unfortunately. Could you give me some of the highlights of your big victory?

—Sure. We were in a bind right away when I discovered I'd left my five wood at home.

—Well, I don't suppose you use a five wood more than a few times a round, do you?

—Are you kidding? I hit that five wood maybe 30 times a round. A drive, a five wood, another five wood, a chip and a couple of putts. That's my game, a nice straight five wood.

—Sounds exciting. How'd you make up for the loss?

—I used my six wood and swung a little harder.

—Your six wood? That's nice.

—Yes. Well, we won the first two holes even though I was in left field on No. 1.

—You had a bad shot?

—Yeah. Like I said, I was out in left field. There's this playground runs alongside the course and I sliced the ball into short left. But Rank came through nicely with a double bogey.

—You won the first hole with a double bogey?

—He sank a long putt. On No. 2, all four of us hit into a pond off the tee, so we said what the heck, and all dropped a ball on the other side and played from there. I took the hole with a five.

—It was a long hole, eh?

—Let's see, what's the card say? Yeah, 155 from the blue tees. Long at that, and tricky, with the pond.

—So you're two up right off the bat. Then what?

—It was touch and go for the next seven. Neither team could break through. I had a chance of the fifth, but my approach caught a sand trap. The one near the eighth green. I had to recover with my six wood.

—A six wood out of a trap? OK, so you're two up at the turn.

—That's when I made a mistake.

—You hit into another trap?

—No, I stopped for a couple of Scotches. I said I'd never do it again, but I weakened and it cost us. We lost three holes in a row to bogeys. It's hard to beat that kind of golf.

—How about your partner? Wasn't he any help while you were shaking off those Scotches?

—Who, Rank? That's why I went into the bar in the first place. To get him.

—OK. So you're through 12 and you're one down.

—Yeah. Exciting, eh? Thirteen and 14 were halved with routine double bogeys, although I chipped in from 80 yards out on 14 for mine. It was a lucky shot.

—Gosh, it doesn't sound lucky to me. An 80-yard chip?

—It caromed off a tree into the hole. But the 15th was the turning point. I had a great drive, all of 180 yards. Then I put everything I had into a four wood and she flew to within six feet of the pin.

—Wow. Did you get the bird?

—No, I was overanxious. I'd never putted for a birdie on a par four hole before and I hit the ball too hard.

—The putt went past the hole?

—Yeah. By seven feet. I was farther away than when I started.

—How did your partner react to this?

—Rank wasn't around. He was in the woods looking for three golf balls he hit off the tee. But let me finish. I banged the return putt in for a par to even the match. They fell apart after that and we won the next two with bogeys. And now buddy, I got a question for you.

—What is it?

—Where's the photographer?

Maybe Pats' offensive line is anti-Mexican

October 26, 1970—Hiya fellas, my name is Joe Kapp.

—Joe, nice to meet you. I'm Jon Morris. Say hello to the rest of the gang. This here's Mike Montler. Here's Tom Funchess. The guy with the receding hairline is Len St. Jean, and the big handsome son of a gun is Tom Neville.

—Good to know ya, fellas. Whadya doing in town?

—We're the offensive line for the Patriots. That's a football team.

—Sure, sure. I knew I'd seen you somewhere. I play quarterback for the same team. You must have caught my act the last couple of weeks.

—C'mon, Joe, you're kidding. I can't seem to place your face.

—I didn't look like this before yesterday afternoon. It's been rearranged a little.

—I still don't believe you're our quarterback.

—Here, I'll prove it. Let me lie down here, curled in a fetal position.

—Hey, it is our quarterback. That's the way you looked in the second quarter, underneath Bubba Smith. Funny, you seem smaller standing up.

—I am smaller. Saturday, I was six-three. I'm only five-ten now, with this funny ringing in my head.

—Like a telephone?

—Exactly. I answered the ringing in the third period, and a voice long distance from Minnesota said "Don't you wish you were back here?"

—Listen, you're gonna love it in Boston, Joe. It's a swinging town, plenty of culture if you dig that stuff, plenty of bistros when you get tired of the art museums.

—Yeah, but what about Sunday afternoons? Sunday afternoons I have to show up and get the tar pounded out of me. By the time the season's over I'll look like Toul-Lautrec.

—Nah, it won't be that way, Joe. The guys are going to get together this week and map out a block. We can do it. We can block somebody, I know we can.

—I'd like to believe that. You seem like good guys, but maybe you just don't like Mexicans.

—That's not it at all. We tried hard yesterday. I remember asking Bubba to be careful not to use his elbows and he said he would. He lied, Joe, he plain lied to me, because he did use his elbows on the very next play.

—Luckily, I was able to ward him off with my cheekbone for a 12-yard loss. But what about Billy Newsome, the defensive end?

—Who ever heard of him? We just figured he was a rookie, not worth worrying about, so we didn't. Did he bother you?

—He interrupted my breathing somewhat. But listen, you did your best. I wish the guys held on to my passes the way you held on to Baltimore's jerseys.

—The way we figured it, Joe, a 15-yard penalty was better than you getting a broken jaw. We operated with you in mind all the time.

—So did the Colts. They were the operators and I was the operatee.

—Things are going to improve. We have to become better acquainted, so we can synchronize our timing. There's more to this game than just blocking your man, you know.

—I'll settle for that.

—No, Joe, before this season is over we're going to be a finely-meshed machine, a thing of precision, a well-oiled unit.

—The Edsel was a well-oiled unit. Who do we play next Sunday?

—Buffalo. They're nothing, Joe, a bowl of ice cream. You'll have enough time to recite the Gettysburg Address back there before you throw.

—I tried the Rosary yesterday, but never got past The Sorrowful Mysteries.

—Stop kidding around, Joe, I went to Holy Cross. Listen, let's start planning for Buffalo now. Let's the five of us go over to The Point After and start mapping strategy.

—Why is it named The Point After?

—Gino owns it. You know, he kicks the points after.

—The points after what?

—C'mon Joe, the points after touchdown.

—What's a touchdown?

Rush story sad all the way

November 4, 1970—Sad. That's the only word for the demise of Clive Rush, the man many thought would lead the Patriots out of the football wilderness.

Rush wound up his tumultuous career in Boston yesterday by repudiating Pats president Billy Sullivan's statement that he (Rush) was taking a leave of absence because of ill health.

"I resign," he told a small group of newsmen in his office. "I resigned last midnight and I'll never coach this team again."

Rush, obviously distraught, had to be restrained from throwing a punch at Clark Booth, sportscaster from WBZ-TV, who had made statements critical of Rush the previous evening.

Nothing in Rush's career in Boston was routine. The day he was announced as new coach, a blizzard hit New England. Rush and Billy Sullivan were forced to take a train from New York and his first Boston press conference was held at Logan Airport.

A few weeks later, at another press conference to introduce general manager George Sauer, Rush was almost electrocuted by a faulty microphone. Only fast work by Pats owner Dan Marr Jr. saved him. Marr ripped out several wires, shutting off the power to the mike.

Ironically, yesterday Rush laid much of the blame for his final plight at Marr's feet, saying, "It's an inaccurate release by Dan Marr Jr. that I'm on a leave of absence. I resign."

Rush got into his first brush with the press even before the 1969 season started, when the Globe's Clif Keane suggested that Rush might possibly not be the messiah to bring the Pats to football heaven.

The coach asked to have Keane barred from training camp.

In 1969's first game, the Denver Broncos humiliated Boston, 35–7, and the Monday morning accounts said so. Rush was upset over this and over criticisms of defensive back Larry Carwell.

Then came a succession of little incidents. Rush lectured young writers on the art of covering a football team. He phoned sports editors several times a week to complain about stories.

He was incensed because Leigh Montville of the Globe wrote a story quoting quarterback Tom Sherman as saying he wasn't being given a fair shake.

Rush fired Sherman as a result of that story.

Rush had two violent arguments with Claude Gibson, backfield coach of the Buffalo Bills. He kept his team off the field against the Bills while he argued with the referees.

Four times in his first season he drew penalties for sideline gestures on arguments. In Alumni Stadium at Boston College he argued with the fans because they were bunching up behind the Patriots bench and shouting criticisms at the players.

When fans put on an impromptu halftime demonstration during a rainy-day game at BC, Rush threw them off the field and later criticized BC for allowing such things to happen.

In San Diego, Rush called a press conference at seven in the morning to protest stories of the previous afternoon's defeat.

He was incensed when reporters kept asking him about Carl Garrett's military status, saying, "Why make a Federal case out of a Federal case?"

Before the Jets game in New York, he was so convinced the room was bugged, he reportedly gave the players a false game plan in discussing the Jets.

This year, things went along smoothly enough until an hour before the first home game, when Rush kicked defensive backs Carwell and John Charles off the team for rejecting contracts.

There were several other embarrassing incidents, particularly on road trips, that have never seen print, and perhaps never will.

Rush and the Patriots were on a collision course and the collision happened yesterday, after an all-night meeting at Rush's house between Sullivan, Dan Marr Jr. and Dr. William Baker, the coach's physician.

When Marr and Sullivan left, they thought they had Rush convinced that their method was the best. Apparently, this was not the case.

The football team will probably be better without Rush. "Eleven guys seem to be going eleven different ways," Len St. Jean said after last Sunday's embarrassment with Buffalo.

It is doubtful 11 guys will immediately look like Super Bowl candidates this Sunday under John Mazur, but there will be more cohesiveness.

This does not make the whole mess any less distasteful or the decline and fall of an imaginative but troubled man any less a personal tragedy.

Sad is the only word for it.

Westie & Red:
A house is not a home

March 23, 1971—The time is July, 1972 and the place, an office in the Boston Garden.

Weston Adams Jr., novelty clerk, pinball addict, fledgling mogul and president of a hockey team is in deep conversation with Arnold Auerbach, television commentator, cigar smoker, Chinese food devotee and general manager of a basketball team.

Adams is speaking.

—Red, I know you'll be pleased to hear we're bringing in our Junior A team from Oshawa for 40 Garden dates next year.

—Gee, that's swell, Westie. This will fit right in with your American League team and the Bruins. I hate to see the Garden dark.

—I thought you'd be excited. You understand, of course, there'll have to be some adjusting of Celtic dates.

—Oh, sure, Westie, just as long as we can stay in your lovely, clean, modern, plush sports palace.

—Ah, well, that's the problem, Red. You won't be able to fit all your games in the Garden. So I've figured out a couple of alternate plans. Some of your early games against expansion teams, when the weather is nice, you can play them outdoors.

—Outdoors?

—I've already arranged to have baskets set up in the parking lot. And there'll be bleachers seating 3200. That ought to be enough room, whaddya think?

—Well, I dunno, Westie . . .

—Tell ya what. The Bruins will foot the whole bill—$650.24. We want to be fair about the thing. Now let me tell you about my second plan. You know the games you have with the Milwaukee Bucks and the Knicks?

—Sure, great games.

—Yeah. Well, here's my plan. You never win those games anyway, so why not forfeit them?

—Forfeit? You can't be serious, Westie.

—I've never been more serious. Just don't show up. I've got a list of alibis you can use. A virus swept through the Celtics, the bus broke down, the snow was four feet deep, your trainer lost his equipment, all the air went out of the basketballs, the referees took a plane to Cuba.

—But we make good money on those games.

—After a couple of forfeits, nobody will show up. Think of the money you'll save on overhead alone. With the outdoor games and the forfeits and the tripleheaders we'll be able to squeeze the Celtics in.

—Tripleheaders?

—Sure. We've booked four tripleheaders for you. Here's one. You play the Pistons at noon, then take on the Bulls at 3:30 and follow with a game against Phoenix at 8. That gives the players time for a snack between the second and third game.

—But my players will be exhausted.

—How can that be? I keep reading that John Havlicek can run all day and not get tired. This is his chance to prove it.

—Gosh, Westie, I don't know if the players will stand for it. They were upset last year when you insisted on them playing during the week the circus was in the Garden.

—What was so tough about that?

—The elephants kept getting in the way. Ever try to work a pick and roll around an elephant?

—I'd just as soon not get into the technical stuff, Red. We all have our problems. Don't forget there was a hockey game last year that didn't sell out.

—There was?

—Sure. The night a tornado came down Causeway St. Scared a lot of customers away. We drew only 13,457. It wasn't all a bed of roses for us either, Red.

—I know it, Westie. I'll tell my guys the tripleheaders are for the good of hockey. They'll take it like pros.

—Good. And one more thing, Red. Don't under any circumstances, make the playoffs.

—But Westie. We've got a young, hustling club. I think we can do it.

—Forget it. There isn't one open date. From March 15 through May 12, it's solid hockey.

—Westie, give us a break. We'll play in the morning, the afternoon, anytime.

—Oh, sure, big deal. Play in the morning or afternoon. Knock the roller derby and six-day bike races right out of the Garden. That's the trouble with you basketball people. You want everything.

What's so great about spring in suburbia?

May 12, 1971—Spring is terrific. Everybody says so. Look how the grass comes alive. See the sidewalk, virginal after the winter slush. See the croci and the forsythia and the tulips.

See Jane. See Jane in a miniskirt. See the breeze do pretty things with Jane's miniskirt.

All very well, but here is what I see. I see a little list, numbered one and two. Number One is Wash the Windows, and Number Two is his nasty kid brother, Rake the Lawn.

These two, Mr. Inside and Mr. Outside, are the most worthless tasks ever inflicted on suburbia.

To wash windows around our seedy mansion, we sneer at commercial products, preferring instead a home mixture of ammonia and water, a spin-off from an old formula for mustard plaster my great grandmother swore by for chest colds.

Now, I have been washing windows, man and boy, since the outset of The Boer War, and have yet to see one pane improved by my handiwork.

The windows look marvelous to begin with. You can see out, which, I think, is the quality that makes them windows.

Ah, but Good Housekeeping says that in order to win a seal of approval, the windows should sparkle like a John O'Hara paragraph. If they aren't scrubbed regularly, by the year 2163 they will be noticeably dirty, and what kind of a legacy is that to leave to our children?

In our house, there are perhaps 20 windows. Not so bad, eh? But they are subdivided into 400 panes. Each pane has four corners, making 1600 in all. Each indoor corner has its outdoor counterpart, so really there are 3200 corners to be dug into.

Thirty-two hundred corners. Put in those terms, the job is insurmountable.

Now, if I could swipe each pane lightly with a cloth and have it look like the Hope Diamond, there might be cause for optimism. But window-wiping cloths have minds of their own. They work like this. Squirt the cleaner on the pane, then rub. Now you've done it. At last, the windows are truly dirty, a combination of moisture, dust and lint. Finally, there is a reason for washing them.

It doesn't matter what kind of cloth you use. Old sheets, jockey shorts, the finest Irish linen, shirts from Taiwan, a pair of socks worn by Erich Segal in the last Marathon—they have one thing in common, an endless supply of lint.

There are, finally, the outside upstairs windows, which are a problem if you (a) don't own a ladder and (b) are a sniveling coward about climbing anything more precipitous than a foot stool.

What you do is try to wash the outside from the inside, leaning out in pretzel-like angles that could earn you star billing with a circus.

Even at that, you can't reach every pane. You push the top window down and the bottom up and there's still some overlap that will, for shame, remain forever dirty.

And it's about that time, when you're leaning out an upstairs window, left arm twisted like a hairpin, that the guy next door comes out, slings his golf clubs into his car and drives away, smirking.

Now about raking a lawn. It is undeniably true that fresh air is involved. But there is an abundance of fresh air in other places, spots that do not involve rakes, old bones, dead tree limbs, flattened beer cans and petrified leavings from every animal that uses our backyard as a latrine.

There is simply no sense of accomplishment in raking a spring lawn. After the job is done, what have you got. The same yellow, formless cabbage patch. It looked better with the dog bones.

Where is it etched in stone that a yard must be raked? Did Julius Caesar rake his lawn? Did Abner Doubleday or Henry Wadsworth Longfellow? Of course not, and they got by. What will it matter 100 years from today?

And yet, people tell each other how good it is for a lawn to be disturbed in the spring, to get rid of dead grass and loosen the soil. It all sounds like a rumor started by a hardware store caught with a warehouse full of rakes.

There is one redeeming factor. If you rake long enough—in my case, for about 10 minutes—you'll develop terrific blisters in the "V" between the thumb and forefinger of each hand.

Properly publicized, these blisters will not only prevent you from doing any more raking, they will also keep you away from the windows. Getting out to the golf course is YOUR problem.

A solid vote for baseball

September 5, 1971—Maybe you think, from what you've read over the winter, that baseball was born in a lawyer's office, grew up in a courtroom and flourishes in a bookmaker's shop.

That's not so. Baseball is more than Bowie Kuhn, Curt Flood, Marvin Miller and Dennis McLain. It's more than franchise shifts and lawsuits.

Baseball is grace and talent under pressure. It's Carl Yastrzemski scooping up a single on the gallop in left field at Fenway and throwing the tying run out at the plate.

It's Frank Howard missing and the crowd going "Ooooooh," and Howard three innings later hitting the ball 450 feet.

It's Harmon Killebrew's tape-measure homer into the centerfield stands and Rico Petrocelli with his short swing sending the ball 316 feet into the left-field screen.

Baseball is Bert Campaneris stealing third on a pitchout, George Scott turning a line drive into a double play. It's a Frank Robinson triple and Sam McDowell's fast ball.

Baseball is also excitement off the field. It's cops on horseback and crowds milling around the players' entrance.

It's kids leaning on a dugout before a game, yelling "Yaz, gimme a autograph." It's a guy in the bleachers with a beer asking "Why do they leave the bum in?" and a lady in a box seat asking "Why don't they take the bum out?"

Baseball is watching the scoreboard for out-of-town results, and fighting for a ball with five people you've never seen before.

It's leaving your seat in the ninth when your team is five runs behind, but lingering in the runway to watch because somehow you think they'll pull victory out.

For a sports writer, baseball is a bunch of memories, most of which have little to do with runs, hits and errors.

It is 10,000 people at an airport to greet a team, and 1000 people in a Cleveland Stadium that seats 80,000. It is Russ Gibson being told that he is not going to make the club and Mike Derrick being told that he is.

It is Tom Satriano standing in a Washington hotel lobby holding his two-week-old baby, no bigger than a shoe box, and it's Mrs. Jerry Stephenson in a bikini, stopping traffic at the Ranch House Motel swimming pool in Winter Haven.

Baseball is writing 20 paragraphs in 20 minutes in order to catch a plane to Cleveland, and paying two dollars for one egg, three strips of bacon and some toast in the hotel coffee shop in New York.

The game is a chance to meet nice guys like Brooks Robinson, spoiled kids like Tony Horton and churls like Leo Durocher.

Baseball is contrast. It's Sparky Lyle throwing his glove in a trash barrel after giving up a game-winning grand slam, and it's Sparky Lyle surrounded by reporters after striking out the side with the bases loaded.

There is plenty wrong with baseball. Club owners are autocratic and players are greedy. The season is too long and the hot dogs are terrible.

A critic once characterized baseball as six minutes of action crammed into two and one-half hours.

Okay, I'll buy that. Much of the beauty of the game is in the mind of the beholder. What if the batter walks? Will he steal? Can he squeeze? Is the pitcher tired? Can the man pinch-hit? There is plenty of nonaction.

Nonetheless, you can have your blue lines, red dogs and double dribbles. Tomorrow the best of sports in a sports-crazy country returns to Fenway Park and I'll eat a hot dog if it kills me.

Franklin Park GC—a city's disgrace

September 13, 1971—Okay class, time for the annual multiple choice quiz. Put away the scratch sheets, stop mumbling about Eddie Kasko's strategy and pay attention.

Mark "x" next to the answer you think best fits each of the following 10 statements. Or scribble a "y" or a "z" or whatever you want. Neatness doesn't count.

Here we go.

1. What is so rare as a day in June?
   (a) Harmony in the Red Sox clubhouse
   (b) A statement from Joe Kapp
   (c) A golf ball washer at Franklin Park.
2. The No. 1 miracle of all time is considered to be:
   (a) The loaves and fishes
   (b) Bobby Orr
   (c) Sinking a 15-foot putt at Franklin Park.
3. A perfect circle is best typified by:
   (a) Leo Durocher's head
   (b) The Patriots' ground game
   (c) The minibike track on the eighth green at Franklin Park.
4. The best crabgrass in Massachusetts is found in:
   (a) Your lawn
   (b) My lawn
   (c) The Franklin Park greens.
5. It is helpful to have one leg shorter than the other when
   (a) Climbing Mt. Everest
   (b) Wearing one elevator shoe
   (c) Teeing off at Franklin Park.
6. The oldest sports equipment in town is
   (a) Bob Dee's helmet
   (b) The Boston Garden
   (c) The cups in the Franklin Park greens.

7. Sandtraps are
    (a) Devices to catch sand mice
    (b) Spartdnas spelled backwards
    (c) What there are none of at Franklin Park.
8. The song "It's Not Easy Being Green" was inspired by
    (a) A Boston Bruins defenseman
    (b) The left field wall at Fenway
    (c) The fairways at Franklin Park.
9. "Fore" is an expression in golf which signifies
    (a) A warning to the group ahead
    (b) The number on the ball you hit into the woods
    (c) The number of people having a picnic on the sixth green at Franklin Park.
10. Three men are usually needed to
    (a) Make a doubleplay from Tinkers to Evers to Chance
    (b) Lift Carl Yastrzemski's wallet
    (c) Hammer a tee into the ground at Franklin Park.

Okay, okay. If you've come this far, maybe you get the drift. The Franklin Park golf course—a potentially fine recreation facility in the center of the city—is shamefully, unbelievably neglected.

It's an insult to charge two dollars to play the place because it isn't worth two cents. Eighteen flags stuck in a meadow don't constitute a golf course.

The tee areas are a disgrace—bumpy, soggy, grassless. If a rake has been put to them in the last 100 years, you'd never know it.

Most of the benches are broken, the one drinking fountain leaks, and there doesn't seem to have been any water on the fairways since the 1955 flood.

The greens? They're brown, and brown, in this case, is far from beautiful.

What business of mine is Franklin Park? you might ask, and rightly so. I don't live in Boston. Until this weekend, I'd never set foot on the golf course.

But what does that matter? The city of Boston has an obligation to do something about the Franklin Park golf course. The obligation involves money and time and perhaps the city doesn't have enough of either to bother with people who chase a little white ball around.

Maybe the problem of supervision—keeping the place free from vandals and molesters and from those who have no qualms about destroying property—is too vast.

If that's the case, plant corn out there or get some taxable industry or turn the joint into a city dump.

But if Franklin Park is going to have a golf course, the city should make it a decent one. The one there now is a disgrace.

Stan Bondelevitch: A very special guy

December 10, 1971—SWAMPSCOTT—The records are there in living, pulsating black and white.

Eight undefeated, untied seasons; one loss in the last six years; never a losing season in 25 years of coaching; dozens of kids with continued football and educational success in college.

This is public testimony to the coaching greatness of Stan Bondelevitch, the intense, enthusiastic driving spirit—is genius too strong a word?—who has made high school football the common denominator in Swampscott for a generation.

Okay. No more statistics. What manner of man is this who can rally a town around kids playing a game, who can worry in equal quantities about a missed tackle and a mixed-up boy?

Grab a seat on the trolley car and take a ride through the world of Stan Bondelevitch. No need to fasten the safety belt, the streets are straight and plainly marked with the virtues and guideposts of yesteryear.

Mr. Bondelevitch will conduct the tour. Speak right up, coach, so the lady in the back can hear, and never mind the X's and O's. Tell them about you:

"I was gonna be a lawyer, accepted in law school and everything, 25 years old and out of the service, and I got this job coaching and substitute-teaching English at Maynard High.

"Five years in the service, what did I know about teaching English, but I got some books and boned up and you know, I could hardly wait to get to school every morning to teach the kids.

"So I said, why should I want to be something else if I love this so much. Some people told me I was crazy, that getting accepted to law school was the tough thing and I was throwing all that away. They said I'd be nothing but a sports bum, but I went to BU and got my masters in phys ed anyway, a lot of theory and dry, but I got it, and I've never been sorry the road I took.

"So I'm doing the same thing I was doing 25 years ago, coaching kids, but my enthusiasm is even greater. Why? New faces, always new faces, and the closeness that football brings you to kids. It's a love affair, you love the ones who've played for you.

"But I don't want to own a kid, I mean a player of mine. I don't want to play God. I'm not a character builder. That's the parents' job. The kids belong to them, not me. But there are things football at Swampscott gives a kid. Confidence and pride and loyalty and I like to think I have a part in that.

"We've got intelligent players at Swampscott, but not everyone's natural. It's a small school, smallest in the conference and we've had kids come out who were so uncoordinated they couldn't walk and chew gum at the same time.

"But very few quit if they made the varsity and even ones without much talent benefit from playing football for Swampscott High.

"Maybe the best thing they did for the team was hold the tackling dummies for the kids who could play better but they were part of the team and at the end of three years of football they had confidence, you could see it.

"Players like to come and talk to me. We have open campus at Swampscott, which means if a kid doesn't have a class he doesn't have to stay on the grounds. But instead of knocking around town, the players drop in to talk to me, about football and other things. They do something wrong, like smoke what I call a funny butt, and the odds are they'll tell me. They'd rather tell me themselves than have me hear it from someone else. And I would never lie to a kid. Lie to one football player and your word is never the same.

"Are they afraid of me? I don't think so. But they have respect and they know I'll listen. And they know the rules and what it takes to be a good football player and a good person.

"We run hard practices, but they're short—say 3:30 to quarter of five most of the time. I've never had a kid run a lap for missing practice or being late. If a kid is going to take laps he should be on the track team.

"What do I do for punishment when a kid is late? I really don't know, I've never had one late without a legitimate excuse.

"Hair? No big deal. I tell a player he gets tackled by the hair, then maybe it's time to get a haircut.

"I call Friday smile day at practice. Nobody gets bawled out because he drops a ball or misses an assignment. The rule is the coaches stay 30 feet away from the drills so they won't spot mistakes. But on Tuesday through Thursday, we chew out the mistakes good. That way there shouldn't be many mistakes Friday or Saturday either.

"The only game we lost in six years was to St. John's of Danvers in 1970. A good game, St. John's earned it. I told my players afterward it was bound to come sometime and that it wasn't the end of the world.

"I told them the easiest thing to do now was to feel sorry for yourself, or go out and drown your sorrows in some beers, but that it would be better to go home, try to relax and don't dwell on the loss."

End of the ride.

Afghan tells all: Hard work reaching blue ribbon stage

December 19, 1971—The dog, an afghan hound, didn't seem nervous. He was a wistful, intelligent looking animal, perhaps 30 inches high and weighing 40 pounds, and he sat there being stroked and combed and fussed over yesterday afternoon at the 58th Eastern Dog Show at the Hynes Auditorium.

In a little while, he would go into the ring to be judged with 56 other afghans, but for now seemed at ease talking to a reporter who wanted to know how he felt about show business.

"It's a job, like any other," the afghan replied. "Oh, sure the glamor is there, but it took hard work to get to the blue ribbon stage."

The dog said concentration was the key to success in his business.

"Everybody has good and bad days," he said, "but I can't afford to let anything upset me. Like today, coming in here, I didn't have my pass and they wouldn't let me by the gate until I made a couple of phone calls. A less experienced dog, that would get to him."

The reporter asked if the competition was tough this year.

"The best in the east," the afghan replied. "No garbage truck chasers in this bunch. But they all put their pants on one leg at a time, to borrow a human expression."

The reporter, pushing aside a mental picture of that operation, wanted to know if the afghan had tips for aspiring young dogs in the suburbs.

"Just be yourself," the star replied. "I mean, if you're a poodle, don't come on like a St. Bernard or you'll get eaten alive. And above all practice and maintain a correct diet."

"Such as?" the reporter prompted.

"Well, stay away from scraps and the in-between stuff. I knew a Bedlington who trained exclusively on pizza and won best-in-breed at a big show, but that's an exception."

The afghan said there are a couple of excellent new books on the general subject of dog shows. He mentioned "Everything You Wanted to Know About the Siberian Husky But Were Afraid to Ask" as being especially good, and also recommended "What to Do Until the Sweeper Comes," a technical book that deals with dog shows from the ground up.

The reporter was curious to know if the afghan had a life of his own outside the ring.

"I'm becoming more and more politically oriented," the hound replied. "I'm head of a nationwide committee working to promote a better image for us. You could help."

How's that, the reporter wanted to know.

"By cleaning up the language. We're sick of reading about dog days and hearing expressions like "I wouldn't feed that to my dog" or "He led a dog's life." How would you like to be bombarded with Elvis Presley singing, "You Ain't Nothin' But a Hound Dog"?

The reporter said he'd do what he could to enlighten the public. Then he thanked the afghan for his cooperation in the interview and wished him well.

"My pleasure," the dog replied, "and when you're leaving, watch out where you're stepping, that's not second base."

Let Santa, the fraud, yield to Peter, de lawd

December 24, 1971—

'Twas the morning of Christmas, all cold, dreary and dark,
Yet creatures were stirring throughout the ball park;
The cables were hung in the stadium with care,
For the NBC peacock soon would be there. (1)
The athletes were nestled, each one in his suit,
With vision of Super Bowl's mind-blowing loot,
And out on the highways the cursing increased,
As motorists hurried to Pete Rozelle's feast.
The officials were ready, the ball was in place,
The players were poised to begin the great chase,
When out on the turf there arose such a clatter
That everyone rose, mad as a hatter,
To discover the itch they already were sick of,
The wastrel who dared stay the opening kickoff. (2)
A short guy he was, with a snowy white beard,
Obviously not a man to be feared;
Less than five feet and terribly fat,
With belly obese and feet that were flat
"Cease and desist," the little man roared,
"Go home and worship the birth of The Lord,
"Meet your family and have some fun
"And dwell no more on the bump-and-run."
Then out of the press box there came a great yell.
"Pay no attention," said Peter Rozelle,
"To the ranting of Claus, the man is a fraud.
"Everyone knows that I am De Lawd.

"Santa's outmoded for various reasons,
"Pro football's become the toy for all seasons.
"Now Staubach and Alworth, now swift Bobby Hayes, (3)
"Go Griese, go Warfield, on instant replays.
"On Eller, on Page, recover the ball,
"Now dash away, dash away, dash away all."
The referee heard the unholy commotion,
And showing the proper football devotion,
He laid a big finger aside of his nose (4)
And gave his tin whistle three healthy blows.
Down the greensward the warriors flew,
Trampling the turf, and Santa Claus too.
They villified Santa and called him bad names,
And penalized him for delay of the games.
They stomped on the man and pushed him around,
They flattened old Santa right into the ground.
But they heard him exclaim as he sank out of sight,
"You've just ruined Christmas, may heaven help Easter." (5)

Footnotes:

(1) This is poetic license, as NBC has put the Peacock on the taxi squad.

(2) Admittedly, this is not a true rhyme, except perhaps in Siberia.

(3) I could find no Donners or Blitzens on any pro roster.

(4) This never made sense in the original, and still doesn't.

(5) You may notice, if you've struggled this far, that the last two lines do not rhyme. This is known as the ultimate unrhymed couplet, first used with great success by Lord Byron in the poem, "Confessions of a Nude Waterfall."

2

1972–1973

I'll miss you, Tony, you were fun to watch

February 28, 1972—A thousand times since that awful August night in 1967, doctors have probed and inspected and peered into the eyes of Tony Conigliaro, professional baseball player.

They did it again last Thursday and told him what he already must have known in his heart: "Put it out of your mind, you cannot play the game for a living."

Tony says he will accept that judgment and try no more to hit a baseball thrown 90 miles an hour by aggressive young men eager to make a fool of him.

I tried to imagine, after reading this latest development in the career of the young man from Boston's North Shore, what it must have been like for him since the night a Jack Hamilton fast ball struck him in the head.

I tried to put myself in his place. How would I have reacted to the pressures? What would my response have been to the hundreds of journalists who followed him like jackals, asking "how's the eye, how's the eye, how's the eye" until it became a banshee howl heard 24 hours a day?

How would I have reacted to the seemingly crude and unfeeling attitude of Dick Williams, or to the crushing realization in the spring of 1968 that every pitched ball was a complete and total mystery?

I don't know. I don't think I could have withstood the pressures, or had the courage to make the comeback. I doubt if many athletes could have accomplished what Conigliaro did in 1969 and '70—play 287 games, drive in 198 runs and hit 56 home runs after a year of confidence-shattering idleness.

It took courage, plain guts to grab a bat and stand at home plate in a major league game after what he had been through in 1967 and 1968.

Journalist Roger Kahn, in a fascinating book called "The Boys of Summer," describes what it was like to stand, bat in hand, while pitcher Clem Labine threw toward him.

"The ball exploded toward the plate," wrote Kahn, "with a sibilant whoosh, edged by a buzzing, as of hornets. I had never heard a thrown ball make that sound before . . . an impossibly fast pitch that made the noises of hornets and snakes."

Then Labine threw curves to Kahn.

"Through a resolute act of will I held my ground. The impulse was not simply to duck but to throw away my bat and throw my body to the thick-bladed Florida grass. I could no more have swung at, let alone hit, one of Labine's pitches, than run a three-minute mile."

This is what Tony Conigliaro, with a blind spot in his left eye, conquered in the spring of '69. And it's what he couldn't conquer in 1971 when playing for the California Angels.

Pitcher Lew Krausse said Conigliaro was pathetic swinging at curve balls in 1971. Krausse said that when Milwaukee pitchers went over Angels hitters the agreement was never to throw Conigliaro a fast ball anywhere near the plate, but to throw a curve anywhere, because Tony had no idea where it was.

I was on the road trip the Red Sox made to Anaheim when the story broke about the Angels fixing up Tony's uniform with bandages and ketchup and whatnot. Conigliaro had been having shoulder and back problems, and as a matter of fact, had been in the hospital, though none of the Angels bothered to visit him.

I remember Lefty Phillips, the Angels manager, dismissing the ketchup gag as just another baseball prank.

"You know how players are," he said. "They have their little joke, but they don't mean anything by it."

I agreed with Lefty. "Sure, just a joke, trying to kid with Tony."

But the more I thought about it, the less it seemed like a simple prank. What right did these people, these bickering nit-picking Angels, have to mock a ballplayer who had shown more courage in five minutes than they had been asked to in a lifetime?

Where was the man among them to stand in the locker room and tell the fun makers to stuff their ketchup and adhesive tape?

Lefty Phillips and his merry men should have apologized to Tony Conigliaro. Well, they didn't and it wasn't long before Conigliaro was home, a victim, finally, of the unceasing pressures.

Tony Conigliaro, in the years I covered him, was often self-centered, ambitious, petty, crude, impatient and opinionated.

But he was also gracious, charming, marvelous with kids (if the kids were polite), witty and cooperative.

And he could play the game, don't forget that. A Tony C. line drive was hit the way a baseball is supposed to be hit.

Tony, you were fun to watch and fun to cover and I, for one, will genuinely miss you.

The brave ones swing at golf

August 22, 1972—Any golfer has heard the tired jokes on the first tee.

Player No. 1 says, "Well, let's make a match. What's your handicap?"

And Player No. 2 replies, "A bad backswing," and thinks he's Bob Hope. Or he says, with a smirk, "My wife. She won't let me play enough."

It's all hilariously funny, but there are a bunch of golfers at the Marshfield Country Club these days who make a mockery of the word "handicap."

Paul Ackerman, for instance. Ackerman lost both hands above the wrist when a steel forging hammer fell on him in 1949. Yesterday, using a unique device that locks his club into an artificial arm, he shot 85 and was unhappy with the score.

Or take Jim Garner. Garner has had 35 operations since being left for dead on a Korean battlefield with a shattered leg and 75 bullet wounds. Yesterday he hit tee shots 240 yards.

Bert Shepard lost his leg in a P-38 strafing mission over Germany. Yesterday his drive off the first tee was about 10 yards behind that of pro Paul Harney.

Corbin Cherry stepped on a land mine in Vietnam and it cost him a leg. Sunday he shot 75 at Marshfield, and yesterday played nine holes in par 35.

Bob Manion, who is 23 and was a star football player in high school, ran into a booby trap in Vietnam. He lost one leg and the other was partially paralyzed and yesterday he lost three bucks in a Nassau match.

Tom Herbert, who is 27 and hasn't had any hands since he was 2, holds a golf club between his stumps, takes a terrific swing and hits drives 220 yards.

You can see these gentlemen and 100 others who have lost limbs in the 24th National Amputee Golf Tournament at Marshfield today through Friday.

It's a sight you won't forget.

Shepard, the ex-P-38 pilot, is defending champion. He's a former professional baseball player, who once pitched 5⅓ innings of a major league game for the Senators against the Red Sox in 1945, a year after he lost his right leg. He came in that game with the bases loaded and struck out George Metkovich.

Shepard pitched batting practice for the Senators for a couple of years, and once in Fenway Park, his foot broke on the mound, whereupon he calmly kicked it off before the horrified early customers as players on both teams fell down laughing.

Ackerman, the man with the locked-in clubs, is a 53-year-old from Canton, Ohio, who never played the game until after his accident.

He practiced seven or eight hours a day and never expected to be any good, but a few years ago in Reading, Pa., shot a 69. He also bowls and averages 180.

Cherry, the man who stepped on a land mine, is an Army captain and a chaplain in a San Francisco hospital. He writes poetry and popular songs and says of his golf: "Heck, I play better than most of my two-legged contemporaries. I've got nothing to feel sorry about."

Garner, the only black in the tournament, is from Winston-Salem and before Korea he played against Charlie Sifford and other top black golfers, and had thoughts about making the game his living.

"I guess being an athlete helped me recover. Now, beating guys with two legs gives me a kick."

Garner and Manion, the young man who once played defensive back, are rooming together during the tournament. Manion, asked if he'd reconciled himself to never playing football again, replied: "I still play it, up here," pointing to his head. "I watch games and think what I would do. It's not as good as playing but it's something, and I enjoy it."

But the phenomenon of the tournament is Herbert, because of the way he holds a club despite having no hands to hold it.

It's enough to make a guy forget about the sore shoulder he complained about all weekend.

Tips to assist Pats in search

December 7, 1972—One cannot quarrel with the Patriots' intention to have the best available coach in America.

The problem now is, how do they go about their mission? How do they obtain this paragon?

As a concerned journalist, I'd like to do my part, so here are a few suggestions.

The Patriots should not overlook the power of the classified ad. Newspapers reach millions of homes, and in one of these homes resides the best available coach in the country, who presumably can read. Something like the following would certainly give him food for thought:

> HELP WANTED: Professional football coach. Experienced in accepting defeat. Bright future, good pay and living conditions. Man we are looking for must be forceful, yet have ability to communicate with 40 young men. Must be able to draw Xs and Os on blackboard, run 16-millimeter projector and deal with vitriolic press. Great opp'y for man who likes to travel. Shorthand, typing not necessary. Our employees know of this ad. We are an equal opportunity employer.

And I think a good investment would be the matchbook cover. Many an office clerk has become a millionaire after filling out the miniature form on the back of a matchbook.

A message such as this might be effective:

> Learn how to cope. The New England Patriots of the National Football League offer on-the-job training. A year with us will put life in its proper perspective. Never again will you snarl at children, get fidgety at traffic lights or complain about mail addressed 'occupant.' Graduates of our program are leading a fuller, more enjoyable existence. Our course is given in pastoral setting, adjacent to horse farm. Send application to Madhouse, Foxboro, Mass.

Also useful would be a short training film, which could be shown at coaching clinics throughout the country.

The film would include a history of the Patriots, showing the team's early sumptuous office quarters on Lansdowne Street, its exquisite practice field in East Boston and its intricate scouting system.

Other features might be the award-winning clips of a traffic jam outside Schaefer Stadium, a montage of holding calls against the offensive line, a rare shot of Carl Garrett at a practice session, and a two-minute section depicting the complete Patriot highlights of 1972.

A boffo finish would be spoken testimonials from Lou Saban, Mike Holovak, Clive Rush, John Mazur, and Upton Bell, with all the bad words deleted.

But of course, it is probably true that the Patriots board of directors has already narrowed its search to a dozen men, tried and true.

These 12 should be sent a personal letter, describing the advantages and challenge of the job. The letter might go something like this:

Dear Ara:

If you are not interested in a million dollars plus a lifetime contract, throw this in the wastebasket. But if you are a man who welcomes a challenge, a man who does the difficult immediately and takes only a little longer to accomplish the impossible, this message is for you.

We are prepared to offer you the position as general manager-coach of the New England Patriots. Perhaps you never heard of us, being involved as you are with winning, but we are a professional football team located in Foxboro, Mass., only a stone's throw from the daily double window.

We are, frankly, a financial success but an artistic failure. The job, if you choose to accept it, won't be easy. Here are the pluses. Well, never mind. Here are the minuses:

Number one, we have no offense. In the second place, we have no defense, and in the third place everybody says bad things about us.

But there are signs of progress. The toilets are working, a fan hasn't been hit by any empty bottle in two weeks and last month we completed a screen pass.

If you are interested, please send a resume, showing the schools you've attended, if any, your coaching record, and explain in 50 words or less why you are applying for the position

Hoping to hear from you soon, I remain

Yours in football
William H. Sullivan, Pres.
New England Patriots

WHS/rf

CC to John McKay, Joe Paterno, Chuck Fairbanks, Darrell Royal, Bear Bryant, Frank Broyles, Joe Don Looney, Dick Cavett and the Philadelphia String Quartet.

Boxing gives lifer hope

December 19, 1972—The whole business was new to Chris Pina, all of it. The weigh-in, the taping, the Vaseline smeared all over the body, the ex-pugs coming in to wish him well, the hangers-on, the trainers, what is left of the fight mob in Boston.

He was fighting his first bout, a four-rounder in Sam Silverman's card in Waltham, but that wasn't the half of it, because what Chris Pina was really doing was making sports history in Massachusetts.

Pina is a lifer. His home is the correctional institution at Norfolk, and yesterday he became the first inmate to be allowed outside the walls of any state prison to be on a fight card.

On May 27, 1968, Christopher J. Pina Jr., then 19 years old, pleaded guilty to second degree murder and was sentenced to life in prison.

One November midnight in 1967, a man was badly beaten outside a bar in Scituate harbor. His body was found the next day in a culvert in Norwell.

The following day, Pina and a friend were arrested and charged with murder, kidnapping, robbery and stealing a motor vehicle.

He pleaded guilty to second degree murder and was sent to Walpole and then to Norfolk. In 1971, he sought a new trial, saying he had pleaded guilty because his original lawyer had led him to believe he would be sent to the electric chair if convicted of first degree murder.

The appeal was denied.

Last night, Pina saw the outside of prison for the first time in 5½ years, except for the ride from Walpole to Norfolk.

"When I first went in the can," said Pina, "it was so weird. I mean I was shut off from the whole world. The whole world. I thought about it all the time, that I was here for life. It was hard to believe it was me. Now I can't believe it's me out here in the world again."

At 10 yesterday morning, Pina left Norfolk with Paul Pender, the former middleweight champion who is athletic director at the prison.

He was "on furlough," the term they use for prisoners given time away from their institution under Gov. Sargent's new plan.

Pina spent the afternoon at Pender's house and by 6:30 was in the IBEW Hall in Waltham, where Silverman tries to keep boxing alive in Greater Boston.

"I think it's a wonderful thing," said Pender. "I don't agree with everything Boone (prison commissioner John Boone) does, but this is good."

At 7:30 last night, Pina, dressed in a short blue bathrobe with white stripes, stood on a tiny bathroom scale for the weigh-in. Dr. Nathan Shapiro put a stethoscope to his chest, and then asked Pina to read a fly-specked eye chart on the wall. "P-K-D-C-F", read Pina, and he was pronounced fit to fight.

Pina was in the second bout of the night, so about ten of eight, Pender began to tape his protege's hands.

"Turn 'em over," said Pender. "Make a fist. Pay attention. Now listen, don't go trying to knock the guy out in the first round. Knock him out early, people will think he's a stiff."

Pender showed Pina how to sit between rounds. "Don't slump back. Sit like this, with your hands here. And breathe in through your nose and out your mouth."

People kept coming in the cramped dressing room and wishing Pina well. One pressed a $20 bill in his mitt.

"Alumni," Pender explained.

The first bout was over and it was time.

"As soon as you land a punch, move away, move to your right," said Pender. "Okay, let's go."

Pina, a middleweight at 155 pounds, was fighting a blond kid from Lowell named Jack Kirk, and it was soon obvious Kirk was not going to do very well.

In the third round, Pina tagged him with a solid left and at 1:40 of the fourth round, the fight was stopped. Pina was a TKO winner.

"He was a little anxious," said Joe DeNucci, "but I liked him."

"When he stuck to what he was supposed to do, he was good," said Pender. "Sometimes he looked a little disoriented out there."

Pina was excited. He'd won, he'd heard people cheering for him, he'd found out that somebody cared about the rest of his life.

And maybe that's what the whole day was all about anyway, the fact that somebody cared.

Ref's lips zipped on Steelers' TD

December 29, 1972—Almost a week has passed since the play that kept the Pittsburgh Steelers alive in the race for Pope Peter Rozelle's Holy Grail.

The deflected pass that Franco Harris returned for a touchdown has been cussed and discussed. It has been dissected and analyzed by every expert from Howard Cosell to Howard Schmidt, our milkman.

Everybody has been interviewed—Harris, John Fuqua, Jack Tatum, Oakland coach John Madden, general manager Al Davis, Pittsburgh coach Chuck Noll, owner Art Rooney, the National Football League office, the supervisor of officials, trainers, clubhouse boys, the man who holds the first-down sticks, a lady who was walking past the stadium.

The only man who hasn't been widely quoted is the one who made the final decision. Nowhere, to my knowledge, has there been an interview with Fred Swearingen, the referee who went to the dugout phone, talked briefly and returned to the field to fling his arms dramatically in the air in the touchdown sign.

So why not contact Mr. Swearingen, a 13-year veteran of officiating in the NFL?

Certainly he could explain the play that's been called the most controversial in pro football history. He could say whether the replay was a factor in his decision and whether using such pictures is a good thing.

He could describe the sequence of events. Did the ball hit Tatum on the shoulder or hands? Did it hit Fuqua at all?

Well, forget it. The ref isn't talking. The NFL silencer is pointing at his head. Loose lips sink ships. Zip it up or the whistle goes in the attic. We'll do the talking, you just wave your arms.

Swearingen, who lives in Carlsbad, Calif., wasn't antagonistic on the telephone last night. On the contrary, he seemed a most pleasant man.

And he knows his place.

"I really don't want to talk about the play over the phone," he said. "The league office has explained the play and I'd be happy to give you their number."

Well, to heck with the league office and official versions, cleaned up so everything is in apple pie order. What happened, Fred?

"I don't think anything is served by discussing the play further. Things get twisted and turned around. It was a tremendous game, so let's let it go at that."

All right, Let's let it go at that, and who cares whether the millions still wondering what went on ever get to know.

Pro football, in its arrogance, has kept its goal line unsullied once again.

Pro sports—with the exception of baseball—don't consider officials as part of the game when it comes to reporting. You can ask a coach when he stopped beating his wife, or a player when he learned to count to 10, but to talk to a football, basketball or hockey referee after a game you need diplomatic immunity.

A few years ago, a Patriots' player named Mike Ballou almost broke San Diego punter Dennis Partee in half with an entirely unnecessary block. No flag was thrown, although it seemed a flagrant infraction.

The 30,000 fans at Harvard Stadium were confused. So was a reporter, who thought it might be a good idea to interview the ref to clear the confusion.

How naive. The reporter was told to get out of the officials' room before he was clapped in irons. Later, he discovered that in order to get information from officials, newspapermen must go through a public relations director, who takes any questions into the officials and emerges with an answer.

If that's journalism, I'm the next Patriots' coach.

Funny, but baseball, considered the stodgiest of sports by the football people, doesn't work that way. If Mike Nagy hits a Tigers batter with a baseball and the Tigers pitcher responds by plunking Mike Nagy in the back and there is bad blood all around, the umpire is available.

He will tell you, syllable by syllable, obscenity by obscenity, what happened. He'll explain who was thrown out and why and will spare no details.

That is the way it should be, because what does an official have to hide? He makes the calls and he alone knows why.

The people who shelled out time or money or both for the privilege of watching the action certainly are entitled to be let in on the secret.

His teacher speaks of Clemente she knew

January 6, 1973—SAN JUAN, P.R.—Maria Isabel Caceres is a history teacher at Julio Vizcarrando High School in Carolina, Puerto Rico. She has been there a long time and will never forget the shy boy who sat in the back of her class and seldom raised his hand or opened his mouth.

Mrs. Caceres was Roberto Clemente's history teacher, but more than that she was a good friend and counselor.

The school—which has a framed, color portrait of the 1960 world champion Pirates hanging in the entryway—is closed now for the Christmas vacation.

But Mrs. Caceres came over anyhow to talk about the young Roberto she knew, the athlete who went on to become one of the great baseball players of this or any other time.

"He was so quiet, so I didn't know him well at first. But his parents traded at my father's store, so after a while I got to know Roberto better.

"Then he played on my husband's softball team. Sello Rojo, it was called. Roberto was a shortstop and he would come to our house to wait for the rest of the players."

Mrs. Caceres gave Clemente a "B" in history. "The classes were taught in English, and Roberto didn't know much English. I was astonished to see him on television later speaking so well and without seeming shy because he was very reserved as a child."

Every year, when Clemente returned to Puerto Rico, he visited Mrs. Caceres.

"One time about 10 years ago," she said, "he came to the school and they told him my back hurt and I was sick in bed. So he went to my house and I told him how bad I felt and he took me in his arms, right out of bed, and brought me to a doctor. Every day until I could walk he would bring me over there.

"I asked once how much it cost, I wanted to pay, and he got mad at me. 'You're offending me by asking,' he said."

Mrs. Caceres got the news of the plane crash at 5 o'clock in the morning on New Year's Day.

A youngster called and said he heard something on the radio that he hoped was not true, but he thought she should know it.

"So I turned on the radio, and of course it was true."

Mrs. Caceres spent that day from 8 in the morning until 10:30 at night helping console Roberto's wife, Vera, whom she had also had as a student.

"I am divorced from my husband," Mrs. Caceres said, "and he was the first person I met at the Clemente's that day. And, oh, so many came."

There is still a Roberto Clemente attending Julio Vizcarrando High School. He is the son of Roberto's brother, and Mrs. Caceres had asked the young nephew to remind his famous uncle to come and say hello to the students, as he did every year. He was going to come after the holidays.

"He was a good friend of all the boys here. He would give baseball clinics in the field over there and bring them presents, and we would give him some, too."

The last time Clemente came to the school he brought Mrs. Caceres 50 pictures to give to the children.

"We gave him some plates and a placard signed with all our names."

Clemente played high school baseball in an enclosed park directly across the street from the school. The fence now is crisscrossed with hand-painted political and inspirational signs, such as "Arribe los de Abajo" (Up with those who are down) and "La luche sigue" (The struggle continues).

The field long ago was renamed Roberto Clemente Park and yesterday black crepe hung from the wire mesh backstop. Black mourning bands also hung from car aerials in Carolina, which is about a half-hour outside of metropolitan San Juan.

The center of Carolina is a hodgepodge of stores and houses around a central plaza. On Munoz Rivera street, facing the square, is San Fernando Church, where Clemente was baptized at the age of 9, and where, in December of 1964, he married Vera Cristina Zabala.

And it was in San Fernando Church on Thursday that the Pittsburgh Pirates came to pay Clemente final tribute at a special mass conducted by Juan Lopez, archbishop of San Juan, and six assistant priests.

Many wives of the players attended, along with three of Roberto's major league managers, Harry Walker, Danny Murtaugh and Bill Virdon. Former teammates Bob Friend and Ron Kline flew in. Bowie Kuhn was there and Marvin Miller. Steelers owner Art Rooney and Steelers players Preston Pearson and Dick Brown came with the chartered plane.

Bob Johnson, a Pirates pitcher who was playing winter ball here, said he was hosting a party at his 27th floor apartment on New Year's Eve and from his window could see furious activity in the ocean.

"It was obvious a plane had crashed, but we had no idea it was Roberto," said Richie Zisk, another teammate.

"We thought it might even be one of those 200-passenger jetliners and we were saying how tough it was going to be for the relatives involved to get the news."

Father Angel Perez, a Cuban exile who came to San Fernando Church two years ago, said that many in Carolina didn't know that Clemente was lost until 10 o'clock that New Year's morning.

"When I announced it from the pulpit, you could feel the shock run through the crowd," he said. "People began crying and shaking their heads. This town was awfully quiet, and even now it is hard for them to believe."

The hold Roberto Clemente had on the people here is overpowering. It began because he was a famous athlete, a man who had struck it rich in America, but his strength has spread over the years to encompass much more.

Carmello Romain Galarzia, a 17-year-old student at Julio Vizcarrando High School, met Clemente once.

"He was so nice. He took such an interest in me. He asked me questions and gave me advice. When I heard about the crash it twisted me all up inside. It was like a brother had died."

Life goes on in Puerto Rico, of course. In the luxury hotels it's standing room only in the casinos, where tourists toss $25 chips around as though they are Necco wafers.

El Commandante race track is back in action and there is a Pro-Am golf tournament at Dorado Beach. The Puerto Rican All-Star baseball game is being held this afternoon.

But in Carolina and on the streets all over the island, the people of Puerto Rico will be a long time getting over the death of Roberto Clemente.

Chamberlain remains the bad man for all seasons

February 9, 1973—He's still the villain, the one most likely to tie the farmer's daughter to the railroad track.

The hate doesn't pour from the stands the way it did when he came to town to battle Bill Russell, but Wilt Chamberlain is still Everyman's bad guy.

He fills an important void in a sports fan's life. How would it be if every superstar was a John Havlicek, a Walt Frazier, a Jerry West?

The continuing passion play that is pro basketball demands there be a Mr. Evil. Oh sure, the referees, but that's too easy. That's like booing sin, or the capital gains tax.

Chamberlain is perfect. He's bigger and stronger than anyone else and, if you go strictly by statistics, is the best who ever played the game.

But he is the lumbering giant, on hand to be made a fool of by the six-foot five-inch Lilliputians who keep buzzing around him.

His presence is so awesome that when a pygmy scores against him it is David beating Goliath, the common man beating the system, the nice kid outsmarting the bully, and the customers love it.

When it was Chamberlain vs. Russell, the hate was pure. It was offense against defense, the individual against Mr. Team.

A fan could relate to Russell, a man who sacrificed statistics for the greater glory of winning. Who could identify with a glutton who shot 50 times a game, played defense with reckless indifference and won a reputation as a wrecker of coaches?

Much of that has changed. Chamberlain plays differently now. A pass to him is no longer a one-way ticket to the basket. Against the Celtics Wednesday he played 48 minutes and took seven shots.

Seven shots. In the old days if you bent down to tie your shoe, Wilt would be in double figures.

Now he lurks around the basket like your friendly neighborhood octopus, swatting away shots and turning the other side's easy lay-up into a calculated risk.

This switch to defense has diluted the hate, and in the finals against the Knicks last spring, Chamberlain almost reached the hero stage. Sweetness and light descended upon him and you could almost hear people saying: "Hey, he's almost human."

But the worship was short-lived and he's a villain again, and that's the way it should be, because Wilt is as type-cast in his profession as Gary Cooper was in his. Making Chamberlain likeable would be like asking Raquel Welch to play Mother Superior.

Wilt is a man of a thousand grimaces. He scowls at referees when they call a foul on him. He leers when they don't call a foul on the man playing him. He shoots pained looks at teammates when a ball goes astray.

The world is against him, this seven-four millionaire, and you wonder how he feels about that. You get the idea he would like to be loved but doesn't know how to go about it and is resigned to his loneliness.

At 36, Chamberlain is an old man in his profession. His knees have crescent-shaped scars and before every game his fingers have to be taped.

His legs are thin for his bulk and have been pounding basketball floors for a quarter of a century, and looking at him after the overtime defeat Wednesday, you wonder how much longer he would keep going, even at $300,000 a year.

Chamberlain was stretched out like a felled Sequoia in the Lakers' locker room and he looked terribly tired.

A radio man thrust a mike in his face and asked a question but Chamberlain said: "Man, I got nothin' to say so you might as well take that thing away."

Reporters stood around, trying to think of tactful questions, but the few that were asked were innocuous and got noncommittal, monosyllabic answers.

After awhile, the reporters drifted away to Bill Sharman, who smiled and talked about the loss, the Celtics and the league.

Other writers went to Jerry West, who analyzed the game and his part in it, answering the same old questions he's heard a hundred times.

Wilt Chamberlain was left alone, lying on the trainer's table and staring at the ceiling. He's been in and out of Boston for 14 years now, but he's still a mysterious, lonely figure.

And maybe that's the way it should be, because if you get to know a villain too well, you might discover he's not a villain at all. You might actually get to like him, and then where would pro basketball be?

You're wrong this time, Georgie boy

February 15, 1973—I was sitting around with the rest of the shills in the sports department yesterday, divvying up the day's spoils from the pro teams in town.

Sometimes it's difficult to give everyone an equal share, the way the stuff pours in. How many sets of registered golf clubs, after all, can a guy use?

"I wonder what's in my package?" murmured Leigh Montville, ripping viciously at a square cardboard box marked "Glass, Handle with Care."

Montville reached his greedy paw into the innards of the box and withdrew a hideous purple drinking mug that had the insignia of the Pro Football Hall of Fame stamped on its side.

"Oooh," marveled Montville in wonder at this latest payoff. "I was gonna write a column about Bill Nelsen the Patriots new quarterback coach, but now I think I'll tell everybody what a marvelous place the football Hall of Fame in Canton, Ohio, is, now that I've been paid off."

All us shills agreed a column on the Hall of Fame would be perfect, and then the talk got around to which sports team in town we would stick for lunch.

That's the way it works with us, see. Sportswriters get free meals and drinks from the various sports establishments in town, and in turn, we write nice things about them.

But you knew all that, didn't you? Listen to any sports talk show and they'll tell you about us locker room Larries, hanging around for the crumbs owners and players throw us.

Or if you don't listen to the talk shows, surely you read George Frazier, who, when he can't think of anything else to write, points the finger of righteousness at the press box.

He did it again in yesterday's Globe, as a lead-in to a criticism of something I wrote—I assume it's me, although I haven't quite reached the same league as Curt Gowdy and Barbara Walters, who get their very names in the column.

George, criticize my thinking all you want. Pat yourself on the back for being out there in the lonely, anti-establishment world, fighting the good fight while the rest of us walk the party line.

But don't call me a thief, and don't call the people I work with thieves unless you have chapter and verse in that nasty black notebook of yours. Don't suggest that I write columns predicated on how I am treated by the establishment.

Integrity did not pitch a tent exclusively on your doorstep.

There most certainly is room in my world for a difference of opinion. You can praise Marvin Miller, and presumably I can write a column critical of him without being in league with the devil.

But let's stop it there, okay? To suggest, for example, that the sports pages of the Globe should criticize the Red Sox management because they released Gary Peters and Ray Culp is to admit you do not know much about Gary Peters and Ray Culp.

Peters was released because he was, from all indications, at the end of a distinguished career. Culp was released because he'd had an arm operation and was a big question mark for 1973. He is going to spring training and will certainly be back with the Red Sox if he can still pitch.

To say that Peters and Culp were released because they were player representatives is preposterous and anyone who writes that simply does not know what he is talking about.

It's possible, of course, that George Frazier would like to be a sportswriter, to get a cut of the subtle payola he is forever writing about. We need a night watchman on weekends to answer phones ("Hey, Mac, who played right field for the Red Sox in the 1946 Series?").

George might be able to work up to a July trip with the Red Sox to Kansas City, where the press room fare—cold cuts, potato salad and raspberry jello running rampant on a paper plate—is hardly comparable to Locke-Ober's, but is, after all, free.

But enough. It does little good to conduct intramural nastiness in the public prints, especially when the man you're jousting with has as facile a pen as Mr. Frazier.

Rip my thinking all you want, G.F., but save the smear stuff for people you know something about.

Is nothing sacred? I should have known it all along

August 24, 1973—I come to you with heavy heart this morning.

My faith in sporting America, which first began wavering when I discovered that George Gipp didn't always attend classes, is now as unraveled as a dime store baseball.

In retrospect, I should have been more prepared. The telltale signs of corruption, the many milestones along the path to sporting disillusionment should have had me ready for the final indignity.

But I kept staring at my world through rose-colored binoculars. "Anyone can make a mistake," I rationalized.

And so I passed over the fact that Yogi Berra wasn't really a wit. I closed my eyes when it became apparent that Joe Namath did indeed drink and chase, as he calls them, broads, attributing his weakness to a deprived boyhood spent in Beaver Falls.

"He really wants to be pure but fate won't let him," I reasoned.

Bill Russell not signing autographs, Derek Sanderson performing in an X-rated movie, the fact that Ivy League football isn't as good as the Big Ten—these were all danger signals but I ignored them.

I can ignore no longer. I can say no more that sports is the toy I knew, the escape from the world of viciousness and deceit. I will continue to write about the men and women who play the games but the tinsel is off the tree.

The Soap Box Derby was rigged.

Even as I write the words I can barely believe them.

The Soap Box Derby, as American as Playboy magazine, H. R. Haldeman and cheating on your income tax, was won by a boy who apparently used an electromagnetic device to give his racer more go power, as we say in advertising circles.

In Akron, the county prosecutor said the incident was "like learning the Ivory Snow girl made blue movies."

Oh, no. It's worse than that. One can adjust if the soap box lady leaps from the laundry room to the bedroom, so to speak. These are permissive times and even Rinso White is not as pure as it once was.

But chicanery in the Soap Box Derby is tantamount to shattering a childhood. It is as though you took the years from eight to 14, said they were all a fraud and dropped them into the Grand Canyon.

Oh, the envy that would creep over me as I looked in the Springfield Union on the lazy summer days of my youth and saw the pictures from Akron, or viewed, on Saturday afternoon at the Park Theater, Paramount News (the eyes and ears of the world) as it showed the freckled-faced kid holding his trophy aloft.

What must it have been like to race down that Akron hill with the crowds lining both sides? What indescribable tingle would come from crossing the finish line first, thus winning about 80 million dollars and the promise of an education that would make you President, or at least a brain surgeon?

Our crowd was too mechanically inept to build a soap box racer, of course. The ability needed to put four wheels on a carton and get it from point A to point B without tipping over was light years beyond our comprehension.

Our mechanical limits were reached in the effort required to draw a reasonably circular ring on a sidewalk with a piece of chalk, inside which we'd play marbles.

So we shot aggies and flipped baseball cards, and did incredibly nifty things that involved sticking a jack knife in the ground from impossible angles.

And all the time we looked at those Akron photos and wondered what it must be like to have enough brains to build a soap box racer.

And now even the last innocence has fled. The Derby for the last two years has evidently been won with the help of a Rube Goldberg-like invention, a magnetic butazolydin pill, if you will.

Devious, devious. Did the 14-year-old winner dream up the ingenious rig all by himself or did he have adult help? How widespread is the device? Was it used at Indianapolis? Were inspectors merely lax and careless or were there kickbacks?

These are disturbing questions that deserve answers and proper investigation will no doubt provide them. But surely the Soap Box Derby as we know it is gone, and with it, a treasured memory of childhood.

Ralph Nader, where were you when I needed you?

Armchair QB, are you ready?

September 16, 1973—It's that season again. You've had fun in the lazy, hazy days of summer, but it's time to get down to serious business once more. It's football-watching time.

Now, there are two ways to watch football on television. You can be slapdash, hit-or-miss about it. "Oh, is there a game on? What channel? I'll catch it after dinner."

Or you can be systematic. You can use the time-tested Fitzgerald formula for football fun for greater enjoyment of a great sport. Follow these 10 rules and you'll not only have a better understanding of the game, you'll also be a better person.

1. *Lock the kids in a closet.*

This may seem cruel and callous, but believe me, in the long run it's best for all concerned. Be firm. There may be cries of anguish well into the first quarter, but when the little darlings discover how little air there is to breath in the average closet they'll quiet down.

The children will probably become hungry before the afternoon is over. What has worked well for me is to slide grilled cheese sandwiches under the door at halftime, and possibly a few Ju-Jubes for dessert.

For extremely difficult teenagers, a promise of a flashlight and a copy of Playboy has always been a pacifier.

2. *Draw all the shades in the house.*

One of the problems in watching TV football, especially in early autumn, is the guilt feelings that come from the knowledge that any normal human being should be outside enjoying the marvelous fall foliage rather than be cooped up in a house watching a dumb game.

Drawing the shades helps ease this feeling. What you don't know can't hurt you. It might be raining out there. A tornado might be flying down the next block. Who knows? Keep the outside world in its place and you maintain peace of mind.

3. *Don't believe the starting time.*

Okay, so it says in the TV magazine, 2 p.m., Redskins vs. Giants. Forget it, unless you are a fan of Jerry Vale singing The Anthem, or are crazy about Pat Summerall's voice, or like meetings at midfield to toss a coin to fake a decision that was made at half past eight. The game will start no sooner than 2:08, giving you time to read three more Sunday comics.

4. *Sit in a hard chair.*

Under no condition should you stretch out on a couch or in a favorite overstuffed chair. If you want to take a nap, go to bed and leave football watching to the tough guys. There is nothing more revolting than a pseudo fan who props his feet on a sofa, settles back for the opening kickoff, and wakes up when CBS Central is into its wrap up.

5. *Watch the ball at all times.*

You've probably read advice from dozens of experts telling you to watch the defensive end or the pulling guard if you really want to appreciate football. That's nonsense. Watch those people and what you see is some big oaf tossing himself at some other big oaf. You can see the same thing in any alley.

Let the intellectuals watch the pulling guards. You watch the quarterback. He gets the ball, doesn't he? He throws it or hands it to people who score touchdowns, doesn't he? That's what the game is all about, isn't it? Watch the ball.

6. *Have your parlay cards within reach.*

How frustrating it can be to have part-time scores come hurtling out of the TV set and you with your parlay card on the upstairs dresser.

Don't go to extremes, however, and flaunt your cards. I know a man who played seven cards each week and Scotch-taped them to the window. This is gauche and should be avoided.

7. *Watch the game alone.*

At first glance, this seems unfriendly and un-American, but experience has shown that when watching a football game, one is company and two is a fist fight. Watching by yourself gives you a chance to vent your spleen, if you're interested in that sort of thing, without anyone else thinking you've gone bananas.

8. *Remove all blunt and sharp instruments from the room.*

Some go to extremes and have anything of a throwing nature removed from the entire house, but the normal viewer's rage is of such short duration that his passion has cooled by the time he has to hunt down a suitable object for throwing, hitting, etc.

I know of a man who once heaved a hassock through a window after his team fumbled on the one-foot line, and since then he has nailed all his furniture to the floor during the football season.

9. *Make sure you have the jersey colors right.*

Admittedly this is basic, but there are cases on record of viewers cheering for the guys in blue only to find out in the third quarter that they had money on the ones in red.

10. *Never watch halftime.*

Turn the set off and get away from it. Do yoga exercises. Write a letter to someone in the service. Bake a chocolate cake. Go to the closet and see if the kids are still breathing.

In other words, forget football for 15 minutes. Never mind the halftime highlights, the replays of the instant replays.

Then stroll casually back into the room and flip on the set just as the kickoff is heading downfield. That is TV cool.

If you can follow these 10 simple rules, yours is the earth and everything that's in it, and which is more, you're ready for the Super Bowl, my son.

3

1974

Mantle: Pain and power

January 16, 1974—If you want to know the truth, I was never a great Mickey Mantle fan. He was a Yankee, for one thing, and for another, he struck out too damn much.

He struck out more than anybody in the history of major league baseball—more than Babe Ruth or Vince DiMaggio or Pancho Herrera or anybody. In 8102 official at bats, he fanned 1710 times.

Once in every five, Mickey Charles Mantle whiffed, as we say in Little League.

Yet, there can be no denying his greatness, and it would be a great upset if the official dispatch later today does not say he's been voted into the baseball Hall of Fame.

Mantle, when he did hit the ball, hit it so far that he was the yardstick for the white baseball-playing youths of the '50s and early '60s.

The kids of the '20s and '30s said, "Who dya think ya are, Babe Ruth?" Those of the '40s and early '50s countered with, "who dya think ya are, Ted Williams?" And the next generation was, "Hey, stop swingin' hard. Who dya think ya are, Mickey Mantle?"

Mantle's greatness was built on power and pain. He exuded the first and endured the second, and rarely was there a feature story on him that didn't dwell on both departments.

Mantle hit 536 homers, lifetime. But he also missed 255 games in the prime of his career because of assorted ailments—torn ligaments, shin splints, bruised ribs, an abscessed hip, pulled muscles, a broken foot and constant bruises and sprains.

When playing became a sometime and not-very-rewarding thing, he said, "It isn't fun when things are like this. I'm only 33 but I feel like 40."

And yet, Mantle hung on for four more years hitting .255, .288, .245 and .237. The lingering knocked his lifetime average below .300, even though he'd been well above .300 for 10 of his other 13 seasons.

Maybe a kid today would look at the stumbling finish and wonder, "Was he any good?"

Well, he was good, all right, and what he was best at, if you'll pardon the use of a word that is currently overworked, was intimidation.

He intimidated pitchers. Get him out twice, make him look bad on that fast ball up and in, but look out if a pitch slipped just a hair.

You wouldn't get touched for a lazy 340-foot home run into the second row. You were more apt to be creased with a drive that would wake you up sweating at 3 a.m. for the rest of the summer and maybe the summers to follow. You didn't see a Mantle home run so much as you heard it.

His most famous homer was the one they measured at 565 feet in Griffith Stadium, Washington, off Chuck Stobbs. There was also the one that came within 10 feet of going out of Yankee Stadium, striking the facade that overhung the third deck,

I saw Mantle hit three home runs in the 1960 World Series, the first one I ever covered and the one with the most exciting finish.

Mantle, batting right-handed, hit two homers in the second game at Forbes Field, one 450 feet to left center and the other 478 feet to right center. In the fourth game, at Yankee Stadium, he hit one 430 feet to right center.

Mantle's ability always brought out superlatives. He hit nine spring training homers at the age of 19 and the writers called him another DiMaggio.

Having been at a spring training or two, I know the art of over-rating young players is not confined to Boston, but this time the journalists had the genuine article.

Mantle didn't get to be a folk hero in New York until late. Even when he was hitting the homers and winning most valuable player awards he was booed. Fans wanted a home run every time from their superman.

And Mantle wanted a home run every time, too. When he struck out, he slung bats, shattered water coolers, kicked cement posts.

Ted Williams never thought Mantle made the most of his tremendous talents. "I can't classify him as a good hitter," Ted once said, "He should be able to run .300."

Toward the end he was a somewhat pathetic figure as a player, not nearly as bad as the last two seasons of Willie Mays, but bad enough.

Still, there were good times, times when everything clicked again and the ball went 400 feet into somebody's souvenir case.

"I never had goose pimples in my life until the day I saw Mick limp up to bat and hit a home run," said second baseman Bobby Richardson.

When a ballplayer can affect another one that way, I guess all those strikeouts don't matter much.

Uncaught in the draft

January 31, 1974—I've never seen my friend Forbush so agitated as he was the other night at the bowling alley.

He missed a dozen single-pin spares and couldn't seem to concentrate on his game.

On the way home, after he'd gone through a red light and nearly hit two kids on bicycles, I asked Forbush what was bothering him.

"You've been my friend for a long time," he said. "I can trust you. It's my son, the one in college."

Oh oh, I thought. Drugs. The kid seemed to be such a straight arrow. Good student, a credit to his parents. Well, you never can tell. They say parents are the last to know.

"Where did you find the stuff?" I asked, "Under the mattress?"

"What stuff?" asked Forbush.

"Well, you know. The funny cigarettes, the pills, the needles."

Forbush pulled the car to the side of the road.

"Whadya talkin' about? It's not drugs. This is really serious."

"What could be more serious than drugs?" I asked.

"I . . . I . . . I . . . don't quite know how to say it," Forbush stammered, leaning against the steering wheel in anguish.

"Your secret is safe with me," I said, patting him on the shoulder for encouragement.

Forbush looked at me. "It's . . . it's . . . my son hasn't been drafted by anybody," he blurted out. "The NFL, the NL, the AL, the WFL, the WTT, the NHL, the WHA, the NASL—every athlete in the country has been picked and my son isn't even on a free agent list."

Sobs racked Forbush's body and he seemed exhausted by the effort of releasing the awful news. Gradually, however, he calmed down and was able to talk about the tragedy.

He said that his son was the only male at school not contacted, except for a 52-year-old World War II vet back for some special courses.

"Even the veteran got a feeler until the pros found out he had an old leg wound," said Forbush. "A four-foot-three exchange student from Thailand signed a two-year, no-cut pro fencing contract. But my boy has been ignored."

Forbush knows that when the newspapers get hold of the information they'll splash it all over the sports pages.

"I'll be the laughing stock of the office," he said. "The other kids at college know about it already, of course. My son wears a false moustache and dark glasses and never leaves his room except for classes."

I told Forbush I didn't realize his son was an athlete.

"Sure he is. He was a halfback on the jayvee football team, 158 pounds but lightning fast. The coach had something against him, but anybody who knows football knew he should have been playing.

"You've seen him in the summers playing kick-the-can in the street. You can tell he has natural soccer ability. But we never had one scout come to take us out to dinner."

I mentioned that I hadn't seen his son play sports since he set a town record for strikeouts in Little League.

"Then you remember the terrific natural swing he had," said the distraught father. "But he hasn't got a nibble in baseball either. If they could only see him throw a snowball, they'd be knocking down the doors to sign him."

I almost hesitated to ask about basketball.

"What a floor general," exclaimed Forbush. "He averaged 7.5 points a game for his fraternity team."

How big is he?

"Five-eight, but quick as a hiccup. You mean to tell me Chamberlain couldn't use him on the Conquistadors? Who's kidding who?"

Forbush thought his son had broken the barrier last week when a lawyer called, but it had something to do with an accident last summer, when the boy totaled the Mustang.

"Sure, he'll probably complete his studies and become a brain surgeon," said Forbush, "but what good is that. This will leave a scar he'll have to live with forever. And it's a social disgrace for us."

It was then I had my brainstorm.

"Your boy can still be a pro athlete," I told Forbush. "Here's what you do. Borrow five million dollars, start a new league and draft him No. 1."

He was ecstatic. "You've got it. I'll get to the bank first thing in the morning."

Forbush wanted to make me president of his new league, but I told him, no, I wasn't looking for any personal glory. Just helping a friend out of trouble was reward enough.

The short and the tall

March 28, 1974—SALISBURY, N.C.—They played an experimental basketball game during the NCAA finals in Greensboro last week, using a basket that was 11 feet 6 inches from the floor.

The game, as expected, was terrible, partly because the teams—Davidson and Wake Forest–weren't very good, but mostly because the added height threw the shooters off.

But the most interesting bit of trivia to emerge was not that the players disliked the experiment. The intriguing information was the fact that the basket has been 10 feet from the floor all these years, simply because that was the height of the molding when Dr. James Naismith got his inspiration to keep students occupied on a rainy day.

Dr. Naismith needed something to nail the peach basket to, something wooden, something that would hold. There was the molding. Whap, whap, whap, whap, the basket was up.

There is, therefore, no directive from on high that requires the basket to be ten feet from the floor. The distance came, not as a result of an extensive survey or from trial and error but through mere chance.

And even though players are a foot taller than they were when Dr. Naismith was double dribbling his way through downtown Springfield, and even though today's athlete can jump 12 feet in the air, the basket remains the same height.

There isn't likely to be a change either, which set me to wonder what the game would be like if the rule makers offered the same resistance to other portions of the original game.

Here's the potential broadcast:

"Good evening, ladies and gentlemen. Welcome to the big game between UCLA and North Carolina State. The start of this crucial clash is only ten minutes away and right now you can see the stepladders being wheeled into place alongside each basket.

"The ladders have the usual five steps and tonight are festooned with the colors from both schools.

"Janitors from UCLA and North Carolina State will man these ladders of course, having acquired the prestigious job through civil service.

"Both men have a simple but important task, namely to climb the ladder and retrieve the ball from the basket after each goal.

"The peach baskets are made of the finest Georgia pine, tapered nicely from 11 inches circumference at the top to eight at the bottom.

"The bottom of the basket is solid oak to prevent a repetition of the wild happening of the semifinal when the ball actually went completely through the hoop and on to a startled participant's head below.

"Scattered radicals among the coaching fraternity have suggested that there is no reason for having a basket bottom.

"'Why not simply let the ball fall through?' asked one coach, who insists on anonymity for fear he will lose his job.

"The obvious answer, of course, is that high schools and colleges would then be stuck with surplus stepladders. But beyond that, it would be difficult to explain the decision to custodians for whom the job is a fringe benefit not to be sneezed at.

"There have been other rule changes suggested. A number of coaches want the double dribble eliminated, and have tried experimental games using that restriction.

"This has resulted in such high scores as 24-20, 22-18 and the like. Basketball is not meant to be a racehorse game, so it is doubtful you will ever see the double dribble disappear, or, for that matter, a relaxation of the rules to permit players to use one hand at a time.

"A few coaches have suggested that guards be allowed over midcourt, but this has also been scoffed at. Guards have a definite job on the court, namely defense, and it is hardly likely they will be allowed to mix in with their own forwards.

"Another idea whose time has not yet come is to allow the player fouled to take the free throw. This penalizes the team which has worked long hours training one man to shoot all the foul shots, and it is difficult to visualize complete novices at the line.

"Well the game is about to begin. The crowd is at a fever pitch, the players are adjusting their knee guards, and for those who are keeping score out there at home, keep in mind that UCLA is shirts and North Carolina State is skins."

Hey, Devil, let's play ball

April 13, 1974—If the Devil knocked on my door tomorrow and said I'd won his lottery and was therefore entitled to one wish—nothing as big as eliminating poverty or war or bigotry, but some personal little whim—I know what I'd ask for.

"Make me 12 years old again for a month in the spring," I'd say. "Give me a ball and a bat and make it the way it was when the greatest man in the whole wide world was Henry Louis Gehrig of the New York Yankees."

Crazy? Well listen. I'm middle-aged and no longer look like Cary Grant and like everyone else I have a feeling the country's going to hell in a locomotive.

And I can remember what it was like to be 12 years old with the smell of spring all around, the ground still wet and kind of mushy, but not too soft to begin playing baseball.

It's a pleasant memory.

Sure, I had a vague realization that there wasn't a pile of money around the house, that there were problems, that there was hash for dinner a lot and I don't recall anybody being wild over hash.

But those were grownup problems. My worry was whether there'd be enough guys for baseball.

Not Little League. That doesn't start until school is over and is big business. Better for a boy than knocking over a drug store, but still big business.

The baseball I mean is pickup baseball, with kids who were really interested, who aren't around just for a uniform or because their parents think it would be good for them.

Without meaning to sound like an old fogey sitting on the veranda whittling whistles, there was a phenomenon then that seems to have vanished from the American scene, at least around my neighborhood.

When a kid went to find out if another kid wanted to play hit-the-bat or something, he didn't ring a doorbell.

He approached to about 10 feet of the other kid's house and yelled.

"Staaaber." (All the kids had weird nicknames.) If there was no response, he'd yell again.

"Staaaber."

Either Stabber would show, or his mother would yell from an upstairs window that Stabber had to beat rugs and wouldn't be out for an hour.

Only seven or eight guys were needed for a game, as long as one of them had a bat and ball. You didn't need umpires or managers or scorekeepers or even bases. Just an empty lot and play until dark and then go home to get bawled out for being late for supper.

I don't know if 12-year-olds play hit-the-bat anymore, but it was big then. The perfect throw from left field that rolled right to the bat but then hopped over it may have been my first realization that life is unfair.

It wasn't just the playing of a game that was fun. It was also the simple fact of being out there, released from the bondage of winter. You got a sense of accomplishment from picking up a throw on the short hop at first base and an indescribable feeling that ran up your arms and across your shoulders when you timed a pitch right and lined it to right field.

Look out, Lou Gehrig, there's a phenom growing up in Westfield, Mass.

This was small-town, middle-class America. Maybe in the city it was different.

I guess there isn't as much pickup baseball any more, what with Little League, and the decline of baseball as a boyhood pleasure. It's spring now, yet I see more street hockey games and basketball shoot-outs than baseball games.

But once in awhile I come across a pickup game, with kids in sneakers and jeans and a motley collection of shirts. They seem to be having fun, although often appear to get more delight out of fighting among one another than they do from the game.

"You didn't touch the base." "You can't wind up like that." "You batted out of turn."

Possibly it's a sign of the times, the influence of television, or maybe we argued, too, and time has clouded that over.

Well, you can't go home again, etc., etc. It's more interesting as an adult (pause for chortle). Certainly spending $40 a week for groceries is much more fun than hit-the-bat.

But listen, Devil, I'll be around the house for most of tomorrow. Just drop by and yell "Fitz" and I'll come out.

If I don't have to clean the cellar.

A fat hit? No, never!

June 13, 1974—I've been depressed ever since I read the remark, tucked away in Joe Concannon's advance story on the National Open, which starts today at Winged Foot in Mamaroneck, N.Y.

The quote is from Jack Nicklaus and goes this way:

"I hit the ball fat," said Nicklaus, speaking of his tee shot on the 16th hole on his final round of the Masters last April. "And it suddenly hit me. I never hit a fat ball in my life before. I said, am I getting old?"

Can you believe it? How many golf balls has Jack Nicklaus hit–20 million maybe, and until that steamy afternoon at Augusta, he'd never hit one fat. Never.

Not flubbed it, or topped it or scuffed it or hooked or sliced it. Hit it fat.

Unless you play the game with a devotion that borders on religion you may not even know what the term "hitting a ball fat" means.

It means . . . well, damn it . . . it's when you . . . well, it's not exactly that, either. Hitting a golf ball fat is hard to describe, but when it happens, you know it, and so will those playing with you.

"Hit that one a little fat, huh?" the wise guy who has just knocked his own shot on the green is apt to say.

It all has to do with a too-big divot, a bigger swing than usual and the vague feeling that a lot of effort has been expended to send the ball very little distance.

It's as though you swung at a golf ball but hit a pillow.

Getting back to Nicklaus, he has become a likeable young man over the last few years, dropping his cold image for a warm, pleasant personality, and even though he still hovers over a putt 'til eternity freezes, he is a most admirable athlete.

And now this. Now he has to spoil it all by telling the world he has hit exactly one (1) fat shot in his life. There are golfers I know who average a fat shot a hole and still think they're having a helluva day.

How does he think the average golfer is going to feel after reading how Nicklaus worried he was getting old because of one miss-hit shot.

After giving the matter a great deal of thought, I've come to the conclusion that Nicklaus simply doesn't want to remember other fat shots in his career.

Everybody has to block out the bad times and concentrate on the good ones, or where will the old confidence be?

Therefore, Jack has conveniently dismissed the fat shots in his past and would like them permanently expunged, thrown down the memory hole into the eternal fires.

Sorry Jack, it won't work, not in free, democratic America. You can dodge and jump and swivel-hip, but the past will eventually trip you up.

After checking with various early acquaintances and relatives back in Columbus, I've come up with three additional documented incidences of Nicklaus hitting fat shots.

One occurred when he was eight years old and using a borrowed set of clubs much too long for him. On a par three hole, he caught a five iron fat, hitting it only 135 yards.

Young Jack turned to his father and asked, "Dad, am I getting old?" But his father calmed the prodigy down and play continued without incident.

Another fat shot came during his sophomore year at Ohio State. Nicklaus, who was much beefier than he is now, was hitting a seven-iron approach during a triangular match with Michigan and Purdue. Just as he went into his back swing, someone said: "Woody Hayes wants you to go out for football, Bear." The result–fat shot.

The final happening was a few years ago when Jack asked for a nine iron but was given a six instead by his caddy. Nicklaus hit the six iron fat, but because the shot called for a nine iron, the result was perfect—two feet from the cup and an easy birdie.

Nicklaus never let on that he had been handed the wrong club, sportsman that he is, and retains the same caddy even today, who walks around with printed instructions: "Loop at the bottom means six, loop at the top means nine."

So have a good Open, Jack. Hit 'em straight and true. But when it looks as though you have the thing locked up, hit one fat for all us guys out here.

Sports isn't fun anymore

July 11, 1974—Every day lately when I arrive at the office my conscience calls a quick conference.

"Listen," it says, "you gotta sit down and write something profound and illuminating about the pro football dispute. Discuss the issues. Take a stand. Sports fans want to know how an expert feels."

And I answer, "Okay, conscience. Today's the day. Let me at that typewriter."

But after a few hours of glaring at a blank sheet of paper, after three Cokes, four cups of coffee and nuisance visits to every desk on the second floor, I write some fluff about elves or mechanical catchers or why Rico Petrocelli should have bunted the tying run to second in the ninth.

Then I go home, vaguely dissatisfied that I'm not doing my job.

And that gets me to the point of this essay. What is my job? What did I sign on for when I passed up the chance to become ambassador of Lichtenstein and went instead into sports writing?

Whatever I thought lay ahead in those dear days beyond recall, it wasn't what now confronts me and my peers daily under the guise of sport. Strike threats, contract jumping, players saying "see my lawyer" and agents promising "I'll get you a million, kid," expansion boondoggling, tax shelters, pampered athletes, head-in-the-sand executives.

And hanging like an evil cloud above all this, the pervading, sickeningly sweet smell of—whisper it—money.

Nope, that's not what I bargained for when I turned my back on the opportunity to become head surgeon at Mass. General and headed for the nearest press box.

I opted for entertainment, the boxed-in drama of the stadium and the locker room. I headed for the toy department of the newspaper because that was where the fun and freedom seemed to be, in juxtaposition to a real world filled with bad news.

Fires, elections, trials, wars, campaigns, strikes—those are the meat and potatoes of a newspaper. Fine. Let somebody else cover them.

I'd write for the odd hour when the citizens wanted to read something else, something that didn't matter and yet really did, because all the pages of a paper can't dwell on important stuff 24 hours a day, 365 days a year.

But now the big issues in sport are the same as the big issues anywhere. Now it isn't who will finish first, but which side will file for an injunction. The stories describe picket lines, not defensive lines. When you talk about the running long jump, you're apt to mean the guy who leaped from the Toronto Maple Leafs to the Vancouver Blazers.

I exaggerate, of course. It isn't all that way, but "the big issues" are all around, nibbling at the cabbage patch.

Somebody should have warned me. Maybe I'd have said, well, if that's what's ahead, make out a transfer. I'll cover the strike at the shipyard, the busing controversy, the slum lords, all of life's inequities.

If I was going to do it, do it where it counted.

Who was responsible for raining on my parade? Who kicked some of the fun out the back door and let reality crawl through the cellar window?

Was it television, with its capacity for overkill? Or did pro sports start to become just another of the world's con games when expansion and spin-off leagues not only lowered the standard of excellence but also poured such a cornucopia of names at us that no one could keep up with it all?

But, then, maybe pro sports haven't crumbled at all. Maybe it's all better than ever—big league basketball in New Orleans and team tennis and King Corcoran throwing footballs for the Philadelphia Bell.

Maybe it's better than ever and I'm simply a stuffy reactionary banging a noiseless drum for the St. Louis Browns and Fort Wayne Pistons.

Okay, conscience. I'll comment on the football dispute. The players have legitimate grievances, but their bleating about personal freedom and the right to do whatever they damn well please leaves me slightly nauseous.

Management has its points, too, but also has an inability to find the word compromise in the dictionary, plus a talent for waiting until the barn burns down before yelling "fire".

How's that, conscience? The players are right. Management is right. Is that wishy-washy enough?

What I truly feel, though, is that the whole business brings one more touch of gray to a canvas once bright and filled with color.

And now, if you'll excuse me, I have to begin research for tomorrow's essay, an analysis of the effects the Taft-Hartley Act had on the infield fly rule.

In a word, he was awful

SPECTATOR—"What's his handicap, 25?"
CADDY—"At least."

August 1, 1974—SUTTON—He was under more apple trees than Isaac Newton. His drives would have cleared Pleasant Valley of all wildlife within a week. If you walked down the fairway, chances are you never would have caught a glimpse of the man who might be our next president.

Gerald R. Ford, Vice President of the United States, did not have what would be called a vintage afternoon at Pleasant Valley yesterday.

If performance in public office is in inverse ratio to performance on sun-swept links, the country will be in marvelous hands if Ford takes over.

He was, in a word, awful. The report was that he is a 16-handicapper at Burning Tree in Washington. If so, the computer at Burning Tree needs a new tube.

There is, of course, the possibility that Mr. Ford simply had a bad day. It happens to the best of us. He didn't get into Washington from California until 5:30 Wednesday morning.

This gave him little sleep before departing for the Worcester Airport. He could well have been suffering from jet lag.

Ford arrived at Pleasant Valley about five after one, just as reporters were wondering if he were going to pull a Richie Allen and not show up at all.

The vice president was greeted with large applause at the front entrance. "There's Gerry," gushed a lady. "Please let me see him."

He went immediately to the locker room to change into a gold shirt, brown checked pants and what appeared to be Hush Puppy golf shoes.

Bob Menne, the pro from Gardner, inadvertently walked into Ford's dressing area, and was confronted by drawn pistols. Menne beat a hasty retreat.

Before teeing off, Ford hit a bucket of balls at the practice area. His swing was deliberate, with a slow backswing.

"Nobody can get in trouble," Bobby Jones once said, "with a too-slow back-swing."

Bobby Jones never saw Gerry Ford hit a golf ball.

Ford was in a foursome that included pro Dave Stockton, Denver industrialist Richard Hanselman (a Sampsonite veep) and majority whip Thomas P. (Tip) O'Neill from Cambridge.

Tip has two l's in his last name, a long cigar in his mouth and 21 clubs in his bag. He had eight woods, so help me, and 13 irons, and during the course of a long afternoon, had plenty of occasion to use them all.

Twenty-one clubs are seven more than the rules allow, of course. It's lucky Tip didn't shoot a 68, because he would have been disqualified.

As a matter of fact, Tip did shoot 68. It occurred somewhere around the 12th hole.

As Ford left the practice tee to begin what was to be an ordeal, radio newsmen crowded around his cart. Ford put them off, saying he'd answer questions when the golf was finished.

One radio man persisted.

"Mr. Vice-President," he said tactfully, "do you think President Nixon will be impeached?"

Ford stared, didn't answer, and the cart pulled away.

"They should shoot all reporters," said a spectator.

"They're what's wrong with this country," said another.

"They won't let up. They won't let a guy relax and enjoy a game of golf," said a third.

I suppressed a retort having to do with who was paying for this game of golf. I also hid my note pad and tried to look as though I'd just come along to see the fun.

Ford, incidentally, was using Titleist golf balls, X-rayed by a machine brought in from Ft. Devens. Tests showed none of the balls had dynamite in them, a fact Ford verified with his performance.

It would be whipping a dead donkey to describe Ford's round, but some of the more memorable moments should be recorded for posterity.

His opening shot, on a par three 135-yarder, screamed into a stand of trees to the left of the green, winding up a foot from the base of a young and suddenly trembling oak.

It was a perfect spot for an Agnew ricochet job off somebody's brow, but Ford smashed it out cleanly—over the green, over an adjacent trap, and into some rough. The next shot was weak and the next was in his pocket.

And so it went. The drive on No. 2 was 150 yards up and 30 yards out. It was into the pocket again on three after a drive out of bounds and a Marco Polo adventure in a sand trap. Stockton gave a lesson on the grip about then, to be followed by Ford's only par on the par five fourth.

Ford's drive on fifth was monstrous. His main problem was that he didn't know what his main problem was. A hook here, a slice there, a push here, a top there. If variety is the spice of life, Gerald R. Ford never had more fun.

On the eighth, Ford hit a drive dead right. It was a shot that Willie Hoppe would have loved—at least eight-cushions. It hit more trees than a lumberjack.

"Geeze," said a kid sitting on the adjacent hillside. "Spiro was never that bad."

Oh, yes, he was.

The CCNY homecoming

September 8, 1974—Irv Dambrot, Al Roth, Ed Roman, Ed Warner, Floyd Layne.

The names are from another generation, out of yellowed, agate-type box scores almost 24 years old, and anyone who recognizes them has a long memory indeed.

But I remember the names. Oh, how I remember. These five comprised the UCLA of my day. They were starters for the CCNY basketball team that in 1950 won both the NIT and the NCAA championships, something never done before or since.

I saw some of those tournament games, and boy, those guys played basketball the way we loved it, slick New York basketball at its best—the give and go, movement stuff the Knicks play even today.

But less than a year after they took New York by storm, these five were in disgrace—guilty of accepting bribes to shave points and throw games.

It was the first college basketball scandal—there would be others—and it rocked a sports-loving public that had equated college athletics with purity, motherhood and fair play.

"The age of innocence was over," wrote a columnist at the time, and it has never returned.

I drag this painful memory out of college basketball's closet only because the other day I read a "where-are-they-now" note about the CCNY team.

Dambrot is now Dr. Irwin Dambrot, a dentist in Queens; Al Roth is a realtor in New Jersey; Ed Warner (probably the best player from that team), a New York recreational worker and Ed Roman a psychologist for the New York Board of Education.

And Layne? That's the biggest success story of all. This week Floyd Layne, expelled from CCNY 23 years ago for accepting $3000 in bribes for his part in rigging three games (one was a loss to Boston College), was named basketball coach at CCNY.

"That stigma will remain with him the rest of his life," the old coach said. "He can't do anything about it."

Holman is right. Even if the kids of today know nothing of those dark days, there'll always be someone—"usually a newsman," says Layne—to bring up Feb. 27, 1951, when two detectives picked Layne up on the CCNY campus.

He led them to his home in the Bronx, where he had hidden $2500 in a soiled handkerchief buried in the dirt of a flowerpot.

After Layne's arrest, CCNY called off its last two games. When basketball resumed two years later, it was small-time gymnasium stuff, and that's the way it's been ever since.

The scandal spread. Players for Manhattan, LIU, Toledo and Bradley were involved. Kentucky coach Adolph Rupp blamed it all on coaches and authorities at Eastern schools.

"Take basketball back to the campus as we've done at Kentucky," he said.

Not long afterward, several former Kentucky players, among them Alex Groza, Ralph Beard and Bill Spivey, were implicated in a fix that had occurred when they were undergraduates.

"We were kids who made a mistake and went on to pay a heavy price over the next 20 years," Layne said yesterday.

"I could have gone into a shell, I suppose. But I directed my energies into regrouping, into getting another start in life. Bitter? Reporters always ask me that. I don't know, maybe they want to portray me as a bitter person. But there wasn't time for that."

After some time in the army, Layne played for the Globetrotters, hoping for a shot with the NBA. But the NBA's memory was forever. It never forgave Layne, or Warner or Spivey or Sherman White—all of whom might have been professional stars.

CCNY had more compassion. Layne returned to school, graduating in 1957. He became a community director, working with kids. One was a skinny little guy named Nate Archibald.

"Floyd Layne," said Archibald recently, "was responsible for keeping me off the streets."

So Layne is back where it all started, back to the scene of his greatest triumphs and his day of infamy.

He was a kid who made a mistake, and 23 years later, he's working to keep other kids from making the same sort of mistake.

Layne will never be able to escape the past, but when people ask him about it, they're not being vindictive. It's their way of saying "you've come a long way coach."

Thank you, Gus Suhr

November 10, 1974—I get dozens of letters asking how I became a sportswriter. Well, not that many. Two a year, maybe. Listen, in my circles, that's a lot.

Anyway, it becomes quickly apparent that the letter writer isn't as much interested in how I got into this business as in how he or she can break in.

The budding journalist seems to be seeking a magic formula that will lead to the great press boxes of our land, a bagful of verbs, adjectives, nouns, clichés and batting averages that will end up in a toy department by line.

Well, most sportswriters will tell you there was no planning involved, that they fell into the profession by mistake—a wrong road taken on the way to a promising career as a hubcap stealer or The Prince of Wales.

But looking back, I suppose there were early indications that I was headed for a life in the box score jungle, a far-off land teeming with the ferocious sabre-toothed fan, the terrifying typographical error, the mysterious three paragraphed misquote and the dreaded collar-tightening deadline.

So, if there are young souls out there searching for guideposts to a career as a sporting journalist, perhaps these remembrances of things past will be of some help.

For example, there was the Gus Suhr fetish. Gus Suhr was a first baseman for the Pittsburgh Pirates when I was a youth, and for some reason The Springfield Union frequently ran a large cartoon of him. Gus had a big smile and looked like a nice guy, so because of him I began to paste sports photos in scrapbooks.

The cartoons always had a central face, and around it, little vignettes of the subject's life. For instance, to the left of Gus Suhr's ear would be a tiny table with a lot of people around it and the caption: "Gus was one of 12 children." And above Suhr's shoulder, a tiny man in basketball shorts and knee guards and the caption: "Gus was all-city three straight years at Aliquippa [Pa.] High."

This collection continued for years and then one day, looking through the scrapbooks, I realized how sick I was of smiling Gus Suhr and never cut out another cartoon.

And there was the business of picking up baseball games from other cities on the radio. No city was too far away, this being before the West Coast made the majors. KDKA, Pittsburgh; WCAU, Philadelphia; KMOX, St. Louis; and what was it, WJR—in Detroit, all within reach of a teen-age dialing expert with the magic fingers of Jimmy Valentine.

I gave the dial-twisting up after almost driving off the road into Quincy Bay one night while trying to pick up the Tigers game. Last July, I think it was.

Then there were the football contests. The Springfield Daily News ran one every week—10 games, with the entrant picking the most winners getting two tickets to one of the New England biggies—Colgate vs. Yale or Tufts vs. Williams.

I always entered, and once got nine out of ten, but that week the winner had 10 of 10, including a pick of a tie game and exact scores on three others. I knew then there was no Santa Claus.

But the Springfield contest was small stuff to the one run by the New York Daily News. Pick 15 games and if you won you got $1000. I sent in a completed blank every day, but so did 87 million others, and the winner was always somebody from Far Rockaway or Queens.

It was while involved with the New York Daily News, incidentally, that I found out about love nests and gang murders.

Fantasizing might also have been an early sign of the incipient sportswriter. I was always on the mound at Yankee Stadium—never Fenway—facing the dread Gehrig. In my grammar school days, I'd kill a dull 10 minutes at Sunday Mass dreaming about the bounce pass I'd throw to set up the winning basket for Westfield High against Holyoke.

I finally got to high school and made both the basketball team and the bounce pass, but the pass was always intercepted.

Even today, if I'm not careful, I slip into the bounce-pass reverie at church, usually at collection time.

There were other indications, such as listening to Notre Dame games while lying flat on my back in the living room and spiraling a football into the air.

You'll never amount to anything doing that, my mother told me, and ha-ha, Mom, look at what a big man I am today.

And there was playing dice baseball when other kids were building erector sets, or reading Baseball Joe Matson books when others were buried in Buck Rogers adventures.

So maybe you are what you eat, after all. As the child is bent so goes the man.

My advice then, to all wondering how to become sportswriters, is this: go to the nearest newsstand immediately and buy all the papers with a photo of Gus Suhr in them.

It's a start.

Dream over for Loudd

December 29, 1974—For Rommie Loudd, a man who had a dream of becoming a powerful force in professional football, life has become a screaming, holes-in-the-pockets nightmare.

Loudd, a former pro linebacker, was coaching the New Bedford Sweepers in 1966 when the Patriots made him an assistant to Mike Holovak.

"Patriots Name Negro Coach" said the Globe headline, the word "Negro" being not quite on its way out. Loudd was a breakthrough into an all-white AFL world.

A couple of years later, Loudd made more history. The Patriots named him director of player personnel, the first black to be part of a pro team's front office.

Time skittered along and Loudd cast his eye on a more distant sparrow. Blacks constituted half of the NFL players, yet no black ran a football team. Loudd made that his goal.

"Personally, I know that if I'm granted a franchise, I can do the job," he said. "I've done it all in this game. I've played. I've coached. I've scouted. I've gone through the growing pains of a new stadium."

Loudd picked Orlando, Fla., as the territory—one of the fastest growing areas in the United States. There were stops and starts and two paces forward and three back, but he kept struggling.

A year ago this big, handsome and powerful looking man was at the Super Bowl in Houston, meeting people and telling them that no, he wasn't Jimmy Brown even though there might be some resemblance, that he was Rommie Loudd, and that things were looking good for his franchise in Orlando.

But things began looking bad, and pretty soon the NFL awarded, for a paltry $16 million, an expansion franchise to Tampa, 80 miles down the road.

Then, just as it seemed Rommie Loudd would have to put his dream into the "out" file, up popped a pie-in-the-sky man named Gary Davidson, selling a toy called World Football League. Wind it up and it would head straight to bankruptcy court.

There was a franchise available, one that had started in Washington, been shipped by slow freight to Norfolk and then been banished from that Virginia city on a vagrancy rap.

Loudd met a man named Dave Williams, about 35 years old, whose "daddy" as they say in Spanish moss country, owned several Holiday Inns in the Orlando area.

Williams agreed to provide the capital—$3.6 million was the accepted figure—and Loudd was named managing general partner, the same title Al Davis has in Oakland. He was to run the show.

What happened after that, like any story of trickery, deceit and failure, has many sides. Loudd had to dish out money to expand the stadium, which, because of construction, was about as easy to get to as Fort Knox.

There were pollution law hang-ups, plus high ticket prices for an unknown product.

Yet, 14,000 came out for the opener and for a game against Jacksonville, there were 25,000.

Then came the fiasco in Atlanta. One version says that Loudd went up there without Williams's knowledge in an attempt to get backing to move the franchise. He got false promises and Williams, when he read the papers, pulled out financial support.

The other version, as told by Loudd's lawyer Robert Deutsch, is that Rommie went up there seeking money because Williams had dropped out after investing $890,000 of the promised $3.6 million.

After the Atlanta debacle, Orlando no longer thought highly of the Florida Blazers or their managing general partner.

Without a sugar daddy, bills piled up. Creditors became more numerous than ticketholders. A million dollar check, displayed on television as a franchise-saver, turned out to be made of green cheese. The Blazers, even though they made the WFL final, weren't paid for the final eight weeks.

"All the promised money," said an Orlando newsman, "came from either bank robbers or car thieves."

Last Monday, Loudd was arrested on a charge of embezzling state tax money, which in reality is a charge that he failed to pay the state sales tax out of gate receipts.

"For two years," said Deutsch, "Rommie worked like a dog, day and night, seven days a week to get a pro team going in Orlando."

As a managing general partner, he's responsible for the dozens of suits pending, and for bills totaling as much as a million and half.

Said an Orlando sportswriter: "He was like a kid who wanted an electric train and couldn't afford it, only he went out and bought one anyway."

4

1975

Talk about busted plays!

January 6, 1975—Around 7 o'clock Sunday morning, the trembling began. Smedley recognized the symptoms immediately—the start of football withdrawal.

Heaven knows he'd prepared the best he could for this wretched, mind-warping malady that struck every first Sunday in January, when there was no football on television.

He'd wrapped himself in blankets, the way it said to do in the manual on how to kick the football habit. There was a pot of chicken soup on the stove, and he'd lit the candles on either side of his 8 by 10 glossy of Pete Rozelle.

Now all Smedley could do was belly it out. He knew that hiding in the closet or sleeping the day away would be impossible.

He'd tried that once and had a nightmare in which a judge who looked exactly like Joe Kapp kept pounding Smedley's head with a gavel, chanting over and over: "No more football—ever."

No, he'd stay awake and show the world he could take it, that there was more to life than a game.

At 7:45, Smedley turned on the television set. Maybe one of the stations was running a pro highlight film.

He got four test patterns, some gospel singers and a man drawing arrows and wavy lines on a blackboard. Smedley brightened. Were they plays? There, wasn't that the Green Bay power sweep?

The man turned to the camera and began talking about stomach acidity.

Smedley snapped the set off in disgust. He felt alternately hot and cold now. This was worse than when he gave up cigarettes and at the end of the first week was found with his arm caught in a vending machine.

His wife came into the room.

"Want some bacon and eggs for breakfast?" she asked.

"Either shut up or talk football," he snarled. "How about Bart Starr getting that job?"

"Is he the one just moved in down the end of the street?" his wife asked.

Smedley glared, and his wife fled to the kitchen, weeping.

"She ought to know better," Smedley muttered. Maybe it would help if he looked over his collection of pro football bubblegum cards, Smedley thought, getting the shoe boxes down from the closet.

He was proud of his collection—the original New York Titans, Red Grange with his helmet on backwards, six different views of Joe Don Looney.

And a complete set of the 1958 New York Giants. Okay, so they lost to Baltimore in the playoff, they were still his favorite team.

Smedley rifled through the cards, ticking off the names even before he got to the picture—Huff, Gifford, Kyle Rote, Rosie Brown, old Charley Conerly, Jim Katcavage . . .

Wait a minute. His Katcavage was missing. He rummaged through the shoe boxes. Katcavage wasn't there. He ransacked the closet, tossing out boots, snowshoes, two cats and a bent umbrella, but no Katcavage.

Smedley broke down then, sobbing and shaking uncontrollably.

"There, there," consoled his wife. "Have some soup and I'll tell you what, let's play a game of electric football. I'll be the San Diego Padres and you can be the Celtics."

Smedley raced from the house, trying to get a grip on himself. He'd go to church, that's what he'd do, and find solace in the service.

But it was no use. He told the usher he'd lost his seat stub but always sat in section 12, on the 40-yard line. When the collection basket came around, he handed it off to a lady in the next pew, whispering "Run to daylight, O.J."

Everything reminded him of football. A row of candles resembled a team lining up to kick off. The hymn book looked like a game plan. The minister was George Allen.

Smedley stumbled home. Try television again. Maybe TV Guide was wrong, maybe there was a Broccoli Bowl they forgot about.

But TV Guide was right. There was only hockey, basketball, tennis, boxing and some superstars running through an obstacle course.

"I'll bet they couldn't climb that wall with a football under their arm," Smedley thought, ramming his fist through the picture tube.

He looked at his watch. One-hundred forty-seven hours until Super Bowl. Could he hang on?

"Let's play that electric game," Smedley said to his wife. "You kick off and I'll have Havlicek and Jo Jo back to receive."

He'd survive. He had to. The draft wasn't until Jan. 28.

Russell—the recalcitrant idol

Feburary 11, 1975—Hey, wait a minute, Russ, you don't have anything to say about it. It's not your Hall of Fame, it's basketball's.

If the people who run the building in Springfield want to immortalize you in a 10-foot high stained-glass window, that's their affair, not yours.

If they want to hang a plaque on the wall that says you're the greatest thing since dark bread, you can't get a court order demanding that they take it down.

If somebody wants to get up on the dais and read 20 minutes of flowery tribute to the man who changed the face of pro basketball, there's nothing you can do about it. Nothing, so be quiet and try to figure out why the team you coach can't win any games.

Hey, there's no law that says you have to be there for the induction ceremony.

You don't have to make any speeches or accept any scrolls or shake any hands or sign any autographs or be nice to one single soul, living or dead.

You can continue to make your living in a sport and at the same time kick it in the teeth, something you seem to be very good at.

People cheered you for a dozen years in Boston and you kicked them in the teeth when they wanted to honor you. You labeled them racists, 13,909 racists who merely wanted to let you know they loved the way you played basketball.

But the name Bill Russell belongs in the basketball Hall of Fame or the place isn't worthy to be called that.

Hopefully, the Hall of Fame trustees in Springfield won't take the "well, if he doesn't want to be in here, we don't want him" line.

An athlete makes a hall of fame for what he accomplished, in and for his game. His personality, his habits, his attitudes, his lifestyle, even his wishes shouldn't count.

What did he do between the white lines, the goal posts, the baskets? That's what counts.

Babe Ruth wenched and drank more than the adult population of Weehawken, N.J., but his habits didn't keep him out of Cooperstown. Nor did the viciousness and meanness of Ty Cobb.

If Lance Rentzel was twice as good a football player as he is, all the innuendos and suspensions wouldn't, or at least shouldn't, keep him from football's Hall of Fame, and the same goes for Duane Thomas.

And likewise Russell, despite his "hell no, I won't go" stance.

Most people have long ago given up trying to figure out No. 6. He is predictably unpredictable. The racism line he used about Boston hardly seems to apply in this case.

Seven black members of the old New York Renaissance team, plus the coach, are already in the Hall of Fame. Russell would be the first black from the NBA because he is the first one retired for five years who is worthy of the honor, with the possible exception of Sam Jones, who, like Russell, also just became eligible.

Super names such as Elgin Baylor or Wilt Chamberlain haven't been inactive for five years. Globetrotter greats Goose Tatum, Marques Haynes and Sweetwater Clifton aren't in the Hall of Fame and maybe they ought to be, but it's doubtful Russell is bothered by that.

WBZ's Jimmy Myers said Sunday night that Russell's uniform was draped over a white manikin in the Hall of Fame building. But director Lee Williams yesterday called that charge "irresponsible."

"It's not a manikin," said Williams, "it's a body form, with no face, and it's black."

Maybe the whole thing is an involved plot to get the Hall of Fame to compromise and have the induction cermonies by telephone, thus putting a few more dollars in the vault of Russell's secondary employer, Mother Bell.

Whatever the explanation, it is apparent that Russell, who once led the nation in rebounds, is now No. 1 in rudeness. They used to make his people sit in the back of the bus and now he won't even come in the front door.

But no matter. George C. Scott refused to show up and he got an Academy Award anyway. Marlon Brando wouldn't come out of his tepee but he still got an Oscar.

So it should be with Russell. And if he insists on boycotting the cermony, get Ron Watts to accept for him.

Bittersweet was the night

April 6, 1975—They could play basketball. Oh, once upon a time, how they could play the game, those middle-aged men tossing the ball around at the Worcester Auditorium the other night.

They had come out of high schools in the New York City area, most of them, to Holy Cross, a school that didn't—and still doesn't—have a home court.

They were playground wise, these kids, with a basketball sense. They knew what made the game click. Pass the ball and expect it back. Give and go. Bounce pass whenever possible. Move, move, with the ball, without the ball, but move. Expect the unexpected.

Holy Cross became a national power. The team was booked into the Boston Garden, to play Kentucky and Valparaiso and St. Louis and the other magic names of college basketball.

For the first time, sports fans in Boston saw that basketball could be more than clump and bump. They saw it could be a game of grace, of interaction and subterfuge, a game of intrigue and hidden subtleties, and they loved it.

Crowds of 10,000 at the Garden were common. Holy Cross won 27 and lost 3 in 1946-47 and captured the national championship.

From there to the middle '50s, the records were 26-4, 19-8, 27-4, 20-5, 24-4, 20-6, 26-2, 19-7, and 22-5.

Most of the players who began that string and many who kept it going got together the other night in a benefit game for the family of James Lonchiadis, a Shrewsbury policeman who had been murdered.

Tickets were five dollars a whack, but the dusty auditorium was filled, a tribute to the Lonchiadis family and also a tribute to nostalgia. There were young people there, but it was predominantly a middle-aged crowd, back for a last look through the album.

"If anybody's looking for nostalgia," said Bob Curran, captain of the 1947-48 team, "there are several pounds of it out here."

Others returning from the 1947 NCAA champions were Frank Oftring, George Kaftan, Bob McMullan, Ken Haggerty, Andy Laska, Matt Forman, manager Frank Dooley, Dermie O'Connell and a man named Cousy.

"I brought some sneakers," said O'Connell. "I hope Cooz comes up with a uniform. He can begin at size 40."

The gray-haired guys tried to act nonchalant in the warmup, tossing dreadful hook shots and two-handed sets, a basketball dinosaur that departed the earth about the same time as bobby socks, saddle shoes and Mairzy Doats.

Father Earle Markey, captain of the '52-'53 team, paused only briefly for conversation.

"I have to get my shooting in," he said. "I'm on the same unit with Togo."

Togo Palazzi, who co-captained the '53-'54 NIT champions with Ronnie Perry, has been hearing that talk for 25 years. He loves it. His idea of paradise would be to stand on top of a mountain with a basketball, shouting down at the world: "Who's first in a one-on-one game?"

Buster Sheary gave the pre-game pep talk, and that's a story in itself, because Sheary has not been around Holy Cross much since he resigned 20 years ago after a 155–36 record.

But these were his "kids," many of them anyway, so he was back. Sheary is a casting director's idea of a coach, a Dublin-faced tactician with a gift for both basketball and the nicely turned phrase.

He faced his team.

"Let's just pay attention," he barked. "Get a little bit organized. This is all in fun . . . (pause) . . . but if you lose, God help you. Frank (to Oftring), is your back okay? Dermie (to the well-fed O'Connell), you'll press. Now, we'll start off with the NCAA team. They ought to last a minute or so. We'll come in with the NIT guys and then we'll put in the third unit, the ones in some sort of shape."

It was determined that the game would not count in Palazzi's lifetime average and then the team charged—filtered might be a better word—onto the court to play a similar group of Assumption College alumni.

Nobody got hurt. There were some laughs. The game proved athletes' reflexes slow down when they hit 40, but the instincts are still there. Jack (The Shot) Foley, who is 35 and has a Rollie Fingers-type moustache, waxed at the ends, can still shoot. George Blaney, Tim Shea, Don Prohovich—they can still pass. Cousy can still see seven ways at once.

With seven seconds left and Assumption ahead by a point, Cousy slammed into Assumption's Herb Dyson.

"As I was falling down," said Dyson in an echo of complaints from 20 years of Cousy defenders, "I knew they'd never call it on him."

Dyson was right. "I was jobbed," was his post-game analysis.

Cousy made the game-tying free throw, and at the buzzer, a Keith Hochstein to Cousy to Blaney play gave HC the win as the crowd went wild.

It was a bittersweet evening, a remembrance of things past and at the same time another nudge from that old sneak-thief, time.

And for those who played the game, it was a brief and happy return to a period in their lives when nothing much mattered beyond next Tuesday's game.

About time I asked . . .

May 1, 1975—Questions I've always wanted to know the answer to, but was afraid to ask:

Why aren't there any dandelions in the Fenway Park outfield?

What does an NBA referee think about while he's standing at halfcourt during a timeout?

Why don't Cokes taste like they used to?

Is there a trick to winning a faceoff?

Why would it be so dumb if the shortstop were left-handed?

Is holding the ball on field goals exciting?

Will a Red Sox outfielder misjudge a fly ball because of the reflection off the new John Hancock Building?

Does a boxer who has been knocked down actually see stars?

What's it like to catch a marlin?

When Yaz moves to Scituate, will he give his back yard back to Tom Yawkey?

What's it like to ride a winner in the Kentucky Derby?

Whatever happened to Ralph (Tiger) Jones?

Is it true that opposing players put on their pants one leg at a time, or does an occasional superstar jump into both legs at once, off a table perhaps?

Who invented the turnstile?

What does it feel like to get hit on the elbow with a Nolan Ryan fastball?

Does Tommy Heinsohn practice making faces in a mirror at home?

Where do all the autographs go?

Would Johnny Wooden have made a good pro coach?

Has anybody actually watched a game from an obstructed seat?

Is a hockey player the only athlete who wears suspenders?

Has the peanut man in front of the Garden ever seen a game?

Does O. J. Simpson take out the garbage?

Would Abner Doubleday have been able to hit the slider?

Whatever happened to Ronnie Knox?

Will Larry O'Brien award an NBA expansion franchise to Hyannis Port?

Is Catfish Hunter sick of his nickname?

Did George Foreman take career-wrecking lessons from Denny McLain?
lines all mixed up?

Who sneaks into the composing room and gets my

Why don't more pro athletes smoke a pipe?

Did Gerry Ford ever get called for clipping?

Why don't they make a bat that doesn't break?

Where did the word "puck" come from?

Why don't the greyhounds catch on to the fact the rabbit isn't real?

Do baseball coaches order from a menu or just flash signs?

Do basketball players comb their hair during halftime?
Do outfielders still spit in their gloves?
When marathoners practice, are they bothered by dogs?
Do any pro athletes drive Chevies?
Has anybody ever been hit by a baseball while walking down Lansdowne Street, and if so, did the person sue?
Is Reggie Jackson an over-rated ball player?
Is Red Auerbach allowed to smoke cigars in the house?
What's Bill Walton really like?
Was George Gipp a good pool player?
When a baseball player comes home after a game, does his wife ask "how did you make out" or wait until he offers the information?
If Connie Mack were alive today, would Alex Johnson speak to him?
Is Tom Weiskopf really James Caan or is it the other way around?
What's it like at school for the child of an NBA ref?
Do circus tigers have bad breath?
How do you end a column like this?

They'll bow to this ref

May 6, 1975—For nigh on to 40 years now, I've watched basketball players stamp their feet and coaches throw tantrums over referees' decisions.

I've read forever and a day about inconsistency and poor judgment, and listened to the screeches of the multitude over what they considered inept officiating, which is to say, any officiating at all.

It's time, I feel, to end the complaining; time for positive action. Basketball is too sweet a game to be torn asunder by senseless bickering.

With this in mind, I put in a call the other day to the one individual with an unmatched reputation for calling them right. His number wasn't in the book, but I have a friend in the seminary. Here's the way my part of the conversation went:

Hello, God? Listen, I'm not disturbing anything, am I? Oh, good, just finishing confessions. Well, there's a problem down here—no, not a big one like whether to keep the designated hitter—but it's bothering a lot of people. You familiar with a game called basketball?

You know a little about it. Good, that's about average. That's right, five to a side. You probably know, then, that the rules are enforced by two men in striped shirts who blow whistles. Uh-huh. Mendy. That's right. I knew it would come back to You.

Anyway, the referees are having trouble. No matter what judgments they make, everyone gets angry. People get furious and turn purple. There's a devil of a time.

Excuse me, Lord, that slipped out, but You can see how agitated the situation has made me.

Have we tried the game without referees? You son of a gun, still the same old sense of humor.

Seriously, the reason I'm calling is to ask if You could possibly come down and work a couple of games until things quiet down. Wednesday and Friday were the nights I had in mind.

You bowl on Fridays, but Wednesday is free? Hey, that's great. We'll send You a round-trip ticket, first class, and . . . oh, You'll get here on Your own? I suppose you don't really need an airplane, at that.

The game is in Landover, Md. That's right, Landover. Just outside Washington. Who? No, he doesn't live there any more, but that's the general area.

While I've got You on the phone, God, I'd like to go over a few of the trouble areas.

First is the charging foul as opposed to the block. When the man with the ball goes toward the basket and is impeded by a defender, it is a blocking foul, unless the defender gets to the spot first, in which case it's a charge, except if the man doing the driving with the ball is a superstar, in which case it's never a charge.

Lord? You still there? I thought we were cut off for a minute. You're right, it sounds complicated, but somebody who made the world in six days should have no trouble telling the difference between a block and a charge.

Now, another problem has been the over-the-shoulder rebounding foul. If this is called on the visiting team, the crowd feels it was a valid and useful decision. But when a home player gets caught, there's hell to pay.

There I go again, but honestly, Lord, the noise would drive you to drink. Just a figure of speech, I didn't mean You.

And here's another headache. The two men in the pivot—the pivot, Lord, that's where the post men set picks for teammates cutting by and . . . what? I am speaking English.

Maybe I'd better skip the explanations. I'd send You some films, but there isn't time. You'll catch on fast enough once You get here.

Oh, I'd better warn You about the coaches. They can use some pretty bad language. You probably think You've heard it all, but there've been some new ones invented since You were here last.

Well, no, I don't think turning them into a pillar of salt would solve anything. I'd say first a warning, and then a plague on their houses.

Okay, so it's settled. Nice to have You aboard. Stay loose and have a good game and keep in mind: no harm, no foul.

You'll be working with Manny Sokol.

The best game ever!

This article was read into the CONGRESSIONAL RECORD *on October 22, 1975, as follows:*

Mr. Brooke. Mr. President, I was privileged to be Commissioner Bowie Kuhn's guest at the sixth game of the World Series played last night and early this morning at old Fenway Park in Boston.

The game truly had everything: suspense, nostalgia, emotion, and incomparable baseball.

One of our outstanding sportswriters, Ray Fitzgerald of the Boston Globe, called it "the best game ever" and suggested that we call the seventh game off and let the World Series stand at three games for the Cincinnati Reds and three games for the Boston Red Sox.

Well, Mr. President, Ray Fitzgerald has a point. But there must be a world champion. And with all due respect to the great Cincinnati Reds team, it must be the Boston Red Sox.

For, Mr. President, the Boston Red Sox are truly "the incredible team."

I ask unanimous consent that Ray Fitzgerald's article, "The Best Game Ever," be printed in the RECORD.

There being no objection, the article was ordered to be printed in the RECORD, as follows:

Call it off. Call the seventh game off. Let the World Series stand this way, three games for the Cincinnati Reds and three for the Boston Red Sox.

How can there be a topper for what went on last night and early this morning in a ballyard gone mad, madder and maddest while watching, well, the most exciting game of baseball I have ever seen.

But maybe my opinion doesn't count. I've only seen a thousand or so baseball games. Reds manager Sparky Anderson has been to a billion and he said when it was over, "I've never seen a better one."

It was a game with a hundred climaxes. Fred Lynn hit a three-run homer and the Red Sox were cruising. Easy stuff, take Luis Tiant out suggested the sages, and save him for the seventh game.

But then opportunities went sliding down the river—bases left loaded, two men on and no outs and no production, things like that, and you could feel it slipping away, into the batbag of the Big Red Machine.

And then the magic began to disappear from Luis Tiant's wand, that seemingly tireless right arm that had been snaking the baseball past the Reds for so many innings.

Snap, crackle and pop and there were the Reds ahead, 5-3, and King Tut's tomb couldn't have been more silent than Fenway Park as Tiant began the eighth.

Why he was allowed to start the inning was a mystery, because it was obvious he had tired badly in the seventh. Maybe Darrell Johnson wanted him to get a final Fenway ovation.

If so, it cost the Red Sox, because Cesar Geronimo hit Tiant's first pitch into the right field stands to make it 6-3.

And in the skyview seats, the sporting bards of America began typing the obituaries, like this:

"Death, as it must to all teams, came to the Boston Red Sox last night at 11:16 p.m. when Rawly Eastwick the 3d . . ."

Or,

"The powerful Cincinnati Reds, stretched to the limit by the tenacious Boston Red Sox, captured their first World Championship since . . ."

Or,

"Time ran out for the marvelous Luis Tiant tonight as . . ."

Ah, yes, there were deadlines to make, so why not get the story started, because Bernie Carbo was at the plate and barely able to get his bat on Eastwick's pitches.

With the count two and two, Carbo was about to let a pitch go past when suddenly he saw the ball clipping into the strike zone. Carbo chopped at it like a man cutting sugar cane, barely fouling it off. The patient was still breathing. But the 35,205 relatives were gathered at the bedside and saw no hope. It was all over, as the saying goes, but the shouting.

Ah, yes, the shouting. The screaming, the dancing, the ab-so-lute bedlam as Carbo hit the next pitch into the center field seats for the game-tying home run.

I sat in on the Bill Mazeroski home run that won the 1960 World Series for the Pirates, and that has always been, for me, No. 1 among great baseball games played under great pressure. Excitement pyramided in that one to where you didn't think there could possibly be any more.

Now the Mazeroski game is No. 2. Last night was a Picasso of a baseball game, a Beethoven symphony played on a patch of grass in Boston's Back Bay.

Here's the kind of game it was. The Globe's Bud Collins was assigned to do a piece on the game's hero. At the end of the 11th inning, he said, "I've already crossed off 19 heroes. Maybe they should play a tie-breaker, like tennis."

Or listen to Pete Rose, who said to Carlton Fisk in the 10th, "This is some kind of game, isn't it?" and later in the dressing room, "This was the greatest game in World Series history and I'm just proud to have played in it. If this ain't the National Pastime, tell me what is."

Rose videotapes each game so he can sit back and watch them later. He was a loser in this one, but he is the sort of competitor who can admire such things as Dwight Evans' catch off Joe Morgan in the 11th that saved the game.

Sparky Anderson called the catch "the greatest I've ever seen. You won't see them any better."

The drama piled up like cordwood. Lynn's titanic homer, the Reds' comeback, Lynn slumped against the fence after crashing into it trying for Ken Griffey's triple, the Carbo homer, the Reds escaping a bases-loaded none-out situation in the ninth, the Evans catch, and finally, Fisk's game-winning homer.

As Fisk came around the bases, fans poured out onto the field and he had to dodge them on his way home.

"I straight armed somebody and kicked 'em out of the way and touched every little white thing I saw," he said.

At 12:34 it was over, but the people stayed. John Kiley played "Give Me Some Men Who Are Stout-Hearted Men" and the fans sang along. He played the Beer Barrel Polka and Seventy-Six Trombones and they sang some more.

Next to me, Peter Gammons began to write.

"What was the final score?" he asked. In such a game, numbers didn't seem to mean much.

Oh, to shut that mouth

October 26, 1975—Somebody—either Confucius or Sparky Anderson—said that just to speak of the devil is to give him more notoriety than he deserves.

Which is why I studiously avoid the mention of What's-His-Name—you know, the Count Dracula look-alike who serves as the pivotman of Monday Night Football on television.

Out of column, out of mind, so to speak.

But there comes a time the keys can no longer remain silent, when they must leap and jump feverishly and type nasty things about this defiler of our Monday night pleasures.

The breaking point was last Monday, when the New York Giants upset the Buffalo Bills. What follows here has been festering in the Underwood ever since, biding its time until the end of the World Series, not that any of the adjectives to be used are the same as those employed for the Series, which was merely marvelous, sensational and unforgettable.

Well, I take that back. What's-His-Name is also unforgettable, in the sense that a shark coming out of your bathtub is unforgettable, or a spider crawling in your cornflakes.

Since Monday Night Football began, I have been a semi-apologist for What's-His-Name.

He would go into some long, name-dropping story about how he had breakfast with the front four of the Minnesota Vikings, and how they had whispered secrets to him that were unknown even to Bud Grant.

My wife would glare at the television set. "Oh, shut up," she'd suggest, and

I'd reply, "He's not so bad. At least he gets the viewer involved," and there would be a coolness between us for the rest of the evening.

Or he would give an opinion of something or somebody, spoken with the finality of a judge's gavel, a god-like pronouncement in echo-chamber tones, using multisyllabled words (hello there, heterogenous and panegyric) to convey the impression: "geez, he talks smart."

My wife would say "excuse me" and go bite the doorknob, but I would smile and say, "Don't let him get to you. Enjoy the game." And the dampness would settle in once again.

What finally drove me over the edge was What's-His-Name's shameless shilling for a new television variety show he hosts on Saturday night.

In the middle of the Giants-Bills game—no, not only in the middle, all through the damned thing – this electronic huckster told about the wonders of Saturday night, when he would have—gasp—Kate Smith and—double gasp—Shamu the Killer Whale as his stars.

Ye gods and little fishes. Kate Smith and Shamu, right there on the very same stage. It staggers the imagination.

Shamu would presumably sing "God Bless America" and Kate would ram a lifeboat for the grand finale.

"Wow, Kate Smith and Shamu the Killer Whale. Isn't that great, Frank, and what about it, Alex, you will certainly be watching, won't you, my corpulent comrade?"

"Oh, ho, Howard, I wouldn't miss it. That is gonna be some kind of program."

Now, I am aware that television pays the freight for modern professional sport. I understand the TV timeouts and the starting of games at sunrise and sunset and other odd hours.

I realize that commercials are the price the viewer pays for getting to see games in the comfort of his living room, and really, it isn't much of a price.

But I'll be damned if that tariff includes having to listen to self-serving drivel from this glib-tongued symbol of 20th Century egomania.

This brazen propagandizing is an insult to the viewer, a slap in the face to his intelligence. He is giving What's-His-Name the courtesy of entering his home and the guy says thank you by polluting the living room air with verbal garbage.

Sell us cars. Sell us breakfast food. Sell us, if you must, antiperspirants, detergents and toilet bowl fresheners. But isn't there anyone at ABC or in the FCC with the good taste and authority to keep What's-His-Name from selling himself, because, believe me, the price is too high and nobody's buying.

There it is. See what I mean about speak of the devil and you give him too much publicity.

Here's a thought. Trade What's-His-Name to CBS for Archie Bunker, even up, a deal that should help both clubs.

Nah, that wouldn't work. Edith would never stand for it.

The summer game—it's sweet anticipation

October 29, 1975—The cheers have died out over the Blue Hills and relative quiet has settled upon our land, a quiet broken only by the crunching sound as Jim Plunkett's shoulder separates once more.

But the wonder remains. What is there about baseball, a sporting anachronism in a future-shock world, that arouses the emotions which bubbled and boiled for the last two weeks.

On the surface, baseball is exceedingly dull. A person in the silliest suit this side of Buckingham Palace stands on a little hill and from time to time throws a hard ball in the direction of another person in a silly suit, who tries to strike the ball with a piece of wood, called a bat. That is, the piece of wood, not the person in the silly suit, is called a bat.

Sometimes this batperson makes no attempt to hit the ball. Instead, he watches as it sails past into a piece of leather on the left hand of a third person, who not only wears the same silly uniform, but who is also draped with a protective covering that makes him resemble a refugee from Frankenstein's laboratory.

Scattered about the pasture are other similarly dressed individuals mostly in a state of repose, with one eye open in case something untoward happens.

The whole thing is ridiculous and not worth the time it takes to describe it, so how come 70 million people went slightly daffy over the 1975 World Series? How, in fact, does the game survive at all, not merely on the professional level, but on any level? What is its peculiar charm?

High on the list of reasons baseball has outlived its obituaries is that, unlike most spectator sports, it is a game of anticipation, rather than constant action. The pretty girl (i.e., a big rally) is always round the next corner. The Christmas present (i.e., a spectacular catch) is hidden away in the attic of the immediate future.

You know it's there and pretty soon it'll be yours. The fun is in the waiting.

There's also the anticipation of the next time at bat, whether you're a player or a fan.

"You got me this time, pal, but I'll have another chance before the day is done, and you'd better not make a mistake."

Or,

"Hey, if Cooper can walk and Doyle can get on, the bum will have to pitch to Yaz, Fisk and Lynn. They'd better get somebody warmin' up."

That's anticipation, baseball's delicious answer to the power play, the long bomb, and the fast break.

Baseball is a game played by ordinary-sized people. Most of us are—or were before calories took command—of average size. We can, as they say on Madison Avenue, identify.

The biggest surprise people get upon seeing Carl Yastrzemski for the first time is his size, or lack of it. He's not big, he's not small, he's just, well, ordinary. One of us, so to speak, although on a somewhat larger pay scale. There but for the inability to hit a curve, go I.

The same cannot be said in regard to Kareem Abdul-Jabbar or Larry Csonka.

The game itself is played in the open, not cloaked in "I'll have to look at the game film" evasiveness or "hitting the open man" jargon.

Because it is all in front of you, the heroes and the bums are easy to spot. When Denny Doyle tries to score after a 240-foot fly ball, there is no need to check the film before suggesting it wasn't very smart of him.

When Carlton Fisk hits a home run off the foul pole, there is no mystery involved. There it is, and you saw it.

Baseball is as much a team game as any, yet within its framework is more an individual game than most. It's batter against pitcher and fielder vs. runner, a set of one-on-ones that brings an infinite variety of situations.

Oldtimers will tell you that no matter how many games they've seen, the next one will quite likely bring up a play that has never happened before.

For me, baseball has always been the best game to write about. It has many more hero-goat possibilities than other sports, which spotlight the big man (basketball), the quarterback (football) and the goal scorer (hockey).

It is the best of all games for the characters in it, for the second guessing involved and for relating what happened today with what happened yesterday and what might happen tomorrow.

It is a relaxed game—at least for the fan—played mostly in the summer, the relaxing time of year. It's the only team game not restricted by a clock, thus there is a relief from a sense of urgency inherent in the others.

The World Series, of course, is baseball's jewel. Citizens who don't know the difference between a foul ball and Henry Kissinger (If you're curious, send a plain self-addressed envelope) were turned on by the Reds and the Red Sox.

Two men from Australia spent hundreds of dollars to come to America to watch the Series, saying, "It's something we've been planning for 21 years."

George Thomas, the resident wit of the 1967 Red Sox, got so excited watching the games on television from his home in Minnesota that he and his wife flew to Boston for the final two games. For three days they waited in the rain, and then flew home, unable to stay any longer.

My brother, who is ordinarily of sound mind, bought a standing room only ticket for Game 6 from a scalper for $25, sat in the aisle and watched, with a transistor pasted to his ear, perhaps to make sure that what he was watching was actually happening.

I'm not sure the 1975 World Series will bring any great upsurge in baseball. I doubt if kids will take to the vacant lots in droves, if only because most of the vacant lots are now condominiums or shopping malls.

There won't be a slew of kids out hitting rocks with sticks, playing a World Series in their minds, or choosing up sides by alternating fists on the bat handle—"no clawsies."

Little League will have to suffice, and that's okay. Meanwhile, baseball will mosey along as usual, a sport able to accommodate both Ty Cobb and artificial turf without getting tied down to either.

"I wish spring training started tomorrow," said Pete Rose after Cincinnati had won the World Series.

So do I.

5

1976

The pain won't stop

March 14, 1976—PROVIDENCE—The coach who had lost took a puff on a cigar and looked at the player who had lost it.

"Gotta lot of studying to do?" he asked.

The kid smiled a little, although to tell you the truth he wasn't feeling on top of the world.

"Some," he replied.

"Okay," the coach said, "because if you didn't I was gonna suggest we go out and get drunk together."

Pete Carril, the bundle of electrons who coaches Princeton, was doing what little he could to ease the hurt in Pete Molloy, his 5-foot-10 reserve guard. Carril knew the lame jokes and the "hang-in-theres" wouldn't do it, but what the hell, you just couldn't stand around as though Molloy had just been caught robbing a bank.

What had happened was that with four seconds left against a Rutgers team that had won 28 straight games, Molloy had missed a foul shot. If he'd made the shot, it would have tied the game and given him another. If he'd made that, Princeton would have pulled the college upset of the East, and maybe of the country.

But Molloy missed. After two Rutgers time-outs, his shot hit the back rim and the game was over.

After situations like this, you give a player time. You give him five minutes, maybe 10, and then you descend on him, the guys with the pencils and the tape recorders. The job's not a great deal of fun then, because nobody likes to ask the loser "what happened" and "how come?" Winners are easier.

But if it's not a lark for the people who write about these things, it's even less a walk along the beach for the kid. What he would like to do is get into a locker, close the door and come out in a week from next Tuesday.

Some athletes do that. Some coaches do that for their athletes, or maybe you think Woody Hayes and Johnny Wooden are "c'mon in, boys, the kid's over there" types?

Anyway young Molloy didn't duck. He stood in a passageway that led from the silent dressing room to the steamy shower, and he talked about what it felt like to see a season end because the basketball he shot from 15 feet away went four inches too far.

No, the two time-outs Rutgers had called hadn't bothered him. Yes, he thought it was a two-shot foul, but the official said he was bumped before the shot.

He'd never been in a situation remotely comparable, he said. Oh, once, at St. Agnes High in Rockville Center, L.I., he'd made a foul shot to win a game.

"Did it win the championship?"

"Nah, first game of the season, against Mt. Vernon."

He said that during the time-out delays he tried to stay loose, tried to concentrate on his job. He hadn't played much all season and had scored only 31 points. Since the sixth game of the season he'd made only seven points. Yesterday, he hadn't taken a shot until his wild, abortive attempt from a melee around the key with four seconds left.

"What were you thinking about during the timeouts?"

Thin smile. "I was thinking about how great it would be if I made both."

Rutgers star Phil Sellers had said earlier, when asked what he was thinking about during those moments, "I thought it was all over. Princeton has a knack for good foul-shooting, so I was worried."

And so it ended, this strange game between the greyhound and the elephant, between a team from the '70s and one from the '50s.

It was Elton John against Frank Sinatra.

Princeton thinks a fast break is a social disease. Rutgers lives by it. Princeton took two minutes between shots. Rutgers came flying downcourt and shot in four seconds. Or faster.

"Sure, the way they play drives you crazy," said Rutgers coach Tom Young. "I don't want any part of it. There's no way I could play that way. You couldn't pay me to play for Princeton. Oops, I shouldn't have said that."

But the way Princeton plays keeps the Tigers in the game. It is difficult, if not impossible to run away from them. Rutgers, which has run away from just about everybody, couldn't do it. Maryland couldn't do it. Alabama couldn't do it. In a day when 90 points a game is commonplace, Princeton this season held its opponents to an average of 52.8.

But Rutgers scored 54, one too many for Princeton, and so young Molloy's basketball career is over.

"It'd be nice if he could forget about the shot in 10 minutes," said the coach.

"I'll never forget it," said Pete Molloy. "It was the last shot of my career, and I missed it with a chance to win the game."

"I'll never forget it."

Cuba si . . . others, ouch!

July 30, 1976—MONTREAL—I spent yesterday afternoon, in case you're interested—and you'd better be because The Globe is spending une petite fortune to have me cover this international barn dance—at Maurice Richard Arena watching Cubans knock people down, not to mention out, out, out.

They won four bouts and, in three, the opponents developed blind staggers before one round had expired.

Flyweight Ramon Duvalon was the only Cuban unable to get a knockout, but it wasn't his fault. He won by disqualification after a Russian named David Torosyan persisted in hitting Duvalon so many times below the belt the Cuban spent most of the fight doubled over in an imitation of Carlton Fisk after a misdirected foul tip.

Andres Aldama of Cuba dispatched Vladimir Kolev with a punch so devastating the Bulgarian lay prone for five minutes and had to be carried out on a stretcher.

Sixto Soria flattened Costica Dafinoiu of Romania in less than a minute, though, to be honest, I got this by hearsay, having made the mistake of spending 40 seconds in the men's room.

The last of the unfortunate chaps to wish he'd taken up needlepoint instead of fisticuffs was Big John ["I Love America"] Tate, a Knoxville, Tenn., heavy-weight.

Poor John was transformed into a folding chair after a minute, 31 seconds had slipped past.

I don't want to suggest the bout was a mismatch, but Tate wouldn't have been a good bet if he'd been carrying a tire iron. Some thought the referee had used bad judgment by not stopping the bout sooner. Like the day before yesterday.

Did I mention the name of the man who did our guy in? It was Teofilo Stevenson, the defending Olympic heavyweight champion.

Tate, who had suffered a cut over his left eye in a previous bout, seemed to start bleeding yesterday when Stevenson glared at him during the prefight introductions.

At any rate, after some early pawing and prancing that would have been a box office threat to a Fred Astaire movie, Stevenson shot a right to Tate's head.

The American staggered to a neutral corner, small butterflies, large gnats and an occasional pterodactyl buzzing about his head.

As Tate reached the corner with the referee counting, he began to cave in, as though someone had said: "Have a seat, John," and he'd answered, "Don't mind if I do."

He sank in slow motion to the canvas like a messed up jigsaw puzzle in about 83 pieces with a vacant look in his eye. Tate was on the floor for only a six count, the first four seconds having been used in getting there.

The outcome was no surprise. It was evident in Big John's early bout that he had no punch, was eminently cuttable, and, though he didn't lack for courage, was a stranger to any of boxing's subtleties.

And in Stevenson he was fighting a veteran, a professional amateur.

Tate several days ago had said he wanted to win a gold medal to "bring home to my momma."

Stevenson's aspirations are somewhat more practical. He is fighting, he said, for the honor and glory of Fidel Castro. According to Stevenson, Castro has made Cuba one great big athletic Camelot, which he said is the reason Cubans are doing so well here.

Our boxers are obviously taking the wrong tack. When we interview an American winner, instead of saying "Hi, Ma, how'm I doin? I'm glad I won for all you folks down there in Three Forks, La.," he should go off on a political tangent.

"I won this gold medal for my leader, Jimmy Carter, who is making boxing safe for democracy in Plains, Ga.," or "I would like to thank our beloved mentor, Ronald Reagan, for giving me this chance to help keep the Red menace from our shores."

Stevenson made his comment about Castro at a nightmarish press conference straight out of Alice in Wonderland.

Before he arrived, a man named Karl Heinz Wehr attempted to answer some questions involving the dismissal and/or suspension of three boxing judges for incompetence. Wehr is chairman of the International Amateur Boxing Federation.

He speaks only German, so the questions had to be translated, and the answers likewise had to be translated into both French and English.

As best I could make out, the session went this way:

Q. Could you tell us something about the referees who were suspended?

A. The pen of my aunt is on the table.

Q. But what are the referees' names?

A. Munich in the spring is very lovely.

Q. What were the specific reasons for the suspensions?

A. The enemy is at the gates and we can't hold out much longer.

Q. Do you anticipate any further suspensions?

A. Thank you very much.

Tate didn't appear at the conference and that's probably a good thing. Stevenson's drivel about Castro would have sent him right back to dreamsville.

Let's hear it for lowly 10

August 31, 1976—No college football season should begin without predictions from experts, and I see that the wire services and Jimmy the Greek have already made public their picks of the best college teams of 1976.

Nebraska will be No. 1, they all say, with the usual juggernauts—Alabama, Oklahoma, Ohio State, Notre Dame, Texas, Michigan—snapping at Nebraska's heels.

Nowhere, though, have I seen the selection of the worst teams of the coming season. It seems to me this would be a worthwhile reference to have on your desk, along with the seating plan for Minutemen home games and a detailed road map of the rest rooms at Schaefer Stadium.

Below is my Bottom Ten, plus some comments. The list was arrived at only after the most diligent of research, which included visits to 594 campuses (campii?), interviews with two coaches (the other 592 said "get that idiot out of here") and an assessment of 22,937 college players, all but three of whom want to be pros and make a million dollars by the time they're 27.

Number one on the list below could mean the team is the worst of the worst. On the other hand, it could mean that No. 1 is the best of the worst. It's easy to get confused in this business. Here we go, with 1975 records in parentheses:

1. **Case Institute (0-8)**—Veteran observers rate the '75 eleven one of all-time worst. Point ratio of 39 to 230 indicated veteran observers knew what the hell they were talking about. All but two of the 39 points scored by Case in '75 came about while opponents were eating lunch.

2. **Morehouse St. (0-9)**—This aggregation disappointed pundits last season by rolling up 145 points in nine games, 144 more than had been predicted in preseason analysis. However, defense lived up to everything bad said about it by allowing 249. Coaching staff has been pleased with tepid team spirit in early practices.

3. **Frostburg (Md.) State (1-10)**—This often-say-die unit will be striving hard to erase the ignominy of the one victory that blackened its 1975 record. The fact that the team it beat dropped the sport half an hour after the game was over won't dull Frostburg's desire for a perfect season. It is given a good chance as many veterans are returning with a season of ineptitude under their belts.

4. **Virginia (1-10)**—Sieve-like defense was talk of college locker rooms in 1975. Cavaliers allowed 428 points and will be hard pressed to duplicate that. However, in setting its sights in that direction, coaching staff announced the other day the club will refuse to receive kickoffs.

5. **Bethany (1-9)**—This school played in game of century in '75 against conference rival Bethel. Game was declared a loss for each team because each used ineligible players. A similar plan this autumn will shoot Bethany to the bottom of the barrel quicker than you can say "Clive who?"

6. **Wooster (1-8)**—Last place finish in 11 team Ohio Conference in '75 was not true indication of how badly a team can play. Coaching staff has emphasized punting off side of foot in recent drills in attempt to assure good field position for opponents.

7. **Cornell (1-9)**—Will be hard pressed to hang on to reputation as worst in Ivy League. However, step in right direction was taken recently by university's board of overseers when it vetoed plan to smuggle all-time Cornell great Ed Marinaro back into school as a second semester sophomore.

8. **Louisville (1-10)**—Have been unable to confirm publicity office quote that went as follows: "We didn't have anybody last year and they're all back." However, if quote proves true, Louisville could do it all again in '76, and just as badly.

9. **Oregon State (1-10)**—Pacific Coast Conference squad underwhelmed almost everybody in 1975. This season is an enigma because the coach's son will be a quarterback. That isn't bad in itself, but what has team down in dumps (and we all know what sloppy football is played there) is that the kid is only in eighth grade.

10. Weber St. (1-9-1)—This Big Sky conference doormat hopes to cut down on 1975 successes (152 points, three and one-half first downs) by practicing less (once a week) and going at half speed on third down. Coaching staff has inaugurated sure-fire morale booster: Painting star on helmet each time squad member reports back to huddle without falling down.

There are undoubtedly graduates of all these fine institutions out there who are now furious because I've dragged their team through the mud of ridicule.

Simmer down, gang. Don't blame the messenger for the bad news. Think of it this way. Making the bottom 10 is better than not being mentioned at all, or having to make excuses for not going to the Sugar Bowl.

Poor Nasty, so abused

September 6, 1976—What is one to make of Ilie Nastase? Is he truly a buffoon from Bucharest or simply a delightfully uninhibited athlete trying to toss a little fun into pro tennis, a game that can be deadly dull when played by such automatons as Bjorn Borg or Chris Evert?

The Romanian has been severely criticized for his deportment Friday at Forest Hills, when he called German opponent Hans Pohmann "a Nazi SOB," and made various and sundry other menacing and obscene gestures.

Those who deplore Nasty's actions suggest punishment ranging from life suspension from the game to beheading.

A tiny minority look upon Ilie as a ray of sunshine and a barrel of laughs in a tight little world that too often takes itself too seriously.

Yesterday, Nastase told Pat Summerall of CBS that he was just kidding around and that the crowd always misunderstands his joking for the real thing. Nastase said that he has no chance and that the crowd boos him before he has done anything.

This interesting rationalization of a tasteless exhibition led me to speculate on what some of the great villains of history might have said if given a chance to come on national television and explain their actions.

Their remarks might have gone like this:

Attila the Hun—Okay, so I sacked a few cities and destroyed a couple thousand houses. Urban renewal always brings temporary discomfort to a few, but one must keep in mind the common good and the long-range goals.

Fagin—Ask the kids if they weren't having fun. I gave them a sense of responsibility and the feeling of accomplishment. If you could have seen the look on a boy's face when he came to me with a rich man's wallet, you'd know stealing was better for them than Little League.

Lizzie Borden—My parents never liked me, everyone knows that. All my life I had to hang around the house, sweeping the floor, doing the wash, never having any fun. My psychiatrist said to me, "Lizzie, you've got to cut yourself loose." That's the last time I'll take his advice.

Marquis de Sade—The public doesn't know the facts. I'm nothing but a whipping boy.

John Dillinger—People pay five bucks for parking and $15 to watch a football game and don't complain. I rob a few crummy banks and the world falls down around my ears. Where's everyone's sense of values today?

Scarface Al Capone—I sold a little beer and the government acted as though I'd poisoned everyone in America. Listen, if the people didn't get it from me, they'd make the stuff in the bathtub. The way I look at it, my work made America cleaner. Okay, so I killed a few people. That's what free enterprise is all about.

Jack the Ripper—I'll never understand the fuss. I was just a lonely guy who liked to walk around the city on foggy nights. I was warned it wasn't safe to go out alone at night but I wouldn't listen. This is a simple case of police harassment.

Lucretia Borgia—I try to spice up lunch and this is the thanks I get. It's not my fault some people have allergies.

Boss Tweed—Some people collect stamps and bubble gum cards and that's okay. I collect other people's money and I'm called a crook. What's a country coming to when a man can't have a hobby without being pushed around?

Henry the Eighth—The department of public works went over my head, if you'll excuse the expression, and bought this expensive guillotine. If I let it sit around the courtyard and rust I'm criticized. I use it and I'm criticized. You can't win in politics.

Scrooge—The guy had Blue Cross, a terrific pension plan and Christmas afternoon off and I'm still called a skinflint. A bad press can kill you.

Benedict Arnold—I played out my option, the same as a lot of guys, and went where the big money was. Catfish Hunter does that and he's called a hero. I do it and they call me a traitor.

Yaz muffles the razzers

Sepetember 26, 1976—Carl Yastrzemski has outlasted three presidents, six managers, a vicious and degrading war and a change in American lifestyle as swift and powerful as a Nolan Ryan fastball.

He's gone through baseball writers by the dozen. Some have died (Hy Hurwitz, Fred Ciampa, John Gilooly, Harold Kaese), some have retired (Roger Birtwell, Henry McKenna, Roy Mumpton, Clif Keane) and some have gone on to other endeavors (Bob Holbrook, Peter Gammons).

He arrived in Boston as an athletic prodigy, of whom Gene Mauch said: "If anyone tells this boy how to hit, he ought to have his tongue cut out."

And no one did mess with him. Oh, perhaps Ted Williams with a suggestion or two in the early years, but Yastrzemski's style now is basically what it was in 1961, his rookie season—bat high and the big "I get my money's worth" swing.

And as the 1976 season dribbles to a conclusion, as the thunder from the great collapse and the dismissal of Darrell Johnson and the contract squabbles fades in the distance, the man in the spotlight, as it has been since T. Wms. Esq. retired, remains No. 8, limping through the cool early autumn nights in search of his 100th run batted in. In a season of turmoil, he's been the one constant.

Yastrzemski's been part of 24 Jersey St. for 16 years now. Kids have progressed from school-skipping urchins to college graduates since he took his first Fenway swing.

But he's really gone through only four seasons in those 16 years—the spring, summer, autumn and winter of Carl Yastrzemski.

From 1961–66 it was springtime for Yaz. The promise of greatness mixed with rainy-day doubts that he would never be the complete player.

His shortcomings, wrote Harold Kaese, were "erratic baserunning and throwing, a modest RBI total for so good a hitter and a tendency to sulk when things went badly."

In the winter of '63, he got into his first big press tangle when, at the writers' dinner, he thanked Mike Higgins "for all you've done for me," ignoring Johnny Pesky, his manager. In 1964, Pesky benched him for loafing and a coolness existed between the two that didn't thaw until last year.

But there was undeniable talent. Billy Herman said, "He has a great ability to remember how pitchers get him out." Kaese compared him to a powerful Pete Runnels as a hitter and to Willie Mays as a thrower.

I arrived on the scene in '66, in time to see both sides of Carl Yastrzemski. The moody side so impressed me that one day—I remember it clearly, at poolside of the Crest Hotel in Anaheim—I went to my trusty portable and wrote that the Sox should trade him for somebody of value. Among those of value I mentioned were Dean Chance, Tom Tresh, Tommy Agee, and John Romano, proving what a sensational general manager I would have made.

In Carl Yastrzemski's springtime, the Red Sox were forever losers, finishing 6-8-7-8-9-9.

"Let me tell you one thing," said Eddie Kasko, a utility man on the 1966 team, "if he ever gets with a pennant contender, he's going to be one helluva player."

Then along came 1967, the summer of his career, when everything bloomed at once, when every day was better than the one before.

There was a traffic jam at the Callahan Tunnel entrance because a driver wouldn't enter until he found out what Yastrzemski did with the bases loaded. Yaz was voted the No. 1 newsmaker in New England. There was Yaz Bread and an appearance on Ed Sullivan and a Yastrzemski night at Yankee Stadium, and all over New England otherwise rational adults wore "Yaz Sir, That's My Baby" buttons.

Three years later, he was booed at Fenway Park merely for being there. Jim Bouton wrote, "Yastrzemski thinks of himself first—and second." His family sat in their sky box along third base, stood up every time he came to bat and tried, sometimes unsuccessfully, to ignore the abuse.

He was paid a lot of money and was called Tom Yawkey's pet. And as his salary increased, so did the boos.

It lasted a long time, the autumn of Carl Yastrzemski, and there was no guarantee it would ever end. Indeed, there were strong indications he would finish his playing days as a prophet without honor, so to speak, in his adopted city.

But once again, winning changed things. The arrival of Fred Lynn and Jim Rice spread the attention around, took the pressure off, changed the customers' attitude.

And so Carl Yastrzemski, at 37 as much a delight to watch on a ballfield as Yaz at 21, has finally become accepted.

Fans (and writers, too) have at last become comfortable with him, and have learned to appreciate his abilities and not expect the impossible.

It was a long time coming, this appreciation, and for Yaz, a not entirely expected bonus to take with him into the winter of his career.

He was wrong about New York: It's a place to write Mom about

October 19, 1976

Dear Mom:

I'm here in New York City to cover the next three games of the World Series and thought I'd let you know I've changed my mind about this place.

About a week ago I wrote some bad things about New York, just after the Yankees beat Kansas City to win the American League pennant.

You probably remember all the people that threw bottles and ran out on the field in that game. Well, it made me angry and I'm afraid I took to the typewriter and went off half-cocked, calling New Yorkers animals and rude and all that.

But yesterday, I found out how wrong I was. New Yorkers can be as friendly as people in any other city.

For example, when I arrived at my hotel late at night, a whole bunch of women outside the entrance couldn't have been nicer. Dressed well, too, in short skirts and boots, and I can't tell you how many of them asked me if I was interested in a good time. They were probably members of the women's auxiliary of the Junior Chamber of Commerce.

I was too busy to take them up on their offer, but appreciated their going out of their way to make me feel at home.

The thoughtfulness of the desk clerks when I checked in at the hotel was beyond expectations. They took time to wire the FBI to ascertain that I had a proper credit rating, and though this meant that the checking-in process took three-quarters of an hour, I was grateful for their thoroughness.

The television set in the room has an extra touch that was useful and reassuring. By merely pressing a button, I received instructions on how to lock and bolt the door so that thieves and muggers have only a 50 percent chance of breaking in.

And the news in New York is so interesting. A subway boost to 55 cents, a $100 million budget deficit, a 10 percent reduction in the police force—the noon news showed me New York was indeed a rollicking, on-the-move community.

The news finished off with a bright little story about a deranged son who killed his aged mother and then was found babbling in the apartment.

Cheered by this, I went to lunch, where the coffee shop gave me a special $4.80 rate for a cheese omelet and coffee. You won't find a bargain like that in Cincinnati.

After lunch, I went for a stroll through Manhattan, but had to cut it short after three strides because of a cinder in my eye.

I went into a rest room and removed this, with the help of a thoughtful attendant who handed me a towel and dusted me off. He blocked the exit until I handed him a coin, but I had the last laugh there, because it was a Boston MBTA token.

Anyway, Mom, I wanted you to know I love it here, and now if you'll excuse me, I'll cut this short, because the bellhop told me that after 6 o'clock, I should put a chair and a suitcase up against the room door, just to be on the safe side, ha, ha, ha.

Love, your son, Ray

The Ballad of Baseball Past

November 21, 1976—

Once
Upon a time the game was grassroots America,
Silk to spin a dream from.

Every town had a team
Sponsored by the hardware store
Or Al's Tavern,
And they played on a field
More often than not
Filled with rocks, not to mention
An occasional cow chip.

After a man got too old to play,
He'd have the memories:
"Remember when we played in Hadley,
and the ump showed up drunk . . . ?"
The clichés were of kids
Fresh off a farm.
Kids who tossed hay and slopped pigs
And when the chores were done,
Pitched a baseball into a bushel basket
Set against a barn,
Until it was too dark to see the basket.

Or they were of the boy
From the small town:
"You know that tree out beyond left field,
Hit one into that last summer, never seen
A longer one."

A legend,
A boy with man-arms
And freckles
And a shock of blond hair,
And a dream of maybe some day
Playing the outfield for the Rocky Mount Red Sox.

Baseball was the sport
Of the people
Of the lunch-pail crowd, for drudges
Wearing green eyeshades and scratching numbers
In thick red ledgers.

At World Series time,
The dock wallopers and the five-and-dime clerks
("Root, root, root for the home team,
If they don't win it's a shame")
Gathered outside the newspaper office
And waited for the man
With elastics around his shirtsleeves
And a cigar in his mouth
To scrawl another inning on the blackboard.

And later,
After Guglielmo Marconi found a way
To bring Guy Lombardo's music
From a New York City ballroom
All the way to Pierre, South Dakota,
And beyond,
Mothers faithfully recorded every World Series play
On blue-lined, eight-by-eleven J. L. Hammett pads,
So when their sons came home from school,
Kicking rocks and scuffing their shoes,
They'd know about Ernie Lombardi
Falling asleep at home plate
And Mickey Owen missing the third strike.

The headlines
Shouted the news.
"Sultan of Swat Has Bellyache"
"Splendid Splinter Spits at Fans"
"Joltin' Joe Hits in 56th Straight."
And Fred Hoey's voice filtered
Through a thousand lazy summer afternoons:
"Another case of Wheaties for Ole Double X."

The guys from Al's Tavern
Now play slo-pitch softball.
Freckle-faced kids from small towns
Build rockets in their cellars,
And the scout
With the hands of an old catcher
Lives in a trailer and fishes every
Day in Bradenton, Florida.

A steakhouse now sits
Where once the fabulous Ed Remorenko
Poled home runs for the Springfield Rifles.

And kids don't play unless they have uniforms
And are driven to the dugout in station wagons.
Baseball is computers, lawyers, agents, board rooms,
Money.

I tell myself that all things change,
That you can't freeze time like an ice cube,
And try to convince myself I haven't
Lost an old friend.

Cards mean they care

December 19, 1976—One of the terrific side benefits of Christmas for a sportswriter is hearing from all his close friends in the business.

I look forward each year with great anticipation to receiving my annual greetings from the sports world.

Just today, for example, one arrived from Carrie and Pete Rozelle. How often I think of them. How many times I've mentioned to my wife that we must have Carrie and Pete over for Scrabble some night.

But the way life goes, with all of us wrapped up in our own pursuits, we never do get together. A card at Christmas keeps everyone in touch.

The realization that Pete takes time to say hello even though he's busy with such matters as totaling up the season's no-shows proves how close we are.

I'll bet Pete and Carrie don't send out more than 100,000 cards, so it's great to hear from them. After all these years, I recognize Pete's secretary's handwriting on the envelope immediately.

Luisa and Bowie also dropped a note in the mail the other day. Well, it wasn't really a note. I mean Bowie didn't say "stop knocking me" or anything like that.

It was more of a warm "from our house to your house" greeting that had the interests of our national pastime at heart.

Here is a man being sued for $6 million by Charles Finley and yet he grabs a few minutes to lick a 13-cent stamp and go down to the post office in the bitter cold to make sure I'm remembered over the holidays. That's friendship.

Don't think everybody in the business receives a card from Luisa and Bowie. I have it on good authority that a writer on a weekly paper in Iowa has always been left out. He's complained to Marvin Miller, but still no greeting from the Kuhns.

And speaking of Miller, only the holiday spirit of forgiveness keeps me from thinking bad thoughts about him. He's never sent me a card after all we've been through together—the Messersmith decision, the 1972 strike, the free agent draft.

But that's OK. Enough old buddies remember. The San Francisco 49ers, busy as they are trying to explain why they fell apart this season, sat down—probably during an end run one Sunday—and autographed a card for me.

The greeting was a team photograph, with the inscription "Seasons Greetings" in the shape of a football. I was going to write back and tell them there should be an apostrophe between the n and the s in seasons, but thought better of it. They've had enough criticism this season.

I sent them return cards, of course, with my autograph. It's good to keep in touch with Gene Washington and Tommy Hart and the rest of my close friends.

Last Christmas, a card, also autographed, arrived from the Black Hawks. So far this year I haven't heard from them. There may be a Bobby Orr influence there.

Ralph Wilson's card arrived the day before yesterday. Ralph owns the Buffalo Bills and has three tons of money, although until he had to renegotiate O. J. Simpson's contract Ralph had four tons.

Wilson and I go back a long way. I bet if you ran into him on the street and mentioned my name, he'd say: "Oh, great fellow, Fitz. Loved him in 'Going My Way.' Isn't he dead?"

Because of the Bills' bad season, I bypassed the usual return greetings and sent Ralph a sympathy card.

The Orioles' greeting is also in hand, showing a cute black and orange bird wearing baseball cap and spikes and swinging a bat. After the card was printed, the bird went to the Padres in the free agent draft for $1.8 million.

I've heard from the NBA's Larry O'Brien (winter pastoral scene), the Bengals (a sweating Santa who looks like Ken Stabler stuffing a Bengal down a chimney), the Tigers (a big Santa cat), and Pro Football's Hall of Fame.

We've been meaning to have the Hall of Fame over for cocktails, but never got around to that, either.

What we do with these cards is sprinkle them casually around the house, so that if any of the neighbors drop in, they'll be sure to spot them and ask: "What's Carrie Rozelle really like?"

I haven't heard from Mr. Finley this season, which is understandable. The poor man has been robbed and pillaged and only the other day was struck another blow when Charlie O, the mule who came to dinner, passed away.

Mr. Finley is undoubtedly in no mood to send out Christmas cards, and frankly, I'm not unhappy I didn't get one.

Chances are it would have arrived postage due.

6

1977

All Arnie did was spoil us

February 22, 1977—We see them on television through half-closed eyes on a sleepy Sunday, walking down fairways a continent away.

Outside the house, the wind may be blowing and the snow halfway up the second-story windows, but there, palm trees are waving softly and the galleries are in shirtsleeves.

Superimposed on the television screen are some names:

Tom Purtzer, 11 under . . . Rick Massengale, 15 under . . . Bruce Lietzke, 16 under . . . Bob Gilder, 8 under . . . Graham Marsh, 9 under . . . Fuzzy Zoeller, 10 under.

Who? What? Is Nicklaus sick? What about Player? Has somebody kidnapped Johnny Miller? Is Trevino retired? Is Arnie off playing somewhere with Jerry Ford, Bob Hope and King Hussein? Who are these people?

The bodies that belong to the newcomers seem to have come right out of a Pillsbury oven.

"Bake me a tray of young golfers, Oscar. Make them slim-hipped, with maybe a lock of hair that won't stay in place. Uh-huh, blond if you want, handsome enough but not too pretty.

"Dress them in interchangeable slacks with interchangeable sport shirts.

"Give them an accent with a tinge of country and tan them all up to look like the Marlboro man around the eyes.

"Make them unflappable, unperturbed by any of golf's little disasters. Never let them throw a club, glare at a spectator, curse out a caddy.

"Give them the ability to hook a ball around eucalyptus trees, fade three-irons over orange groves, flip a shot out of a trap to within two feet and make a five-iron spin backward four yards.

"Have them baked and ready for delivery in time for the Gabby Hayes classic next Thursday."

They are so damn talented, all these names. Their swing seems to have leaped out of a computer. They slug drives 270 yards and, when faced with a 175-yard approach shot, casually ask the caddy for a six iron.

And they are so forgettable. Today it's Tom Purtzer and last week it was Rick Massengale and last year it was Forrest Fezler. Tomorrow it may be Howard Twitty and next year Barry Jaeckel.

The names come and go and the owners of the names make more than a comfortable living, but they can't capture our imagination.

The trouble is, we're spoiled. Arnold Palmer spoiled us. He coincided with televised golf and was perfect—the common man with an uncommon athletic ability.

We could watch Arnold Palmer fling down his cigarette and hitch up his trousers and we could fantasize. We could say: "A break here and there and that would have been me."

We watched Arnie kid with the gallery and smile his hometown grin and he was one of our family.

The media fashioned the image. Newspaper stories headlined Palmer's flair for coming from behind—Arnie's Charge, they called it, converting four hours of hit and wait into high drama.

Television commentators emphasized Palmer's boldness, the good old American way of risking all to gain all.

And so we became spoiled, and when Arnold Palmer proved to be only human and faded from the leaders after 20 years, we started looking around for the new Arnold Palmer.

We see the next superstar coming over hill, 22 under par in the Covered Dish Open at Tucson, and we say: "Could this be the one? Is this the next Arnie?"

And we are always disappointed. Several years ago, Tom Shaw popped up, a personable lad with winning ways, a charming smile and always a quip. The next Palmer, perhaps? No dice.

No dice either with Johnny Miller, who won a zillion dollars but lacked fire, nor with Ben Crenshaw, even though he's a college sensation who has done well as a pro.

Tom Watson has been the most recent candidate, a terrific player, modest and well educated, and one who seems to rise to the challenge.

Maybe Watson's the one, but the fact is, Diogenes had an easier time seeking the truth with a lantern than we have looking for a new Palmer.

The criteria that made Palmer unique, that made him the right man for the right time, are no longer valid. Today's top young tour golfer is an accomplished athlete and a prolific moneymaker and maybe that should be enough.

We shouldn't ask him to be another Arnold Palmer. We shouldn't ask the impossible.

The Rocky road of sport films is no longer full of clunkers

March 1, 1977—"Rocky" has been nominated for 10 Academy Awards. "Slapshot" has opened to acclaim from critic and hockey player alike.

"Pumping Iron," about weightlifters, has been described as "excellently done." "Brian's Song" touched the hearts of millions, even those who think the Chicago Bears is a rock group.

"Bang the Drum Slowly," a story of a baseball player dying young, avoided mawkishness and was done with compassion and humor.

What's going on here? Where are the sports clunkers of yesteryear? When did the film industry begin treating sports as a legitimate human endeavor rather than as a treacly, cliché-ridden, one-dimensional version of life in an arena?

Except for an occasional boxing movie, Hollywood, until recently, had not distinguished itself in sports.

When I was old enough to attend the Strand Theater without my mother, I was thrilled by a race-driving epic called "Burn 'Em Up Barnes."

This was done in serial form, that is, in 15 weekly episodes. At the end of an episode, Barnes, the fearless and gritty driver, would be seen crashing his burning auto into a pole to avoid hitting a cluster of young children. It was obvious to all that Barnes had been fried to a crisp.

But, miracle of miracles, the next show would unveil what you'd missed the week before—Ole Burn 'Em Up leaping free of his racer just before it was consumed by flames.

In those days, the action in sports movies took place on a mythical college campus, populated by elm trees and kindly professors.

Every kid in the school either played football or was a cheerleader, and spent 90 percent of his or her time at the malt shop, saying things like "Gee, Connie, why won't you go to the hop with me?"

Most of these movies starred either Joe E. Brown or Jack Oakie. Oakie looked about 35 years old, which didn't deter Hollywood from casting him as a football flash.

One of these Oakie classics showed up on television recently, with Oakie in the role of Boley Bolinkewicz, a big, stupid halfback in danger of flunking out.

The student body, appalled at this possibility, taught their star to spell such puzzlers as YMCA and SPCA and got him through the final exam.

Whereupon Bolinkewicz went out and personally defeated State U, the hated rivals, tucking the football under his arm like a loaf of pumpernickel and running 90 yards as the gun went off.

In the Forties a bunch of autobiographical films appeared, with one thing in common. They were all terrible.

Ronald Reagan was Grover Cleveland Alexander, the great but sometimes drunken pitcher. Jimmy Stewart played Monte Stratton of the White Sox, who lost a leg in a shotgun accident but who continued to pitch. Gary Cooper got off a horse long enough to play Lou Gehrig in "Pride of the Yankees."

William Bendix starred in "The Babe Ruth Story," a picture so excruciatingly hokey it makes me squirm just mentioning it.

Pat O'Brien was the coach, and Reagan was George Gipp in "Knute Rockne," a movie that was required viewing in a freshman's first week at the University of Notre Dame.

The worst casting was Tony Perkins as Jimmy Piersall in "Fear Strikes Out." Perkins threw a baseball like Little Lord Fauntleroy and swung a bat like the Queen of England—and that was after weeks of practice.

Car-and horse-racing films always starred either Mickey Rooney or Frankie Darrow, and sometime in the movie they were approached by gamblers or beat up in an alley.

Boxing, however, often escaped the clichés. "The Harder They Fall," based on the rise and decline of Primo Carnera, was excellent. So was "Body and Soul" with John Garfield, "Champion" with Kirk Douglas, and "Requiem for a Heavyweight" with Anthony Quinn.

Sports humor has always been hard to capture, on either paper or celluloid, being ribald, ethnic and cruel. Comedy films have leaned toward the slapstick ("Caddy" with Jerry Lewis) or fantasy ("Rhubarb" about a cat who owns a ball team).

Sports musicals haven't been sensational, although "Damn Yankees" was enjoyable. A Gene Kelly-Frank Sinatra thing called "Take Me Out to the Ball Game" featured a song about a double-play combination called "O'Brien to Ryan to Goldberg," a toe-tapper that fell somewhat short of becoming a standard.

So it's nice to see sports coming of age in films, although if the language in "Slapshot" approaches that of the average locker room—and I understand it does—you'd better dress your kids in asbestos suits.

I think Hollywood is ready to make an honest movie about a sportswriter, not a sloppy klutz like Oscar Madison of The Odd Couple, but a decent, family-type guy.

If Paul Newman is tied up, I'm available.

Ah, fishing—ain't it the life

May 8, 1977—Driving along Wollaston Beach the other day, brain awash with such imponderables as how to pay for the new clutch and whether Fred Lynn will play before Labor Day, I noticed an elderly man standing next to a battered Plymouth, baiting a hook.

My steel-trap mind deciphered the action immediately. The man was about to go fishing.

The scene triggered the usual double-pronged, wistful reaction, namely: (a) people who fish seem at peace with the world and (b) one of these days I'm going to try it.

The response was predictable in the manner that a World War II song called "I'll Be Seeing You" invariably triggers a smoky remembrance of a long ago summer, a remembrance so strong I have total recall of street names and faces.

No matter where I am, when I see someone fishing, the reaction is the same. During spring training in Florida, driving along busy Cypress Gardens road, I'll see folks fishing along the shores of one of those picturebook lakes, and I'll think, "These people are on the right track. They aren't caught up in the rat race."

I'll see oldtimers on a bridge in St. Pete, bait can at feet and fishing pole in hand, and wonder why I'm driving 70 miles per hour to a ballpark to interview a ballplayer who's sulking because he's been offered only a $300,000 contract even though he batted .238 last season.

I'll be heading for a golf course, where for four and one-half hours I'll fuss and fume over an impossible game and I'll see, way out on a pond, a rowboat with a lone fisherman in it, hat slouched over his eyes and undoubtedly a six-pack alongside.

"He's found the secret," I'll think, and be depressed for at least five minutes.

In my heart of hearts, I realize I'm romanticizing the fisherman.

The ones fishing along the edge of that Winter Haven lake are not doing it because they've dismissed modern life as contemporary madness.

Like me, they're literally fishing for their supper, but whereas I attempt to catch something with a pen and notebook, they're trying with a worm and hook in Lake Lulu.

Different methods, different fish, same motive.

The oldtimers dangling a line from the St. Petersburg bridge are more than likely there out of boredom, or because it's not their day for lawn bowling or shuffleboard. Contentment may have very little to do with it, other than the satisfaction that comes from still being able to be up and about.

And the guy in a rowboat? Peaceful, maybe, but he could be there for 100 other reasons—to avoid creditors, a nagging wife, bawling kids, an overgrown lawn, employment, whatever.

Still, I envy him his apparent happiness, and always make a mental note to take up the sport. But it won't happen.

I grew up in a western Massachusetts town rich in trout streams. My brother would head for Jack's Brook at the crack of dawn, the better to stalk the wily trout.

I would get on my bike, loop a first baseman's glove around the handle and head for the ball field, or, if it was raining, rearrange my baseball cards for the 124th time.

Even then, fishing frightened me. It still does. Not the worms. I figured out long ago worms don't bite. No, it's the esoteric stuff—all those mysterious flies neatly laid out in compartments, the unfathomable reels.

The jargon turns me off as talk of swing weights, hitting from the top and pin position paralyzes the non-golfer.

I've never fished a river, brook or pond, although once an acquaintance, much to his eventual regret, talked me into an erratic cast upon a stream in upstate New York.

Bits of the line may still be found in an overhanging maple.

I've been deep sea fishing twice, if going four miles outside a harbor can be categorized as the deep sea. The first time, as my companions alternately guzzled beer and yanked haddock out of the depths outside Rockport, I became violently seasick and was convinced—in fact, hoped—I would die in 10 minutes.

The other time, in two hours on a 24-foot boat, I caught a sand shark and a sunburn, one of which I threw back.

Monty Montgomery, the Globe's outdoors typist—that is, he writes about the outdoors, but as far as I know, types indoors—keeps threatening to take me fishing.

He insists there's nothing mysterious about the sport and that I'll take to it like a fish, as they say, takes to water.

However, perhaps it's better to avoid reality. The actuality would never measure up to the romanticized version.

Like my visit to Puerto Rico, being there wouldn't be twice the fun.

A Florida paper vs Rommie Loudd—and the suggestion it was wrong

June 6, 1977—Few institutions are more adverse to admitting it might have made a mistake than the daily newspaper.

I don't mean the type of mistake in which John L. Doe's photo is published with John Q. Doe's name in the caption.

No, those bloopers are duly noted, if caught, in a correction box usually prominently displayed.

I'm talking about possible errors in judgment, errors of excess, errors brought on by the pressure of deadline or by misguided zeal.

And so, an editorial the other day in the *Orlando* (Fla.) *Sentinel-Star*, plus a long story in that paper's Sunday magazine, are worth mentioning.

Both the editorial and the story are about Rommie Loudd. I've written about him before. Maybe you're sick of reading about the case. You shouldn't be, not if you care about simple injustice.

Loudd is serving 14 years in a Florida prison on a pair of drug counts, being sentenced after a bizarre couple of years of trying to put together a pro football team in Orlando.

The intricacies of the case are more involved than the plans for building Apollo 14, but Loudd and those who feel he was railroaded have always contended that one of the principal forces behind the railroading was the *Orlando Sentinel-Star*.

The paper in March 1975 ran a story saying, "Rommie Loudd was sought . . . as the leader of a cocaine distribution ring . . . as the No. 1 man in a widesweeping organization trafficking in drugs from Florida to New England."

The *Sentinal-Star* quoted an unnamed district attorney as saying: "Everybody told us it was there, moving pounds of the stuff (cocaine) in lobster crates. Yes, players would come in and tell us about it, and so would other people."

Since then, the *Sentinel-Star* has acquired a new editor. His name is Jim Squires and last week Squires wrote a bylined editorial headlined—"The Rommie Loudd drug case; if he did it, he paid the price."

In the editorial, Squires observed: "The *Sentinel-Star*, through its political clout and by its coverage of the Loudd case, systematically created a climate in which there was no way Rommie Loudd could get a fair shake from the law."

A pretty strong admission from a newspaper.

Squires added that the paper's investigations do not prove that Loudd was framed, or otherwise trapped into selling the four ounces of cocaine that led to his arrest.

However, he does say the investigation "leaves no doubt that the drug investigators set out to get Rommie Loudd and got him."

Squires concludes that, "The *Sentinel-Star* is probably guilty of nothing more than shoot-from-the-hip journalism and a failure to demand proof and clarification of some rather outrageous statements by county investigators."

Those "outrageous" statements presumably include the "lobster crate" quote mentioned above.

The truth, according to *Sentinel-Star* Sunday magazine writer Diane Selditch is that "everybody was not talking about crates filled with cocaine."

These rumors, she said, "derived from a few investigators' interpretations of conversations" taped between Loudd and a man named Steven Cox.

Cox posed as Loudd's friend and as a potential WFL investor, but in reality he was a federal agent.

"They and the *Sentinel-Star* couldn't go all the way and admit they helped with the frame," remarked Bill Clark, the paper's former sports editor, who was fired for his unyielding support of Loudd.

"As good as the story looked," said Clark, "the *Sentinel* printed perhaps 40 percent of the full truth."

Perhaps, but even 40 percent seems to be about 39 percent more than was previously admitted by the paper. Please, by all the above, don't picture Loudd as a Sir Lancelot riding into Orlando to slay dragons. He made a carload of mistakes.

But he feels the news coverage "built me up as a killer, that's what got me 14 years. I was a bad sinner . . . but I'm not a drug dealer and I'm not a killer."

Writes Jim Squires: "In retrospect, it seems quite clear that had the general manager (Loudd) been a soft-spoken young white man, he could have bought four ounces of cocaine and no one would have cared . . . but because Loudd was black, had a big mouth and made himself a ton of enemies, he attracted the scrutiny others might have avoided.

"Under any circumstances," Squires continues, "the sentence he is serving seems grossly out of proportion to the harm Rommie Loudd did society."

There's a way to right that wrong—commute the sentence. Tomorrow would not be too soon.

Now that Silverman's gone, who's left to talk up boxing?

July 12, 1977—Miss me? Say you did. Say the last two weeks have been hell on earth. Tell me you've been pacing the floor, refusing to take any nourishment other than an occasional beaker of bourbon until I returned from vacation.

You didn't even realize I'd gone? May the Great Free Agent in the Sky grant you an unconditional release.

Anyway, I'm back, like it or not, and wish to thank Alan Richman, Monty Montgomery, Leigh Montville, Arthur Colinski, John Powers and The Mormon Tabernacle Choir for filling this space with witty words and heavy thoughts in my absence.

I'm back, but Sam Silverman isn't.

It's strange and sad to realize that Sam won't be walking into this office any more with news of his latest phenom.

In an era of high-powered public relations, when press releases are churned out on Xerox machines and come through the mail addressed to Occupant, Silverman still operated on a "me and you" basis.

He figured that if his stuff was going to have a chance of getting in the papers, he'd better deliver the goods in person. And so he'd come into the *Globe* with these godawful press releases, filled with more misspellings and misinformation than a fourth-grader's term paper.

Not much ever did make the paper, but a million rebuffs never dulled his enthusiasm. He just kept on coming down.

Sometimes we'd duck when we saw Sam coming, because he was a man who wouldn't take no for an answer. Thin-skinned he wasn't. Persistent he was.

"How about me bringin' in young Jimmy Corkum? The kid is a natural. You'll love him. Make a great column."

"Well, gee, Sam, I'm tied up all this week."

"How about two weeks from next Tuesday?"

"Gosh, I don't know."

"We can go down to the gym. You'll love the kid. Straight A student, but he hits like a truck."

As so many said yesterday, Sam's final house was a sell-out.

The Stanetsky-Schlossberg-Solomon Memorial Chapel in Brookline was filled as relatives and friends said goodby to boxing's Last Hurrah in New England.

Rabbi Daniel Kaplan's eulogy was excellent, especially his perception of the paradox that was Silverman's love of boxing.

Rabbi Kaplan pointed out that Silverman was not a 9 to 5 guy, and that time meant nothing to him. Yet he was in a business in which time was everything—the 10-second count, the three-minute round, even the split second timing of a jab.

Al Romano was at the funeral. Romano fought and lost Friday in Geneva, N.Y., and afterward he and Sam drove back to North Adams, Romano's home town.

"Usually after a fight I curl up and sleep in the back seat," said Romano, "but this time I drove. Got stopped for speeding. Isn't that somethin'? Me a cop and I get caught speeding."

Romano said he and Sam laughed and told stories and the ride from Geneva didn't seem long at all.

When they arrived in North Adams, Romano suggested to Sam that he stay overnight, rather than finish the lonely ride to Boston by himself.

"Nah, I'll be all right," Silverman said. "See you around." A few hours later came the accident that cost Sam his life.

My first prolonged encounter with Silverman was several years ago when he drove Larry Claflin and myself to Muhammad Ali's training camp in Deer Lake, Pa. That was some ride, 488-plus miles in Sam's Caddy, an unobtrusive chariot with the Massachusetts license plate, B-O-X-I-N-G.

We'd traveled about 60 miles down the Mass. Pike and the conversational level had never gone beyond who knocked who out in what round.

Sitting in the back seat, I thought: "I don't know if I can talk boxing for 488 miles. I'll get the conversation on a higher plane."

"Look at that," I said, pointing to a clump of trees infested with tent caterpillars. "The gypsy moths are really doing a job on the foliage around here."

Sam, with the speedometer hovering around 83 miles per hour, swung around and looked at me.

"What are you," he asked in astonishment, "some kind of outdoor nut?"

We talked about nothing but fights and fighters the rest of the way.

Now Sam is gone, and I'm not sure there's anyone left who wants to do that.

Jackie had courage plus

July 19, 1977—NEW YORK—"I put myself in his shoes," said Harold Reese, a Louisville businessman. "I think about what it must have been like for him. I think of myself trying to make it in an all-black league, and know I couldn't have done it."

Pee Wee Reese was the captain and shortstop of the Brooklyn Dodgers when you and I were young, Maggie. He was one helluva ballplayer, maybe even better than Bucky Dent.

He was talking yesterday about another man who played with the Dodgers of those innocent—at least in retrospect—years of the '40s and '50s.

He was talking about Jack Roosevelt Robinson. The 1977 All-Star game is dedicated to Robinson's memory, and yesterday a few of those who knew him best gathered at a luncheon and remembered what it was like when he broke into organized—that is, Caucasian—baseball.

Roy Campanella was at the head table in his wheel chair. Campanella has spent the last 54 weeks in a hospital, lying flat on his stomach. He looks old and drawn and not terribly well.

"There is no way I would have missed this luncheon," he said. "I think about those days often. What would have happened if we'd lost? What would have happened if Mr. Rickey had brought the blacks to the Dodgers and we'd fallen on our faces? Gee, it was great that we won consistently. We showed we could play."

Around him, black reporters took notes and black photographers snapped pictures. Thirty years ago, it hadn't been like that. Thirty years ago, only the waiters would have been black.

Branch Rickey signed Campanella and Don Newcombe and wanted to send them to Danville, Ill., of the Three-I League.

"If you do that," said the president of the Three-I League, "I'll disband the league."

Rickey then contacted Buzzy Bavasi, who was running the Nashua team in the New England League.

"I've signed two Negroes," he said to Bavasi. "Will you take them?"

"If they can play baseball, send them up," replied Bavasi.

But Newcombe and Campy weren't the first. Jackie Robinson was first.

"Jackie Robinson," said a press release from the White House yesterday, "changed the face and soul of baseball."

I doubt Jimmy Carter personally came up with that line, but whichever of his PR men did think of it didn't go far enough.

Robinson changed the face and soul of not only baseball, but of all America. Nobody is naive enough to say that race relations in this country are one great big smooth superhighway, but before Robinson arrived, there were very few roads out of the wilderness.

We often misuse the word "courage" in sportswriting, saying a relief pitcher showed great courage in striking out the side with the bases loaded. That's not courage. What Robinson did was.

"I was on a ship returning from Guam," said Reese, "and a guy said to me: 'They've just signed a black to play for Brooklyn.' Only I'd have to say that the word the guy used was not 'black'."

The information puzzled Reese. Like most of white America he had notions of what a black athlete was like.

"I just assumed they weren't good enough for the big leagues. I heard the talk, you know, that if you threw at them, they backed down. They couldn't stand the pressure."

Robinson spent 1946, his first year in pro ball, in Montreal, where he burned up the International League, took eight tons of abuse, and kept his mouth shut.

Reese first saw him in spring training in 1947.

"We looked at him. Everybody looked at him. They were curious. He was big and . . . well . . . he was black. You know how guys would stop to watch Williams hit? That's the way it was with Jackie."

He was vilified in 1947. Both opponents and teammates let him know what they thought of his uppityness. Fans called him "nigger" and "watermelon eater."

"Mr. Rickey," Robinson said at one point, "are you looking for a black man who's afraid to fight back?"

Replied Rickey: "No, I'm looking for a ballplayer with enough guts not to fight back."

Reese remembers when the passivity ended. In a Florida exhibition game in '48, Pee Wee threw a ball to Robinson, who took off his glove and shook his hand in pain.

"Oh, poor little Jackie Robinson," mocked the rival third base coach, "he hurt his poor little nigger hand."

Robinson walked from second base to the coaching box. He shook his finger in the coach's face and said, according to Reese: "Don't you ever talk to me that way again. If you do, you'd better be ready."

From that moment, Turn-the-Other-Cheek Robinson became Put-Up-Your-Fists Robinson. He was a black who knew his place, and his place was in a major league box score.

It's all ancient history now, the changes Robinson wrought. Perhaps time would have brought about the changes anyway, but in 1947, a catalyst was needed and he was it.

Somebody asked Reese if Robinson was the best man for that job.

"I don't know," replied Pee Wee. "There might have been better black players available, but none was a Jackie Robinson. Best man? He might have been the only man."

Fifteen ways to spot the Sports Nut at a cocktail party

August 1, 1977—When I get introduced to somebody and the small talk gets around to what we do for a living, I generally say I'm a certified public accountant or mumble that I travel for IBM in Vermont, New Hampshire and Western Massachusetts.

I try to keep my true occupation a secret, because as soon as it's discovered that I write about sports, the conversation goes like Hiawatha's arrow right to that subject.

It doesn't matter that I might like to toss out an opinion on an important issue, such as the philosophy of Erica Jong, or the hidden meaning in punk rock.

No, when the word goes out that "that guy over there is a sportswriter," I get hit with "can the Patriots do it this year?" and "what's Bill Lee really like?"

I'm not exactly sure why this is so. At a cocktail party, people don't show a dentist their latest cavity, or ask a stockbroker if this is a good time to get into soybean futures.

What I've found, though, is that once the talk has switched to life's sandbox, people can be separated into two categories—the sports nut and the casual fan, on the ratio of about 50 to 1.

For instance:

The sports nut knows who's leading both leagues in doubles. He knows Steve Grogan's career passing yardage and the uniform number worn by Bad News Barnes.

The casual fan knows Rod Carew was on Time Magazine's cover, but isn't exactly sure why.

The sports nut watches the Hall of Fame football game on television Saturday afternoon.

The casual fan isn't aware there is a football Hall of Fame.

The sports nut, when he's in a car at night, listens to the Orioles on WBAL-Baltimore if the Red Sox are rained out.

The casual fan, when driving, listens to music.

The sports nut brings a transistor radio to the ballpark.

The casual fan rarely brings himself to the ballpark.

The sports nut turns down the sound while watching the Red Sox on TV and listens to Ned Martin and Jim Woods do the radio broadcast.

The casual fan may watch the game for a while, but then either falls asleep or switches to an Abbott and Costello movie.

The sports nut spends 20 minutes a day reading the Globe Scoreboard.

The casual fan goes from the headlines to the obits.

The sports nut knows who Doug Dumler is.

The casual fan doesn't know who Ray Hamilton is.

The sports nut goes into convulsions when Johnny Most's name is mentioned.

The casual fan thinks Johnny Most is hilarious.

The sports nut, at halftime of a televised football game, switches to another channel to see if the first half of the other game has ended yet.

The casual fan, at halftime of a televised game, takes his kids for a ride and doesn't return until supper.

The sports nut knows the height, weight and time in the 40-yard dash for the top 20 college prospects.

The casual fan may have heard of Tony Dorsett, but doesn't know whether he played for Penn State or Pitt, or both.

The sports nut will watch a delayed tape of the UMass-Holy Cross football game at 9 p.m. on Channel 27.

The casual fan thinks Holy Cross dropped football 15 years ago.

The sports nut lingers in the runway at Fenway Park even though the Red Sox are losing, 12-3, with two out and nobody on base in the ninth.

The casual fan, attending his one game of the year ("because the kids have been on my ear") leaves in the seventh inning of a 4-4 tie to beat the traffic.

The sports nut listens to every sports talk show in town.

The casual fan thinks Clif and Claf is a dance team.

The sports nut will watch a Monday night baseball game between the Reds and the San Diego Padres.

The sports nut thinks the America's Cup trials are a crock of chicken fat.

The casual fan thinks the America's Cup trial races are a crock of chicken fat.

And now, if you'll excuse me, I must get home to watch the Philadelphia Golf Classic on Channel 44. If I turn the set so it's facing south, the double vision won't be so bad and I'll get nice clear pictures of John Listen and Rod Curl and all the immortals.

What they really think

August 4, 1977—Sports are filled with strategy, we all know that. There are team meetings, conversations on the mound, crucial time-out situations where subtle and important decisions have a direct bearing on the outcome of the contest.

But what are the participants really thinking? In their heart of hearts, what would they really like to say? I've done some research on this and would like to present some this morning.

For example, there are men on first and second in a close game. Out comes manager Don Zimmer from the dugout. Over comes shortstop Rick Burleson. Catcher Carlton Fisk walks slowly to the mound, mask in hand.

Here's the conversation:

ZIMMER: He'll be bunting. Give him some high heat and be ready to bounce off the mound.

FISK: If you got a chance to get him at third, I'll yell, so listen up.

BURLESON: I remember this guy from the International League. He likes to push the bunt towards first.

But here's what they're thinking:

FISK: Gawd, I'm tired. If you throw one more baseball in the dirt, chase it yourself.

BURLESON: With the meatballs you're throwing, if I was the manager I'd have everybody swinging away and to hell with the bunt.

ZIMMER: For crissakes, fiddle around with the resin bag until Campbell says he's ready.

The Patriots are behind by six points, but have a drive going. The ball is on the enemy 33, third and six, with 43 seconds left. There is a time out and Steve Grogan trots to the sidelines to confer with Chuck Fairbanks.

Here's what they say:

GROGAN: The linebackers are blitzing and the corners are rotating. I think they're ripe for the 34 draw on a quick count.

FAIRBANKS: The word from upstairs is that in a similar situation last week, their linebackers dropped back and flip-flopped and the cornerbacks folded under. Better try the 82 fly.

What they're thinking:

GROGAN: We don't have a Chinaman's chance with the 82 fly. That play hasn't worked since training camp. I'll call it off at the line of scrimmage and run with the ball myself.

FAIRBANKS: The 34 draw is a terrible play, but so is the 82 fly. I hope he calls it off at the line of scrimmage, so I can blame him when the game is over.

With 12 seconds to go, the Celtics have the ball. They are one point behind, call a time-out and huddle around coach Tom Heinsohn.

Here's what Heinsohn says: OK, now we'll go to the six play. David, you pick for Sidney. Charlie will be the outlet, and if that doesn't work, go to the option for Jo Jo.

Here's what Heinsohn is thinking: Please, Lord, make 'em give the ball to Havlicek.

Harry the Hacker is in the left rough, 170 yards from the green. He is uncertain as to whether to hit a four or five iron, so discusses the situation with his caddy.

HARRY THE HACKER: If I really jump on the shot, a five ought to be enough. But maybe a smooth four will be better, because the ball will fly out of the rough. What do you think?

CADDY: I'd go with the four. Nice and easy does it. If you give it a left to right fade, the ball should move in there nicely.

What they're thinking:

HARRY THE HACKER: This kid doesn't know a four-iron from a flatiron. The last time I took his advice I played my next shot from the clubhouse dining room.

CADDY: This guy couldn't reach the green from here if he had a mortar in his bag. His idea of a good shot is a double Seagrams in a short glass. Close your eyes and pray, dummy.

The bout is ready to start, and the fighters are gathered with the referee in the center of the ring for instructions.

REFEREE: OK, you both know the rules. No gouging, no butting, no hitting below the belt, no hitting after the bell. There will be a mandatory eight-count on knockdowns. Upon a knockdown, the other fighter will go to his corner until ordered to resume fighting. Good luck and come out punching.

What they're thinking:

FIGHTER NO. 1: First chance I get, I slice this stiff with my laces.

FIGHTER NO. 2: First chance I get, this stiff gets an elbow above the eye.

REFEREE: I'm glad I didn't have to pay to see this swindle.

7

1978

Good wasn't good enough

January 8, 1978—The sword of dissatisfaction always has hovered there, about four feet above Joe Yukica's head.

In 10 years as the Boston College football coach, his teams had only one losing season. They won 68 games, an average of nearly seven a season.

The 68 wins are 20 more than any other coach chalked up at BC since football began there in 1893.

Yet the sword always has hung there. Joe Yukica never was quite good enough for what the zealots demanded. Perhaps 11-0 might have swayed them, but not 8-3.

Yukica and his BC teams have always been hemmed in. On the one side were alumni who won't forget Frank Leahy and the Sugar Bowl glory if they live to be 105. Never mind that this is 1978 and if Frank Leahy were alive and coaching the Eagles, he'd be thankful for an 8-3 record, given the same conditions as Yukica.

Yukica was hemmed in on the other side by a "damned if you do and damned if you don't" scheduling syndrome.

It has not been enough to play Texas, Georgia Tech, Texas A&M, Penn State, Pittsburgh and the rest of the big-timers that dotted Yukica's schedule—schools that have much freer recruiting methods and less stringent entrance policies.

Yukica's teams have played some exciting and interesting games against these national powers, but that hasn't been enough. Only victories would have been enough.

The rest of BC's schedule always has been with teams the Eagles were either even with or better than, from a manpower situation.

Victory then became humdrum, expected, and defeat a disgrace.

"Oh, yeah, BC beat Temple. So what? They should beat Temple. They should beat Villanova, UMass, Holy Cross. Who cares? They lost to Texas, didn't they? Yukica's a bum."

If the schedule had been different—if, for example, BC would schedule Boston University, Colgate and Rutgers instead of Tennessee, Stanford and Pittsburgh in 1979, BC might go 11-0. But it wouldn't matter, because the cry would be: "Yeah, but who did they play?"

There really, truly was no way Joe Yukica could win as coach of Boston College.

And so, the other night driving back from a meeting with Dartmouth athletic director Seaver Peters in Hanover, N.H., Yukica made a decision.

"The closer I got to Boston, the more sure I was that I ought to take the Dartmouth job," he said.

Joe Yukica says he's not going to Dartmouth to get away from the never-

never land of BC football. He says it's not to retreat from the rat race or out of the mainstream of big-time football.

He says the pressures of coaching college football will be similar at Dartmouth, and the recruiting even tougher.

Maybe so. But at Dartmouth, he knows what's expected of him. Dartmouth has a football tradition equal to Boston College's, with one big difference. It is in a league.

Dartmouth has something to shoot for—the Ivy League championship. There is a constancy, a goal, a target, that BC will never have as an independent. You don't have to win every game to be Ivy League champion. You just have to finish better than anyone else in the league, a realistic task.

If you are a big-time independent, you think about bowls. You think about national exposure. You think, in the case of Notre Dame or Penn State or Pitt, of being the best college football team in the country. BC, betwixt and between big-time and ordinary time, can never think in those terms and has no conference championship as an alternate target.

Yukica has been criticized by the media for being conservative and for not getting enough out of the studs who have gone on to the pros.

But he has punched no photographers, lashed out at no detractors. He says he understands how the alumni feel when his team loses and why the media write harsh things.

He's a gentle man, but a tough-skinned one who knows right from wrong. Probably the hardest time of his 10 seasons with BC was the Ken Smith situation this fall.

Yukica could have told the wobbly quarterback to take a shower and be ready for Syracuse on Saturday, and nobody would have been the wiser. But that would have been the easy way out. Suspension was the rough road, and the one Yukica took. It cost his team a ballgame.

Yukica is a great recruiter, terrific at remembering names and with parents. He had the respect of his players but was no dutch uncle to them.

"No player ever called him Joe," says a man close to the situation, "but if they had a serious problem, they could go to him."

What makes a good football coach? Some say the win-loss record tells it all. I say it's a man who goes at his job in a professional manner and who keeps what he does in perspective. I say a good coach is someone I'd like to have my son play for.

I'd have no reservations about my son playing for Joe Yukica.

Yours truly confesses he isn't THAT much of a sport

February 7, 1978—I write this in an attempt to purge myself of a cartload of guilt I've been dragging for years. Let me explain.

Back when kids wore knickers and anyone wearing white sneakers was considered strange or a tennis player or both, sports meant team sports.

Kids played football, basketball, baseball and hockey. Golf was for rich people, tennis for guys who liked to wear white sweaters with a red and blue V-neck, bowling for the working man on his night out with the boys, and boxing for underprivileged kids in big city gyms.

Everything was structured and sports-minded people knew their place.

A metamorphosis has gradually taken place. Affluence, increased mobility and more leisure time have allowed sports enthusiasts to seek new horizons and now there are almost as many participatory sports as there are human beings. Team games are out and sports for the individual are in.

Everyone I know seems to be involved in something offbeat. This one is going to the club for a game of racquetball. That one is heading for a comfortable jog around Lake Erie. The other one is thrilled over the new ski lift at that darling mountain in New Hampshire.

All this leaves a traditionalist with a feeling that time has passed him by. I say, as I turn on the television set to watch the Bruins, that I'll get with it tomorrow, but of course tomorrow never comes.

However, I'm sick and tired of feeling like a decadent reactionary. I have my rights. If I want to curl up with a good book instead of risking frostbite fishing for perch through the ice I shouldn't feel guilty.

And so this morning, I'd like to share with you some thoughts on why, if I live to be a thousand, I won't participate in any of the following sports:

Orienteering—Until the day before yesterday, I thought one had to go to the Far East for this, but I'm told you can do it in any convenient woods. It has something to do with following maps with compasses, but since I can't find my way from Norwood to Dedham without a police escort, going into the woods without a rope tied both to my waist and my back porch would be tantamount to suicide.

Sailing—I was 14 years old before I learned to tie my shoes, and know that if I had to handle ropes—excuse me, lines—I would so foul up a sailboat it would take a squadron of Eagle scouts a month to undo the damage. Besides, I get seasick in the shower.

Skiing—Remember Jimmy Piersall's book, "Fear Strikes Out"? In the matter of downhill skiing, fear strikes me out, on three pitches. Under no circumstances will I slide down a hill on anything more exotic than a Flexible Flyer.

It is possible I might try cross-country skiing. A friend told me anyone can do it. "Just strap two boards to your feet," he said, "and walk like Groucho Marx." Since I already walk like Groucho Marx, half the battle is won.

Hunting—If I shot a deer, I'd be so filled with remorse I'd turn myself in to the nearest police station and ask to be committed as an incorrigible murderer. I wouldn't mind firing at a duck and missing, except that one of the requirements for this seems to be that the hunter stand in water up to his clavicle. As for big game hunting, no thanks. Even if I brought down a kudu or a rhino, the only spot in the house big enough to keep it is the bath tub, and there's already a Labrador retriever sleeping there.

Jogging—I've done some research on this sport, and have discovered it was invented by a surly wire-haired terrier who became bored with chasing car wheels, so developed a fetish for barking at humans and biting their ankles.

Fishing—I might relent on this if the fish would cooperate and emerge from the water filleted and broiled to a golden brown. As for deep sea fishing, I've never been able to figure out how they stuff those big tuna fish into those little cans. I know you think that if I had a million bucks I'd buy a 120-footer and seek out the wily marlin. Wrong. If I had a million, I'd buy the Oakland A's and move them to Braintree.

Sky Diving—The reason I will never try this is that one can't say, in midair, "Oh, I don't feel like playing, my knee hurts."

Other sports I will never, under pain of death by firing squad, attempt, include pole vaulting, bobsledding (Fear Strikes Me Out, Part 2), snowmobiling, fencing, diving off the high board (FSMO, Part 3), skeet shooting, mountain climbing and drag racing.

You can have them all. Give me a can of beer, an easy chair and the NFL highlights and pray that my soul doesn't shrivel into the world's largest prune.

Time passes Ali by

February 17, 1978—Time beat him. The noiseless foot of Time overtakes everybody. You can spar for a long while and win some decisions, you can trick Time with rope-a-dope gimmicks and tiptoe through a lot of years with slick talk and razzle dazzle and a mountain of ability.

But sooner or later, there are no more pages in the ledger. Time is the winner, not with a dramatic knockout, not with the jarring left hook to the jaw, and the thundering right cross to the side of the head, but with subtle jabs and counter-punches.

The legs can no longer dance for 15 rounds. The arms, pistons no more, are instead unliftable logs attached to shoulders that have a thousand rounds weighing them down.

The instincts are there, but the reactions aren't. The difference may only be a second—no, a split second—but the difference is enough.

Time over the last 17 years was David with a slingshot, sending stone after stone at Muhammad Ali. Wednesday night in Las Vegas, Ali fell.

The problem with the Muhammad Ali era of boxing—an era that stretches from his dramatic victory over Sonny Liston in 1964 to Wednesday's equally dramatic loss to Leon Spinks—has always been that it's impossible to tell the flim-flam from the genuine article.

When was Ali kidding? When did he mean it? How was one ever to separate the precious metal from fool's gold?

For all these years he's been the consummate con man of sports, a carnival barker working an around-the-clock shell game, the card shark saying "pick a card, any card."

The customers have flocked to his booth, sure they could find him out, certain they'd discover the shell with the pea under it.

And just when they thought they'd unmasked him as a fraud, just when they said: "That one, it's under that one," he'd grin and reply: "Gotcha again, sucker," and pocket another million.

Even in the fight Wednesday night, which ended with Ali so exhausted he could barely stand up, the doubts persisted.

"So he lost," said a cynic. "So he fights the guy again and makes another $3 million. It's the best thing that could have happened to him."

Before the fight, Madison Square Garden matchmaker Teddy Brenner commented: "Ali can't get in shape anymore. All he can do is control his weight."

And Angelo Dundee, Ali's trainer since it all began in 1962, said: "This is the hardest he's worked in seven years. He knows what we have to contend with. He's 36 years old. This could be the end of the rainbow. He remembers a guy named Cassius Clay, an 8-1 shot that wasn't supposed to beat Sonny Liston. For this fight, the positions are reversed."

We should have believed Brenner. We should have believed Angelo Dundee. We should, as a matter of fact, have believed what our eyes have been telling us for the last couple of years.

The man was hanging on. His talent was only a fraction of what it was in his prime.

When Joe Louis was on the downside of his career, all those who followed boxing knew it. They didn't have to be told that the Louis, who was knocked out in the eighth round by Rocky Marciano in 1951, was only the shell of the kid who tore Max Schmeling apart in one round in 1938.

Time had done its job on Joe Louis, so why should we think Muhammad Ali was immune?

But Ali's career has been such an amalgam of flim-flam and talent, such a mixture of shill and skill, that he mesmerized us all. He yelled out: "What's the total of two and two," and we all screamed back: "Five, Ali, five."

Now there will be an outcry that Ali retire in dignity. "Go out in style," the experts will say, "so that we can remember you in all your greatness." As if everything he accomplished would somehow be wiped out of the record books and out of our memories if he keeps fighting.

I've written these words in other times about other athletes, and about Ali, too. It's a presumption I will not repeat today.

The decision belongs to Ali. He needs no advice from those of us who have never been exposed to the smell of big money and the roar of the crowd.

Yesterday, the papers played up big the dramatic photo of Leon Spinks, arms outthrust and mouth in a gap-toothed smile. A man who has had only 31 rounds of professional boxing, a man who stumbled to a draw with a mediocrity named Scott LeDoux is the new heavyweight champion.

The papers should have run a three-column picture of an hourglass, with the sand running out. Time is the new champion.

You know it and I know it, but until Muhammad Ali knows it, let him keep going, if that's what he wants.

Too many bad actors

April 25, 1978—This is grouch day. This is snarl-at-the-world day. My golf ball spent the weekend in Sherwood Forest. My car is coughing like Greta Garbo in "Camille." My wallet is flatter than Kansas.

Today, my cup isn't half full, it's half empty. There is poison in the typewriter, and so you can have these people connected with sports:

—Ballplayers who blame their glove, the sun, the soft outfield, a pebble or weak biorhythms when they make an error.

—The misguided genius who invented the electronic messageboard.

—Weekend golfers who linger over each shot as though the ball might explode if they hit it.

—Pro football referees who are unavailable for comment after controversial plays.

—Baseball fans who slosh down beer, pay absolutely no attention to the ballgame and think their ticket gives them a license to spout obscenities for three hours.

—Alumni at big-time athletic mills who not only insist on winning, but on winning big.

—Little League coaches who tell a kid to go up to the plate and wait out a walk.

—Highly paid professionals who say it's impossible to be up for every game, thus insulting the sap who paid 12 fish under the delusion he was going to see something interesting.

—Spikers, dancers, knee-wigglers and other end zone exhibitionists.

—Pro players who hide in the trainers' room after a bad performance.

—Liquored-up exhibitionists who start fights in the stands.

—Tennis players who argue over close calls. Their shot is never out, and the other guy's is never in.

—People who put down Ivy League football simply because it doesn't supply the pros with a carload of talent every season.

—Golfers who think a fairway is their own private sandbox and never replace a divot.

—Basketball players who would swear on a Bible they've never committed a foul.

—Fans who lean over the railing to grab fair balls hit down the lines.

—Agents who take advantage of athletes.

—Athletes who take advantage of agents.

—Agents and athletes who think the paying public has bottomless pockets.

—Lame-brain television moguls who think switching from game to game is giving the viewer what he wants.

—Basketball coaches who prowl the sidelines.

—Weekend tennis players who show up for a match with three racquets.

—Fans who can think of nothing more inspiring than to chant "We're No. 1," when their team wins a championship.

—A permissive society that allows 14-year-olds to get wacked out on beer at noon on Lansdowne street waiting for the bleacher gates to open.

—Little League parents who criticize umpires but would crawl through a sewer before they'd volunteer for the job.

—College basketball stars who think the world is a free ride, taking all and giving nothing but the ability to throw a leather ball through a basket.

—The fiends who built the rest rooms and concession stands at Fenway Park, both of which look like a cattle drive whenever the park is full.

—Guys who tell me that if you see the last five minutes of a basketball game, you've seen it all.

—Cretins in the stands who throw nuts and bolts, oranges, tennis balls, pennies, rubber chickens and other debris onto playing surfaces.

—Fans who leave their seats two minutes before the end of a hockey period so they can get to the beer line or rest room before the crowd.

—Players who tell me, "What difference does it make what I say? You guys write what you want anyway."

—Natural athletes who don't get the most out of their talents because of dissipation, lack of desire or bad attitude.

—Entertainment celebrities (is there really a Robert Conrad?) who live out their jock fantasies in TV trash-sports.

—Everyone around Leon Spinks, a bewildered kid on the greasy road to nowhere.

A little girl is now a doctor

June 12, 1978—The litany of names had begun.

Sharon Elizabeth Akrep . . . Jeffrey Austerlitz . . . Peter Alexander Bevins . . . Morris Jay Birnbaum . . . Paul Howard Bromfield . . .

The father looked at the faces that went with the names. Strangers. Each was flesh and blood to some other father. Each represented love, hope, ambition, memories.

But to this particular father, they were just stick figures, walking through June sunshine. The selfishness of parenthood, the father thought.

The father and mother and brother and grandmother and aunt were peering through a window on the second story landing of an administration building at Brown University.

They'd come to see a daughter, a sister, a granddaughter, a niece graduate from Brown Medical School.

They'd come to see the little kid who'd spent part of the first year of her life with her foot in a cast become a doctor.

Alan S. Brown . . . Richard Amblard Browning . . . Sheila Elyse Buchbinder . . . John Richard Cangemi . . . Rick Allen Chamberlain . . .

The father could see her at last, shuffling along in line with her classmates, wearing the brown gown with green cowl that signified medical school.

Two weeks before, the father and mother had sat in a leafy courtyard in the middle of Philadelphia and watched their son graduate from law school. It had been a proud moment. So was this a proud moment, and also a bittersweet one, because this was the last of their four children to complete college.

A busy corner of life had been passed, to be seen again only in photo albums or memories, and the father felt happy and sad at the same time.

Maybe I should go down there, he thought, and as she gets her degree, run up on stage and say, "Th-th-th-that's all, folks," like Porky Pig.

William Harry Cooper . . . Joel Michael Corwin . . . Marc Lemay Cullen . . . Edward Vincent Cyburn . . . Kenneth Robert Dawson . . .

Tevye, in Fiddler on the Roof, sings: "I don't remember growing older. When did they?"

Ah, when did they? Wasn't it last year the lawyer had fallen out of bed and cut his nose on a toy telephone? Wasn't it last week the doctor had welcomed the soldiers at the Highland School Veterans' Day pageant?

She'd begun her speech "Dear Vethrens," and everybody had giggled.

Wasn't it yesterday the lawyer had been confirmed by Bishop Weldon with a slap across the face heard in the back row at St. Mary's Church?

Wasn't it 10 minutes ago the doctor had wanted to know if it was okay if she lived in a co-ed dorm and her parents had said "sure," but they weren't so sure.

Charles Denby II . . . David Van Diamond . . . Edward Stanley Domurat Jr. . . . David Steven Egilman . . . Eileen Claire Fitzgerald. . . .

The father got this funny feeling in the pit of his stomach, and suddenly his eyes didn't seem to work right.

His daughter, the doctor, would know why.

He looked; justice hid

September 3, 1978—A little more than a year ago, Don Reese and Randy Crowder, linemen for the Miami Dolphins, were sent to jail for selling 21 ounces of cocaine to an undercover agent.

This afternoon, Reese and Crowder, already released from prison, will be back on the NFL playing fields. Reese is a defensive lineman with the New Orleans Saints and Crowder an offensive lineman with Tampa.

Now for a little contrast.

In July of 1975, Rommie Loudd, once an NFL player, once a coach, once a personnel director, once a general manager, was sent to prison for arranging the purchase of four ounces of cocaine for a man who turned out to be an undercover agent.

This afternoon, Rommie Loudd will be where he's been every Sunday for the last three years and two months—inside the walls of Avon Park Correctional Institute in Central Florida.

Reese and Crowder spent a year in jail for their 21-ounce sale of cocaine. Loudd got 14 years for his involvement with only four ounces.

And Loudd's involvement contains circumstances so murky, so ill-defined as to make his guilt, four years later, a matter of continuing debate and doubt.

There is no begrudging here the release of Crowder and Reese after a relatively short incarceration.

But one wonders what tree justice is hiding behind when Loudd still languishes in the backwoods of Central Florida, victim of a tangle of half-truths and legal inertia.

"I'll probably watch some of Oakland against Denver in our television room," Loudd said yesterday over the phone from the chaplain's office, where he serves as aide and chief liaison with the inmates.

He said he tries to keep up with the Patriots, a team he once served as assistant coach and later as personnel director in the bad old days.

"I'm very happy things are turning out so well for Billy Sullivan," said Loudd. "I have a great love for that man."

Loudd long ago became resigned to his role at Avon Park and has built a new life for himself.

He's made 60 speaking appearances outside the prison to rehabilitation groups, talking about the principles of living according to Christ.

"I didn't have a chip on my shoulder when I came here," he said yesterday "but I wasn't the happiest man in the world either. But in here I've met people a lot worse off than I am, people who need help. There are worse things in life than not having Saturday off."

Loudd's biggest regret is that he's never been able to share the college experience of his son, Rommie Jr., a senior at Washington University of St. Louis.

"I've never had a chance to walk the campus with him. But he's gonna make it. He could graduate this December."

His daughter, Cheryl, is a sophomore at Rollins College in Winter Park, Fla.

There's a good chance, said Loudd, that he'll be paroled in October.

He's applied to Florida parole examiner Howard Sullivan and the application has been forwarded to the parole board in Tallahassee.

But a parole, though it sends a man into the outside world, does not exonerate him. It does not shout, "This man was wrongfully committed. This man was railroaded."

And so Loudd will continue, when he gets out, to work at proving that he was not guilty but was a victim of entrapment by an overzealous narcotics agent.

The entire Loudd conviction, from square one, was as flimsy as a paper airplane. He was put away mostly on evidence given by Steven Cox, the undercover agent who said Loudd arranged for him to buy four ounces of cocaine.

But Cox has since been shown to be the most unreliable of characters, and recently was fired by the sheriff of Orange County, the third law enforcement job he has lost.

Mel Colman, the sheriff, said Cox "ran amok in this community" (Orlando) and conducted himself in an "irresponsible and unprofessional manner."

Rayburn Wood, an agent who worked with Cox during the Loudd episode, told an attorney recently that Loudd "definitely was entrapped," and was also quoted as saying, "I never saw or heard of Loudd selling or using dope."

Other deputies now reportedly say they wouldn't believe anything Cox says under oath.

Loudd has been offered three jobs when the ponderous Florida judicial system finally decides to release him. One is with evangelist Bill Glass, the former Cleveland Browns lineman, another with Campus Crusades and the third with a detoxification center in Stuart, Fla.

He is leaning toward the last one.

Loudd was asked if he worried about the "dope peddler" whispers and pointed fingers he might encounter in the real world.

"I've had fingers pointed at me all my life. If I had to worry about them now, I wouldn't leave the house," said the man who reached out for justice in Florida and instead was given a handful of indifference.

Lunacy and Sox fan

September 25, 1978—The ambulance crew brought the man into the emergency room of the hospital at 7:40 p.m. They'd answered an anonymous call and found him wandering aimlessly on a Back Bay street, talking to lampposts and trying to interest a wire-haired terrier in a game of cribbage.

"Lay him on the cot," said the doctor on duty. "Any identification?"

"Not much to go on," replied the ambulance driver. "Just some loose change and an American League schedule in his pocket. And he was wearing this tag around his neck."

The doctor read the inscription on the tag.

"I am a Boston Red Sox fan and no longer responsible for my actions. If found, bury me at home plate, next to the team's pennant chances."

The doctor shook his head.

"Another one of those. It's close to an epidemic. We're running out of room here. If they keep coming in, we'll have to set up some cots in the state armory."

The doctor motioned to a nurse.

"Give him the usual. Twenty cc of pennant fever. Maybe he'll revive enough to tell us his name."

The nurse plunged a needle into the unfortunate's arm and the man began to stir.

"Never . . . should . . . take out . . . Willoughby," he muttered.

The doctor nodded.

"He's the same as the rest," the doctor said. "As soon as the serum takes hold they begin talking about the seventh game of the 1975 World Series. Here, help me sit him up."

The nurse and doctor gently propped the man into a sitting position. He immediately began shaking uncontrollably and chanting: "Bernie, Bernie, Bernie, we need you."

The nurse grabbed a nearby blanket and threw it around the man's shoulders.

"Steady," she said. "You're among friends. Try to relax and say anything that comes into your mind."

The man opened his eyes.

"You look like Don Zimmer," he said to the doctor and tried to punch him.

It took two orderlies to get the man under control. The doctor stayed at a safe distance as the man lapsed into a stream of consciousness.

"They come into a game they gotta win and it's that stiff Torrez on the mound again. Five-hunnert and 40 grand he gets. Twenty-five grand every time he starts a game. Right away he throws up some meatballs and we fall behind, 3-0. We go ahead, 4-3, but blow a hunnert chances to put the game away. We play as though the Blue Jays was the 1955 Dodgers. Then we blow the lead in the eighth. Absolutely blow it, ya hear me. Campbell gets two strikes on Mayberry and grooves one. It's the beard. Why don't he get rid of the beard? Last year he didn't have no beard and he done good. Campbell gets the next two guys and then here comes Zimmer to take him out. He brings in Stanley. He's gotta know the guy's tired. He's gotta know the kid's got nothin'. Second pitch, two-run double, ooh, my head hurts. . . ."

The doctor frowned.

"This is as bad a case as I've seen," he said. "Give him the never-say-die pill, the big green one with the tadpoles in the middle."

The nurse forced the pill down the man's throat and he babbled some more.

"We get a million breaks in the ninth. Walks and a balk and their first baseman boots a doubleplay ball and we tie the score. We got a chance to win it, guys on first and third with one out and we fall on our faces. Zimmer orders a squeeze. I'd like to give him a squeeze under a steamroller. It don't work, naturally, and we don't score no more.

"Then Zimmer orders an intentional walk to load bases. Twice he does it. He gets away with it in the 11th so he does it again in the 13th. Walks the bases loaded to pitch to Velez, and then that line drive down the left field line and we lose. . . ."

The man began frothing at the mouth.

The nurse whispered into the man's ear.

"They won the game," she hissed. "Velez' liner went foul. The Red Sox won in the 14th."

The wretch threw off the blanket.

"Aw right," he yelled. "We're still alive. One game back and it's a six-game season, all at home."

The fan stood up, combed his hair, straightened his tie and walked jauntily out the door.

The doctor watched him go.

"And they call penicillin the miracle drug," he said.

Yaz still chasing that elusive prize

October 3, 1978—The ball had floated into the air, the laziest sort of a pop up and a certain out, whether the third baseman was Graig Nettles or the kid next door.

And as Nettles grabbed the ball, amid the stunned silence of Fenway Park, you thought, this isn't the way it should end. Not like this. Not with Yaz making the final out.

Somewhere there should be a film director, wearing a beret and shouting through a megaphone: "Another take, gentlemen, and this time, let's get it right."

"Yaz, this time look for the pitch to move inside. Rick, be ready to run when the ball goes through the first base hole. All right, places everyone. Second take, Red Sox American League East playoff victory."

But that's not the way it works. The Back Bay is not Burbank. The passion play that is baseball is one time only before a live audience. You can't erase the tapes and start over. There are no second takes.

And so it's finished, the crazy-quilt 1978 Red Sox season. And the final irony is that the man who had the last swing in that season is the man who most wanted to keep it going—the man still chasing the one prize that has eluded him, the honor of playing with a world champion.

"I wanted New York to win," said a teenager waving a Yankee pennant, "but he was the last man I wanted to see make the last out."

After every game, win or lose, Yastrzemski gets a beer, lights up a cigarette and sits at his locker, thinking about what has just happened on the field.

Not yesterday. He came down the runway, up the stairs to the clubhouse and went into the trainer's room, to cry away his disappointment.

He is 39 years old, and perhaps 39-year-olds should not shed tears over the loss of an athletic contest.

But few of us go at our profession with the intensity of Carl Yastrzemski, therefore few of us are so devastated when what we reach for slips from our grasp.

Later, Yaz came out to face the forest of microphones and the white lights of the cameras and the ballpoint battalions.

He talked about the Rich Gossage pitch that got him out. He'd had no extraneous thoughts, he said, as he walked to the plate, no extra pressure from the crowd noise. He hears no noise, he said, his concentration is so complete.

He knew what he wanted to do—hit a ground ball between first and second for the tying run. Just a single, not a home run. He knew where the pitch would have to be for him to do that and he guessed wrong.

He looked for the Gossage fast ball that tails away and instead got the one that moves in on a batter and he popped the ball off the handle of his bat.

Yastrzemski talked about how similar yesterday's game ("a fantastic game" he called it) was to 1974, when Luis Aparicio slipped twice rounding third and the Red Sox lost the division title.

"Today," he said, "Lou Piniella loses Burleson's hit in the sun and sticks up his glove. The ball lands in there on one bounce.

"And how could Piniella possibly be playing Freddie Lynn where he was in the sixth? Freddie's not a pull hitter and Guidry's throwing him sliders all day and there's Piniella, way over in right field deep, in the right spot when Freddie hits the ball."

For 40 minutes he answered questions, an elder statesman explaining how and why the election was lost.

"My insides are eating me up right now," he said. "It's hard to express how I feel. But in a couple of days it'll wear off. I'll go fishing for a couple of weeks and start getting ready for next year."

Next year? Yastrzemski has been a major leaguer almost half his life. He's chased a million baseballs, swung at a couple of million pitches, seen all he cares to of Cleveland and Milwaukee and downtown Detroit. Looking toward next year?

"You bet. With the talent on this club, it's easy to do."

A reporter standing on a chair leaned over three people and asked: "Do you think you're always destined to be close but no cigar?"

"Someday," Yaz replied, "we're going to get that cigar. Before Old Yaz retires, he's going to play on a world champion."

Like Hemingway's Old Man, Carl Yastrzemski won't quit until he catches the biggest fish in baseball's ocean.

Lee will be missed

December 10, 1978—Miss him? You bet I'll miss him. I write about sports and the people in sports for a living. I write about the way they play, certainly, but also about the things they say, and Bill Lee said plenty of writeable things.

I'd miss anybody who said of Bowie Kuhn: "Bowie's all right, but I know he put eight of us to sleep the last time he spoke to the team."

Who wouldn't miss somebody who fielded ground balls behind his back, who ran to Fenway Park from his home in Belmont on nights he was to pitch, who rehabilitated a torn shoulder by hanging from MBTA train straps, who called Billy Martin a neo-Nazi, who played softball with fans in the bleachers, who stood in parking lots and handed out leaflets, who suggested the powerless California Angels could take batting practice in the lobby of the Sheraton-Boston?

In the hot summer of '79 I'll long for the man who, when asked what he was thinking about during a 27-minute rain delay in the '75 World Series, replied: "I was thinking about asking Kissinger where all our wheat was going," and who described the Reds' bench as "a drill team of Marines from Parris Island. Jack Webb should be their manager."

Oh, yeah, I'll miss him all right. But he went too far, didn't he? Bill Lee got so far out on the limb he reached the point of no return. He burned all his bridges.

For a long time, Lee got away with murder in a business that takes itself more seriously than General Motors, but in the end he committed athletic suicide, at least as far as staying around here was concerned.

The freedom of speech that made him delightfully different was his undoing. His utter disregard for the rules of the game shot him down.

He had always criticized management, which was his prerogative. For a long time management said: "Hey, you know Bill Lee. Don't get too worked up over what he says." But, finally, management talked back. And what management said was: "Here's a ticket to Montreal and be careful going through customs."

His managers never understood him, or liked him very much, except of course for the two and one half hours it took for him to pitch a complete game victory.

Eddie Kasko didn't like him. Darrell Johnson didn't like him, and Don Zimmer . . . Zimmer . . . well . . . we know about Don Zimmer.

Lee said what he thought, but often, especially in later years, was intolerant of the opinions of those at variance with him.

And if a man says what he believes, he also must be ready to pay the price for his principles, especially if the remarks concern those who pay his salary or control the way he makes a living.

He called Haywood Sullivan "a gutless sonofabitch." He called Don Zimmer a gerbil, which the dictionary defines as "any of numerous old world burrowing desert rodents that have long hind legs well adapted for leaping."

Okay. If I walked into the sports editor's office and called him a gerbil, chances are he would not laugh and say: "Hey, that's just good old Ray Fitz's way." Un-uh, especially if my sports editor was as old school as Don Zimmer.

And if I walked into the publisher's den and suggested he was a gutless slob, he might laugh, but it would be as he handed me a broom and a pink slip, not necessarily in that order.

Perhaps if I were Ernest Hemingway or Red Smith, other arrangements could be made, a compromise could be found. And if Bill Lee had been Sandy Koufax or Warren Spahn in their prime, a way out might have been discovered.

But I'm not and he's not.

For several seasons, Bill Lee had his cake and ate it, too. He refused to play the game off the field but still was able to play on the diamond.

He came out of the dog house and into the guest room more often than my pet Schnauzer. He walked the tightrope of athletic irreverence like a champion.

Yet all the time he was operating on a death wish, and this week the guillotine fell.

Nobody should have been surprised, though to judge from the phone calls to The Globe and to the talk shows his fans never thought it would happen. Or if it did, the Red Sox should have received the entire Expos outfield and a couple of starting pitchers for him, instead of a lifetime .230-hitting utility infielder.

But the Red Sox had said in September that Lee would not be with them next season. They had dug a "we'll-have-to-take-what-you-want-to-give-us" hole.

Neither Lee nor Zimmer could backtrack. Lee had walked out on the team in the Bernie Carbo stickiness. Zimmer had buried him in the bullpen. Too much had been done. Too much had been said.

Asking either the pitcher or the manager to change would have been asking for the sun to rise each morning out of Park Street station.

Nobody wins this argument. The pitcher-hungry Red Sox are without a lefty who might still have helped them. Lee is gone from a baseball-mad area that cared deeply about him, one way or the other.

Saying the Red Sox could or should have held onto Bill Lee is like saying you could stop the 20th Century Limited with a toothpick.

His departure for a nonentity was a sure thing, and perhaps the best thing for both sides.

But, yeah, I'll miss him. Miss him a lot.

8

1979

Too bad he couldn't wear his skates

January 10, 1979—Bobby Orr came back to the happy highways one more time last night. He came back to be honored, to be toasted, to be literally praised to the rafters.

But he didn't come back to do what he would give the world to do. He didn't come back to strap on his skates, pull the No. 4 jersey over his head and make poetry out of a game.

Orr is not an athlete dying young, not in the true sense of the phrase, but we all know how much went out of his life—and ours—when, barely past 30 years old, he had to quit because of knees with little but air left in them.

Dan Canney has it right.

Dan Canney is the Bruins' trainer. He was the Bruins' trainer a dozen seasons ago when crew-cut, 18-year-old Bobby Orr showed up at the Boston training camp, a phenomenon in search of an arena.

"Last week in Chicago," said Canney yesterday, "I saw Bobby come out of his office, dressed like an executive, a front-office man.

"But I don't see him that way. To me he'll always be Bobby Orr, the hockey player. That's all. The hockey player."

Boston honored Bobby Orr the hockey player yesterday. There was a reception at City Hall and a press conference at the mayor's office and then a dramatic, emotion-packed half hour at the Garden before the Bruins-Soviet Wings game.

But politicians were not a big part, and, in fact, the crowd made so much noise for Orr at the Garden that the governor and the rest of the celebrities were forced to pass up their little speeches.

Orr's closest friend in Boston is State Treasurer Bob Crane, but Orr was a player of the people, not the politicians.

He was every middle-aged fan's ticket back to youth, and every kid's fantasy.

"No. 4? Sure, I wore it in the Pee Wees," said the Bruins' Bob Miller. "Everybody did."

Last night, the fans gave Orr what master of ceremonies Tom Fitzgerald called "A Guinness Book of Records standing ovation."

It lasted six minutes, five seconds and might still be going on if Orr hadn't stepped to the mike and quieted things.

During the ovation, the crowd chanted "Bobby, Bobby" and Peter McNab slapped the boards with his stick.

At last, Orr's number was hoisted to the ceiling, to hang there with those of Eddie Shore, Dit Clapper, Lionel Hitchman and Milt Schmidt.

And then came the impromptu thing that tugged at everybody. John Bucyk presented Orr with a No. 4 sweater, and Orr stepped to the microphone to begin his acceptance talk.

"I've been thinking for a week to try to think of what to say," he began, and out of the balcony came the shouts: "Put it on. Put the shirt on."

Orr smiled. He hesitated, then took off his suitcoat, the front-office garb, and slipped the white and gold No. 4 shirt over his head as the crowd went wild.

"I was going to try to be sort of formal," he said. "When I get back to Chicago and the Black Hawks see . . . ," and he laughed at the thought of a Black Hawks assistant general manager standing at mid-ice in Boston with a Bruins' uniform top on.

"I love you so much," he said. "I spent 10 years here and they were the 10 best years of my life." He glanced at his wife Peggy, who was sobbing.

"I shouldn't have looked at you, Peggy," he said, wiping his eyes.

Finally it was over, and Orr, still wearing the jersey, went over to shake hands with the present Bruins, hugging old teammates Gary Doak and Gerry Cheevers.

Then he went through the gate and out of the arena, this artist whose artistry was halted suddenly and too soon.

Don Cherry has a video tape of a Channel 38 production of Orr's greatest moments, with Barbara Streisand's "The Way We Were" in the background.

"I have a few beers at home," he said, "and I go down and put the tape on and watch. And when she sings that phrase "the way we were" and the young Bobby is doing the things on the ice that he could do, I just sit there and cry. Every time I cry."

Cherry says he was criticized when he first became coach of the Bruins because he seemed in awe of Bobby Orr.

"Of course I was. So was everyone who ever played with him or against him."

So were we all.

Fairbanks—the organization man gone askew

February 24, 1979—He was the most organized of men. Efficiency should have been his middle name. Charles Efficiency Fairbanks.

When he became coach and general manager of the Patriots in 1973, he inherited the NFL equivalent of the city dump. He brought order out of chaos, made prime ribs out of chopped liver.

His public words were always calculated, measured, and weighed before being packaged for the consumer. His practices were crisp and by the numbers, without a moment squandered.

Shortly after his arrival, Fairbanks made an analysis of every player in the NFL. He and his assistants graded every one, so that if a certain player became available, the Patriots would have a line on him.

He set up a spring camp in Tampa, something that cost a good deal of money, but something Fairbanks considered absolutely essential if he was to get to know his personnel.

In Tampa, he handed out illustrated brochures, outlining the physical fitness routine each man would follow. Report cards were issued every two weeks.

Fairbanks didn't coach so much as he administered. They called him Zeus, looking down from his 25-foot high-power tower.

His assistants drilled the players on blocking, tackling, running. Fairbanks, always organized, always cool, listened. Then he'd talk over what he'd seen and heard, and evaluate.

Like most organizers Fairbanks was a workaholic—8:30 to midnight, looking at films, planning, plotting. "We're going to try to be perfect in the little things," he once said.

He rid himself of the malcontents, those who stepped over the line, made too much fuss. No room for emotion in these decisions. Just goodby, Mack Herron, see you later, Reggie Rucker.

He talked in cliches—"we'll draft the best athlete available," "mistakes killed us"—but he did it. He fashioned a playoff contender, brought respectability and sellout crowds to a franchise that had been down to its last pair of pants.

He did it. Not Billy Sullivan. Not Bucko Kilroy. Not anybody else. He was the architect.

And now the whole damn building is falling in on him. Hardly a week goes past that more information doesn't surface to chip away at his credibility.

And the most mystifying part is that his trademark, which was a talent for not having a single hair out of place, not having a single blade of crabgrass to spoil the lawn, seems to have vanished.

The business in Miami before the Patriots' final game was so disorganized and uncharacteristic of Fairbanks that Denver's Red Miller was hard put to believe it was the same man who had been his boss a couple of seasons ago.

Since, Fairbanks openly has recruited for Colorado even though there has been a temporary restraining order prohibiting him from signing as coach.

This week Fairbanks revealed he'd invited four Eastern Mass. high school coaches and seven top players to his house Jan. 10.

During the meeting, which lasted almost two hours, Fairbanks talked to the youngsters about attending Colorado. Soft drinks, potato chips and pretzels were served.

Norwood High coach John Doherty, one of the coaches at the meeting, used the word "innocent" to describe the get-together. And perhaps under normal circumstances it would have been, even if the NCAA has a rule that does not permit the representative of any college to entertain off campus.

A coke and a pretzel, after all, aren't the same as a Cadillac and a trip to Acapulco.

But Fairbanks is not operating under normal conditions. He is under scrutiny for everything that has happened since that ill-fated day in Miami.

The old Fairbanks, the organized one, would have examined the idea of a meeting with schoolboy athletes. He would have looked at it from all angles, a jeweler checking out a diamond for possible defects.

He would have perceived that such a meeting, in what are for him perilous times, might jeopardize not only his future but that of the University of Colorado football program, and would have backed off.

The new Fairbanks, the one who showed up on Dec. 18, just plows straight ahead and damn the torpedoes. I never quite understood the old one, but I certainly can't make head nor tails out of the new one.

It's as though, inside this Felix Unger of coaching, an Oscar Madison was seething to escape, and finally has, leaving cigar and ash and dirty linen wherever he goes.

OK, 385 yards—but not the 26 miles

April 8, 1979—A week from tomorrow is the annual Boston Marathon, our city's contribution to the legend of sport, a day when all America pays homage to the shin splint.

To get ready for this magic afternoon of agony, lean and hungry types everywhere are loping around ponds, pounding city pavements, legging it through wooded glades.

They are doing upwards of 100 miles a week in anticipation of Heartbreak Hill, and to prepare for the tortured lungs, puck-sized blisters and all-round misery that is required payment for the two final rewards—a bowl of beef stew and bragging rights to 26 miles, 385 yards of asphalt from Hopkinton to the Prudential Center.

You can usually tell serious marathoners from run-of-the-road joggers. Joggers wear warmups. They are often large and overweight and tend to wear basketball or tennis shoes. They run as though they are either wearing leg irons or have just missed a bus.

Marathoners are almost always slight and skinny. They wear short shorts and head bands and have legs that are 100 percent sinew and ligament and no percent fat.

Often they are bearded, and in their eyes is a faraway, almost mystic look. If a dog snaps at them, they snap back. They are always running as though they are trying to beat the bus.

As someone who reaches the brink of physical exhaustion merely by driving from Boston to Springfield, I find the thought of running 100 miles a week simply inconceivable. You might as well tell me they ride a bicycle to the moon for a bottle of milk.

Even 26 miles is tough to absorb. Three-hundred eighty-five yards I can deal with. That's 3.85 football fields. I can visualize that distance. Never will I attempt to run it, even if a deed to an Iranian oil field was at the far end. But at least I can understand the distance.

However, the thought of running 26 miles with nothing at the finish but a bowl of canned stew and a corner to get sick in is enough to send one into a permanent catatonic state. So about three years ago I made a vow not to run 26 miles, total, for the rest of my days.

So far, the pledge is working out OK. Every time I've been forced by circumstance or impulse to do a bit of running, I've noted the distance and jotted it down in the same little black book in which I also keep track of my oil changes. Or rather, my car's oil changes.

Anyway, since making the vow I've run a total of three miles, eight yards, which averages out to 4.9 feet a day. At that rate, it will take 23 more years to go the 26 miles, 385 yards.

But even the three miles, eight yards I've piled up so far is distressing. That yardage could have been avoided with a little discipline, but it's amazing how instinct and reaction can overpower even the strongest of resolves.

For example:

One Saturday about two years ago, I forgot myself and ran downstairs to see if the mailman had delivered the paycheck. He hadn't come through the day before and if it didn't show up by the weekend, the budget would be out of whack, not that it's ever in whack.

That little job consumed about 50 feet and brought a shortness of breath usually associated with reaching the summit of Mt. Everest.

Too many times I jogged across intersections on "do not walk" signals, to avoid Cadillacs, Pintos and Rabbits bearing down on me. I'd say that altogether this misdemeanor amounted to 85 yards of running.

There was also the dreadful moment when I thought I'd missed last call at the neighborhood saloon. How many feet are there in a normal city block? Whatever the number, it was an all-out burst—successful I might add—that I traveled the distance in Guiness Book of Records time.

And, of course, the golf game in Florida. I'd just stepped from the golf cart and entered the woods in search of an errant drive when I stumbled upon what at first glance appeared to be a section of garden hose, but which upon closer examination was something much more sinister.

The sprint that followed surely was of Olympian caliber.

The mere chronicling of these exercises has exhausted me, and I must go home and rest a bit. I plan to walk, not run, to the nearest exit.

Where that red flag flies

July 1, 1979—Robert Trent Jones Sr. and his son are in Moscow making final preparations for the clearing of a 170-acre wooded site that will become the Soviet Union's first golf course—News item.

"Hah, Boris, shall we hunt the wild boar as usual this Saturday?"

"No, Vladimir, put aside rifle. There is new sport I want you should try with me. We will play golf."

"Do you not have it spelled backwards, Boris? Should it not be F-L-O-G, flog. That is truly great sport. Go to Siberia and flog poor wretches in prisons, then turn wolves loose on them."

"Oh, you make poor joke, Vladimir. This is golf. G-O-L-F. You swing savagely at target with club."

"Sounds like flogging to me."

"Perhaps, Vladimir, but you will love this game. It is very big in capitalist America and on British Isles."

"Tell me more, Boris, and I will decide. How much does it cost for clubs you mentioned?"

"You buy them from commissar for about 500 rubles."

"Five-hundred rubles for pieces of wood? I will go into birch forest and cut my own."

"Is not allowed, Vladimir. Clubs must be shaped in expensive factory. Some are wood, some are metal at one end, with grooves in them."

"What are grooves for?"

"To impart English on ball."

"Sshh. Never use forbidden word for fear of reprisal. Describe game to me."

"Certainly, my dear Vladimir. You push wooden peg into ground and on it you balance little white ball with dimples."

"My heart is pounding just listening to you, Boris."

"There is more. Then you take wooden club and attack little white ball."

"Is more like it. I keep striking, then, until ball is vanquished for glory of The Motherland."

"Not exactly. If you use club correctly, white ball flies 280 meters through air and lands on grassy meadow."

"Then what?"

"Then you walk to where little white ball lies and strike it again."

"Let me get this straight, Boris, my comrade. We attack ball with club, then walk until we once again come upon ball, and strike it again?"

"You are correct."

"You have cuckoo game, Boris. I would rather seek out the wild boar."

"But wait, Vladimir. It is not without purpose that you keep striking little white ball."

"Let me guess. I keep hitting ball until it falls off edge of earth."

"You continue to jest, Vladimir. Purpose of game is to hit ball with such accuracy and force that it rolls into hole 440 meters away in fewest blows possible. You do this for 18 holes and you have played round of golf."

"Sounds like the biggest challenge since the day the secret police wanted to know where I got my Mickey Mouse hat. How do I know in which direction is hole?"

"Ah, you are getting interested. Hole is indicated by long pole. Waving from pole is big red flag.

"Is first good thing I've heard about game."

"Is not only good thing, Vladimir. In Russia all 18 holes will be what is called in America doglegs. They will be dogleg left."

"Good, good, Boris, but does not one become wearied by carrying heavy clubs over one's back like bundles of charwood?"

"No, clubs are put in bags and carried by caddy."

"You drive capitalist American automobiles onto Soviet soil?"

"No, no, Vladimir. Caddies are human beasts of burden. In America, children are often used. In Soviet Union, we will employ worthless people, such as physicists and poets. Solzhenitsyn, if he should return, will caddy double."

"Let me sum up, Boris. I hit ball with club, chase it, try to put it into hole in ground, the fewer hits the better. I spend all afternoon at this task."

"Except for Saturdays and Sundays, Vladimir, when you spend all day."

"And when the game is over, Boris, what then?"

"You go to the clubhouse."

"To hunt the wild boar?"

"No, to become one."

A Knight who's tarnished

July 10, 1979—We sent the wrong person to the Salt II talks. We should have kept Jimmy Carter home to pump gas and shipped Indiana basketball coach Bobby Knight to Vienna.

He'd have straightened out the Soviets before the first quart of vodka had been downed. Kiss Leonid Brezhnev? Knight would have cuffed the Soviet premier about the jowls and ordered him to keep his mouth shut or we'd drop a hydrogen bomb on Minsk by nightfall.

If Knight is a U.S. ambassador of goodwill, so is typhoid fever. He makes the Ugly American seem like the village philanthropist.

Knight is coaching the American basketball team in the Pan-Am games in San Juan. So far, he's been as welcome in the Caribbean as a piranha in bean soup.

He was ejected from one game when he protested a call with his team ahead by 35 points. He was reprimanded by the International Amateur Basketball Federation and scolded by Pan-Am officials.

And over the weekend he was involved in a skirmish with a San Juan policeman following a dispute over practice facilities at Roberto Clemente Stadium.

But these indelicacies are not what make Bobby Knight a disgrace. What makes him a walking, talking embarrassment is the way he treats those who play for him, though "play" is hardly the word.

Play is defined as recreational activity, an act intended to amuse oneself, a frolic. Frolic does not quite describe what occurs when you are under the thumb of this athletic despot.

In San Juan he humiliated an 18-year-old kid named Isiah Thomas, who last year was the best high school basketball player in Chicago.

"What the hell's the matter with you? Do you think I'm going to put up with this bull----?" Knight screamed at Thomas, so loudly he might as well have been hooked up to the public address system.

When the half ended, Knight grabbed Thomas and let fly with another stream of invective. The kid, who incidentally will begin what should be a marvelous educational experience this fall at Indiana University, did not play in the second half.

What is Knight's tirade supposed to do for an 18-year-old—toughen him up? Make him aware that life's a jungle and nothing comes easy? Is it supposed to discipline him so he won't make the same mistake? Let him know who's boss? Keep him mentally alert?

Will it make Isiah Thomas a better person to be whipped in public, as though he were an adulterer from the Middle Ages?

I remember, a long time ago, a high school coach who employed Knight-like tactics. He harangued his players during timeouts, cursed and humiliated them.

Enough townspeople thought this was not the way to coach; so after a few years the coach was dismissed.

But it was surprising how many others said: "Hey, he's a little rough with the kids; but let's face it—he wins."

I wouldn't have cared if he'd won every game 100-0. If I'd had a boy in that high school, he wouldn't have played for that coach. Even then I knew the difference between a disciplinarian and a bully.

Knight also wins. His Indiana team has been the NCAA champion once and is usually in the thick of the fight.

But if it is generally agreed upon among civilized people that winning, while worth fighting for, is not the only thing, it is also not worth the candle that lights up Bobby Knight.

"I don't need all this," Knight was quoted as saying last week. "I've won everything a college coach can win. I don't have to prove myself."

"I, I, I." The first person singular prevails. What about the third person plural? What about them? What about the players? Does their dignity count, or are they just available to feed one man's insatiable ego?

It's been said Knight is an intelligent person. Therefore, he must have decided that if he had an athlete for a son, the same tyranny would be appropriate. It would be perfectly okay for a coach to humiliate Bobby Knight Jr. in front of 15,000 people.

Those who know Bobby Knight say he can be charming, warm and witty. I don't know him, don't want to and don't have to. His actions speak for him, and his actions are despicable.

His teams could go undefeated for the rest of his life and he'd still be a loser.

No vote yet for Munson

August 12, 1979—I don't know quite how to express this without sounding as though I'm dancing on the man's grave. I suppose the best way is to just say it, flat out, so here goes.

In my opinion, Thurman Munson was not a Hall of Fame baseball player.

In the emotional wake of the tragic plane crash that claimed the life of the captain of the New York Yankees there have been suggestions that a) Munson should go into the Hall of Fame immediately or, b) failing that, he is a sure thing for Cooperstown when the five-year waiting period is up.

"In January of 1973," noted Rev. Robert Coleman at the funeral services for the catcher, "Roberto Clemente went to Nicaragua to help earthquake victims—and crashed. He went right into the Hall of Fame. Perhaps for New York Yankees' captain Thurman Munson there can also be an exception made."

And in his heartfelt eulogy at those same services, teammate Bobby Murcer said, in part: "Thurman Munson, who wore the pinstripes with No. 15 . . . No. 15 on the field . . . No. 15 for the records . . . No. 15 for the halls of Cooperstown."

One certainly can't fault either the Rev. Coleman or Murcer for their statements. Both were close to Munson and greatly affected by the tragedy.

But if the Hall of Fame is to have any meaning at all beyond a publicity gimmick for baseball, those who are elected to it should be there by logic, not sentiment.

The five-year ruling was rescinded for Clemente and also for Lou Gehrig in 1939 not because they died years before their time but because they were so obviously going to be voted into the Hall of Fame anyway.

In 18 years, the Pittsburgh outfielder had 3000 hits, batted .317 and played right field like a virtuoso. Gehrig . . . well, there is no point in going into his career. If you don't know about him you'll believe it when I tell you baseball was invented by the Soviets on a field near Minsk.

But if a case cannot be made for voting the late Yankee catcher into the Hall of Fame immediately, can one be made for electing him when he becomes eligible five seasons from now?

Perhaps. Anybody who saw him play knows how valuable he was to the modern-day Yankees. His death brought many tributes, many of them hyperbolic and yes . . . hypocritical. But one that wasn't was the statement of so many in baseball that he was the heart of the two-time World Champions.

He scrapped, he played when he was hurt and could have asked out, he played positions strange to him—left field, right field, first base, third base—when injuries prevented him from catching.

And for five seasons—1973–77—he was the most consistent offensive force on the ball club. From 1975 through 1977 he drove in 307 runs, hitting .318, .302 and .306 in those seasons.

But when we talk about the Hall of Fame we are talking about the best baseball players of all time. We are talking about Cobb and Ruth and Wagner, about Simmons and Ott and Frisch, about Musial and DiMaggio and Williams, about Mays and Mantle and Spahn.

Oh, certainly players of lesser greatness than those have plaques on the walls at Cooperstown. There are even some, it could be argued—with statistics, or lack of same, to back the argument—who shouldn't be there at all.

Ralph Kiner, for example, who played only 11 years, hit .279 and made it on the wings of a few big homer seasons. Or Rabbit Maranville, who had a lifetime average of .258 but was voted into the Hall in 1954, presumably because he invented the vest pocket catch and was in the majors for 24 seasons.

Or Jerome (Dizzy) Dean, who won only 150 games but who rode a couple of sensational seasons and a colorful personality all the way to Cooperstown.

But because there are a few in the Hall of Fame who shouldn't be there is not an argument to add others whose qualifications fall short.

Phil Rizzuto is not in the Hall of Fame, nor Pee Wee Reese nor Enos Slaughter nor Marty Marion nor Duke Snyder. In my mind, it would be hard to justify voting Thurman Munson in while keeping those players out.

When Munson was killed he was in the middle of his 10th major league season, the minimum time to be eligible. Aches and pains and injuries had diminished his effectiveness the past season and a half. There is no way now of knowing whether he would have been the same force on the field for the rest of his career as he was during the championship years.

Many kind and thoughtful things were said about Thurman Munson in the days following his death. He was a player I admired, one I would have wanted for a teammate.

Perhaps when five years have passed and it comes time to take another look at what he accomplished in baseball, I'll change my mind about his Hall of Fame qualifications.

But if there were a ballot in front of me right now and I was honor-bound to vote with the facts at hand and not with my heart, I could not, in all conscience, vote Thurman Munson into the Hall of Fame.

Rap session with Lynn's bat ends with smash

August 21, 1979—The game against the White Sox was over and lost forever, and now Fred Lynn's bat was leaning against the locker room wall, waiting to be packed away for the trip to Minnesota.

The bat looked frustrated and tired. There was a glob of mud on the barrel and a small nick three inches up on the handle.

"Tough afternoon," a reporter said, just making conversation.

The bat shrugged, the way bats do.

"Yeah, tough," it replied, "but nobody said hitting a baseball would be easy. I've had so many good games lately, maybe I was due for a bad one."

The visitor nodded.

"You're the hottest bat in the majors right now," he said. "As a matter of fact, you're going like a bat out of hell. People are asking where you came from, how Fred Lynn treats you, what it was like for a bat growing up in America."

The bat gave a wooden smile.

"Anyone who knows me knows I'm a private creature," it said. "I let my work do the talking. As a matter of fact, you're the first one I've ever said a word to."

"I appreciate that," the reporter said, "and I'd like to interview you before you go into the bag for the flight to Minneapolis."

The bat fell silent for a moment, obviously mulling over the request.

Finally it answered.

"I'll give you 10 minutes," it said. "Then I have to hit the road."

"It's the only thing you haven't hit in the last couple of weeks," replied the visitor. "First, I need a little background. Where did you come from?"

"My roots were in a forest in southern New York state," said the bat.

"What was it like growing up?"

"It was a jungle out there. Thousands of us crammed onto a mountainside. A tree had to be tough to survive. So many didn't—burned up at an early age, or forced to become fenceposts or telephone poles.

"In that environment, it was easy to make an ash out of yourself, or, in plain words, be a son of a birch. Some of my childhood chums even took up a life of crime and became pencils for sportswriters."

The reporter asked when the first break came.

"Never say 'break' to a bat," scowled the slugger, shifting his 34-inch, 32-ounce frame into a more comfortable position.

The reporter apologized.

"Let me rephrase the question," he said. "When did the opportunity arrive to escape the forest primeval?"

"One afternoon," the bat reminisced, "a bunch of us were hanging around the corner, whistling at the sugar maples and murmuring at the hemlocks, when some people from the Louisville Slugger Company came around.

"They said I had a terrific willowy build for a sapling and asked if I'd given any thought to becoming a baseball bat. I told them my mother wanted me to pursue a musical career. She had her heart set on my becoming a grand piano and playing at Carnegie Hall."

The bat said the Louisville offer was too good to pass up. It signed, was sent to instructional school in a lumber mill just outside Baton Rouge, La., and emerged all shiny and polished. Shortly afterward, it became Lynn's first draft choice.

"I was lucky," the bat observed. "I could have been made into a fungo bat and done nothing but hit grounders to George Scott. Even worse, I could have been picked by a National League pitcher. I could have spent my whole career hitting into double plays, striking out and being pinch hit for."

"If you had any advice for a young bat, what would it be?" asked the reporter.

"I'd say go out and meet the baseball. You can't hang back and wait for the ball to come to you. Make your contacts and good things will happen. Too many promising young bats think the world owes them a living. They look good in practice but when the game starts they become petrified."

"How does Fred treat you?" the reporter wanted to know.

"With respect, and that's all a bat can ask for. Shaves my handle once a week, gives me a little pine tar massage once in a while, goes easy with the dirt rubdowns.

"After I do my job, he drops me gently on the ground. I've seen some hitters, they strike out and slam the bat on the plate or against the dugout wall. That's not right, and Marvin Miller is looking into the situation. A bat has feelings too, you know."

The bat reached out and shook the reporter's hand.

"You'll have to excuse me," it said. "It's time to pack my trunk."

"That's okay," replied the reporter. "I gotta split anyway."

The bat smashed the reporter on the big toe.

"That's just a little reminder," it barked, stalking away to the bat room. "Never—positively never—say 'split' to a baseball bat."

Say a few words, Coach . . . very few

September 2, 1979—Coach Spike McBullitt, cagey and respected football mentor of the Stegy Prep Bulldogs, has never been one to mince words with the press.

And so it came as no surprise yesterday when the veteran coach answered some hard-hitting questions about this year's squad with his usual candor, pulling no punches.

"Let the devil take the hindmost, let the chips fall where they may," smiled the venerable tactician. "Fire away with your questions and the nastier the better."

"What kind of season do you foresee, coach?"

"It's going to be a rebuilding season," replied McBullitt, drawing on his ever-present pipe. "We are starting virtually from scratch, not to mention from the ground up."

"Do you have many returning veterans?"

"Of course. All our veterans are returning veterans. If a player returns he is automatically a veteran. Otherwise, he wouldn't be returning, he would be joining us for the first time. Do you follow my line of reasoning?"

"I guess so. But what I meant was, did you lose many players through graduation?"

"We were decimated by graduation. In fact, graduation left many holes that will be difficult, if not impossible, to fill. Graduation left, if you will, a tremendous void."

"How would you characterize the athletes who graduated?"

"I'd call them key losses. Everyone who graduates is a key loss, even though when he was around he might not have been good for . . ."

"I get the picture. So what does that leave you with, coach?"

"A team of question marks. Every position is not only a question mark, it is also up for grabs. Wide open, so to speak."

"The situation sounds bleak."

"Yes, we will be fighting an uphill battle. We will be underdogs in every game we play. But we do have a nucleus, or to be more specific, a solid nucleus. Any team that plays us will know it's been in a game. We'll come to play, you can count on that."

"Any promising freshmen?"

"I assume you mean heralded freshmen. Of course, all freshmen have potential. That's because they haven't played a game yet. The way I express it is my freshmen student-athletes are talented but inexperienced."

"Could you assess last year's record?"

"Certainly. Early in the campaign we gave a creditable performance, but then several players—key players, of course—got hurt."

"You mean . . . ?"

"That's right, we were riddled with injuries."

"What did the injuries do to you?"

"They killed us."

"What were you left with?"

"Nothing but walking wounded, not to mention a shell of a football team."

"Would you ever send any of those walking wounded into a game?"

"Good heavens, no. A boy's health is worth far more than the winning or losing of a mere game. Of course, if certain medication will make the pain go away, well, that's for me to know and everybody else to find out."

"Okay. So what is your prediction for 1979?"

"We have no place to go but up. We are pointing toward a bowl, because as you well know, a football takes funny bounces. We hope to vacate the cellar, to become competitive, to prove to the cynics we belong, to surprise a few people, to see the light at the end of the tunnel, to chalk up a first down, to . . ."

"That's enough. If you could have your players the way you like them, how would you want your quarterback?"

"Cool and poised. A coach on the field."

"Your halfbacks?"

"Explosive."

"Your cornerbacks?"

"Fleet."

"Your linebackers?"

"They must love to hit and definitely must throw caution to the wind."

"What about your pass receivers?"

"Soft hands are a must. Receivers must lock the football into those soft hands and run like hell to paydirt. They should not hear footsteps and must get a step on the opposition's fleet cornerbacks."

"And your defensive linemen?"

"Pursuit is paramount. And they must not be suckered on trap plays."

"In the final analysis, where are games won and lost?"

"In the trenches, young man, in the trenches. I thought everyone knew that."

"To sum up, coach, would you briefly state your football philosophy?"

"Certainly. Football is only a game. It's not life and death. It's not war. On the other hand, it's the way I make my living. I've had a good thing going here for 42 years, and if any of these young punks don't shape up, they get shipped out. We're not running a nursery here, we're building character."

"Thank you, coach, and have a good season."

If Pope tuned in to Monday Night Football

October 1, 1979—If Pope John Paul II were staying at my house tonight and he had just rung the doorbell:

"It's an honor and pleasure to welcome you to our humble dwelling, Your Holiness. Wipe your feet on the Chuck Fairbanks Memorial doormat and come on in.

"At last, Holy Father, you're able to relax. It's been quite a day hasn't it? The long flight from Ireland, the great tour of Boston, the marvelous mass with the huge throng on the Common.

"If I may be so bold, Your Holiness, why don't you just slip into your red slippers, put aside the mitre and take it easy for the rest of the evening. A person of your dignity and prominence doesn't have many such opportunities.

"Let me get you a small glass of wine, something not overly naughty but with just a hint of impertinence. Perhaps some Mogen David, in keeping with the ecumenical spirit.

"Ah, there we are. Now, isn't that grand? I have an idea, Your Holiness. It's been written many times that you are truly a man of the people. I think you'd enjoy watching a game of professional football, which is the sport of the American people.

"Here, let me turn on the television set. The New England Patriots are playing the Green Bay Packers. The Patriots are almost a religion in these parts, ha ha ha. In fact, they have a Bishop playing in the defensive line.

"If you'd like, I'll explain things as the game moves along. Feel free to break in at any time with questions.

"The man talking on the screen now is broadcaster Frank Gifford. No, I don't think he'd mind if you called him Giffer. Howard calls him Giffer.

"Howard? He's the one with the ears, the one who keeps shouting 'incredible' and 'unbelievable,' even though the game hasn't even started. Right now Howard is saying he had breakfast with you last Thursday.

"Incessantly, Your Holiness. Sometimes louder. Certainly, if it bothers you. Second knob on the right.

"Who do I think will win the game? The Packers, begging Your Holiness' pardon, don't have a prayer. They can't hold a candle to the Patriots.

"The teams are coming out on the field now. The ones wearing the red and white vestments are the Patriots. It's too bad the team from St. Louis isn't playing tonight. You'd really take to them.

"The team in the green and gold vestments is coached now by a man named Starr, but a long time ago it was led by St. Vincent Lombardi, and was the best in the land. St. Vincent, I believe, was the first to say 'winning isn't everything, it's the only thing.'

"It wasn't St. Vincent who said that first, it was Attila the Hun? There you go. I'm always getting the two confused.

"I'd like to explain, Holy Father, why the huge crowd is on its feet, or collective feet, as Howard might phrase it. The fans are about to sing the Star Spangled Banner. No, it's not named after the Green Bay coach, but how quick you were to note the similarity.

"Isn't it a catchy melody? Fourteen people in the United States have the range to sing it correctly from beginning to end. What's that, Your Holiness? Yes, I suppose that if football is our national religion, it's proper to refer to what you just heard as the opening hymn of the Monday night service.

"Now the teams are lining up for the kickoff. No, that's not a Gregorian chant, Your Holiness, it's the hometown fans shouting 'kill, kill, kill.' Just a cute little cheer that makes everybody feel like part of the action.

"The point of the game, if I may say so here during the deodorant commercial, Your Holiness, is for the team that has possession of the football to advance that football down the field across that wide stripe.

"How do they accomplish that? Well, by violence and insidious deception, of course. See No. 67 of the Green Bay team sitting on the ground holding his broken knee? The Patriots' special team got him good on the kickoff.

"You feel strongly that violence and deception are unchristian? Well, I couldn't agree with you more, Holy Father, when it happens on the street. But in the arena, violence is rewarded, as is only proper and right, with a long term, no-cut contract. Not as long term or no-cut as we all hope and pray yours will be, Holy Father, but long enough.

"But you find the violence extremely repugnant. No problem. We'll simply tune into something more intellectually tasteful and stimulating.

"What'll it be—Kojak, Three's Company or Charlie's Angels?"

Here's a toast in rhyme for Christmastime . . .

December 22, 1979—

The 25th is round the bend,
So this corner wants to send,
With much ado and endless hollering,
Season's greetings to the follering:

To the Sull'vans, Bill et al,
Who watched their team decline and fall;
To Fargo Erhardt, Bucko K.,
(And of course to Leon Gray).
To a party let's invite us,
Sam and Russ and Bill Lenkaitis.
Many joyous hallelujahs,
For Adams, Sam and Adams, Jullyahs.
Gee whiz and wow and also whee,
For Bishop, Grogan and McGee.
Decorate a yuletide bannah,
For Jackson, Morgan and John Hannah.
Reducing pills for fat Sam Hunt,
And Lord, send down a man to punt.
A happy yule to Gilbert Santos,
And all the Foxb'ro elephantos.

Let's also do some celebratin'
For Harry Sinden, Freddie Creighton.
Order Christmas, over easy,
For Gillie, Cash and also Cheesy.
Blow a horn and ring a bell
For Pete McNab and Jean Ratelle.
Pray for Park and Don Marcotte,
Brand new knees would help a lot.
A hi, a ho, a derry-O,
For Middleton and Terry O',
For Jonathan and Gary Doak,
And all the other Bruin folk.

And all we longtime Boston scribblers,
Send a card to Fitch's dribblers.
Not to mention some a capella,
For Roundball Red, the smartest fella.

Pile high the groaning festive board,
For Bird and Dave and Three-Point Ford.
Trim a tree and touch a star,
For Nate the Skate and M. L. Carr,
For Robey, Chaney, Cornbread Max,
And all the other Celtic acts.
Merry Christmas, you're the toast
Of fans at least, and Johnny Most.

And no big day would be complete,
Without a drink to Jersey Street.
Oh dear me, I went astray,
I meant, of course, to Yawkey Way.
To Haywood S. and Buddy L.,
Who swear that things ain't gone to hell.
Light a candle for Don Zimmer,
Nineteen-Eighty can't be grimmer.
Let us hope that once more Yaz'll,
Turn the fancy plays that dazzle.
Let us pray that Campbell's arm
Is just a winter false alarm.
Please make a list and check it twice,
For Fisk and Lynn and Jim Ed Rice,
For Butch and Rick and also Dewey,
And dare I breathe it—old friend Looie.
For Eck and Mike and also Jerry,
Christmas warm and Christmas merry.
An AL pennant, tied with bows,
For each and every Carmine Hose.

And now some added miscellany,
Wrapped in Christmas cellophany,
For Marvin Hagler, Prince of Punch,
And all the Petronelli bunch.
Pour a foaming king-sized brew,
For Crowl and Nate and Howie McHugh.
Let's yell for Kiley at the organ,
And the pen of Timmy Horgan.

Break a fancy wine carafe
On Ding and Dong and Clif and Claf.
Before we're done, let's raise a beakah,
To Eddie Chlebek, Joe Yukica,
Wilson, Pierson, Freddie Cusick,
Who make such pretty hockey music.

Croon an oldtime HC chorus
To Blaney, Perry, Cooz and Morris.
Sing out loud for Clark the Booth,
And all who seek to know the truth.
Here's to Rico, Ken and Hawk,
Here's bah and humbug to New Yawk.
And this verse would be just rotten,
Without a toast to Nedso Mahtin,
Havlicek and Bobby Orr,
Jeffrey Cohen and dozens more.
But that's enough, I call it quits,
Goodnight, God bless from R. M. Fitz.

A dark side to sports—another ugly eruption

December 25, 1979—The wonderful world of sports, they call it, and certainly it is often exactly that.

The grace of a double play, the exhilarating downhill flight of a skier, the pounding of two great thoroughbreds down the stretch—to a sports fan they are as great as anything by Picasso or Rodin or Nureyev.

I've seen the determination of Earl Campbell and the fluidity of Julius Erving and the hustle of Pete Rose and the magic of Bobby Orr and the magnetism of Arnold Palmer, and, if you want an all-inclusive adjective, "wonderful" is about as good as you can find.

But there is a dark side to the wonderful world, and I've seen that also, too much of it. Firecrackers thrown at outfielder Ken Harrelson in Detroit and ball bearings bounced off center fielder Mickey Rivers in Boston. A dart sticking out of Chris Chambliss' arm as he pulled into third base at Fenway Park and a near riot at Shea Stadium.

I've seen drunks falling out of box seats, and heard abuse from potheads and boozebrains at Schaefer—abuse that pushes the principle of free speech over a cliff and into a dismal swamp.

I've seen a whiskey bottle fly out of the stands in Minnesota and hit a football official on the head, and a mental midget fly out of the stands at Boston Garden to wrestle with referee Richie Powers.

I've seen eggs splatter on the ice and the basketball court, and I've seen team buses attacked by angry mobs who separately might be afraid of their shadows, but together constitute the worst sort of sports ugliness.

Sunday night at Madison Square Garden, ugliness rode again. The Bruins had come from behind to beat the Rangers in an emotional game marked by controversial officiating.

The game had an exciting finish, with Gerry Cheevers stopping Phil Esposito's breakaway shot only five seconds before the final buzzer.

An argument arose among the players, principally New York goalie John Davidson and Boston's Al Secord. During the milling about, an alleged fan reached across the glass and punched Stan Jonathan.

Jonathan raised his stick, the goon grabbed it away and began hitting the Bruins player.

Jonathan's teammates went to his aid. Terry O'Reilly vaulted into the stands. Peter McNab, normally the mildest of men, climbed several rows up and tackled somebody who had gone at O'Reilly from behind.

A Bruin—the majority opinion is Mike Milbury—pulled the guy's shoe off and hit him with it.

Yesterday morning, Rangers president William M. Jennings said, according to the Associated Press: "We've been told not to talk about this, but you can quote me; the referee caused this whole problem."

The referee caused the problem? The referee? The referee caused a customer to act like a three-year-old who has just been told he can't set the cat on fire? The referee was responsible for the mob that rocked the empty Bruins' bus, forcing police to bring the bus inside to let the players board safely?

C'mon. Blame alcohol or pot or the violence of the times or a permissive society if you want. Blame the curdled brain cells of a few frustrated cuckoos who twist a simple game into their own personal vendetta.

But nailing the referee for what went on in the Madison Square Garden stands Sunday night is like blaming the Chicago fire on a guy who lights a cigar in Des Moines.

Every time something like this happens in hockey—and it is not uncommon—I try to envision myself as a player. I think about what my reactions would be if I were on the ice and fans got into the act.

And I always come to the same conclusion. I'd do exactly what McNab and O'Reilly and the rest did Sunday night. I'd go over the boards and into the stands and confront the enemy, seeking to convince him this is not a game of backgammon he is getting into.

I might feel embarrassed afterward, and realize I should leave punishment to the proper authorities, but if it happened again, over the boards I'd go again.

Nowhere in the price of admission is there any mention that it is OK for a customer to grab a player's hockey stick. The back of the ticket does not say it is perfectly proper and within the spirit of the arena to spit in a player's face or punch him in the nose.

Enough is enough. Parliamentary procedure is no longer on the menu. Robert's Rules of Order are no longer valid.

It would be more proper and civilized, I suppose, to turn the other cheek, return to Boston and await a memo from the league office. One should, after all, think things out, take the temperate approach.

But we are not talking about proper and civilized people here. We are talking about airheads disguised as fans.

We are talking about the dark side of the wonderful world of sports, and it is always at our elbow, even on Christmas Day.

Five who had the talent but couldn't hack it

December 29, 1979—You got lists, he got lists, all God's chillun got lists, compilations of the best and worst of the 1970s, a decade that even now is waiting in the train station for the midnight express.

Well, I have a little list of my own. Call it a roll call of squandered talent perhaps, or a litany of lost souls of the '70s.

It's a small list. Just five names—a football player, a baseball player, a basketball player, a hockey player and a sportswriter. The athletes have Boston connections, the writer doesn't, but the common denominator is that they all leave a legacy of what might have been.

Here they are:

1. He was only 5 feet 5, but hard to hurt and harder to catch. He'd been a star halfback at Kansas State, but no NFL team would take a chance with him.

So he played for the Winnipeg Bombers of the Canadian Football League. But he got into a drug mixup, and the CFL blackballed him. However, Patriot coach Chuck Fairbanks remembered him from his college days and, desperate for a kick returner, took a chance.

As an NFL rookie, the little guy was a sensation. In 1974 he set an NFL record for total yardage (rushing, receiving and returning).

Then, in November of '75, he gave a birthday party for Leon Gray, a party in which it was rumored drugs played a part. An enraged Fairbanks coldly sold him to Atlanta for the $100 waiver price.

He did little with the Falcons. Then he was arrested in the airport on a drug charge, was found guilty and sent to Fulton County, Ga., prison.

Mack Herron, when he was paroled recently, was 31 years old.

2. Thin as an exclamation mark, he came from Guayamas, Puerto Rico, and could throw a baseball through concrete. He first pitched for the Red Sox in 1970, but didn't blossom until 1974, when he won 13 and lost only 2.

He was nicknamed "Six and Two-Thirds" by writers because he had difficulty getting past the seventh inning, but he showed flashes of brilliance, such as a one-hitter against the White Sox.

He was always smiling, always polite, but inside the demons were gnawing at him. The Red Sox gave up after he was involved in a 4:30 a.m. car accident in 1976 and sent him to Atlanta. The Braves sold him to Texas.

He had a nervous breakdown in 1978, climaxed by a chilling locker-room scene in which he went into a catatonic state for 40 minutes.

He was out of baseball in '79 and now is pitching winter ball in Santurce, hoping for another major league chance.

Rogelio Moret, 47-27 lifetime, is 30 years old.

3. Trouble was his middle name. No one ever denied his basketball talent, but no one yet has found out what makes him tick, or the name of the drummer he marches to.

He was one of Providence College's all-time greats, but is remembered as much for a tire-iron incident as he is for any basket he made.

He signed for a couple of million dollars with St. Louis of the ABA. He was outstanding for them, but he also missed plane flights, practices and games.

He left St. Louis for the Pistons of the NBA, where he missed more flights, practices and games, and also violated probation.

For that, he spent a year in a Rhode Island prison. Upon his release, he signed with Buffalo and then was traded to the Celtics, where he missed more planes, practices and games.

This fall he failed a tryout with San Diego. He's still there, out of shape and out of a job.

Marvin Barnes is only 27 years old.

4. He wasn't a great hockey player, but a terrific penalty killer with the Bruins and a personality perfect for his time.

He took no back talk from anybody and is said to have once told Gordie Howe: "Do that to me again, old man, and I'll slice your head off."

He jumped the Bruins and signed for $2.65 million with the Philly Blazers of the new WHA. He bought a 28-room mansion complete with a maid and valet, and a $32,000 Rolls Royce with chauffeur.

A bad back and arrogant attitude alienated him with the Blazers. Management bought up his contract for a million bucks, whereupon he re-signed with the Bruins for more big money.

He became part owner of three Boston singles bars. But he couldn't stand peace and quiet and was suspended after a fight with teammate Terry O'Reilly.

The Bruins traded him to the Rangers. The Rangers traded him to St. Louis. He spent some time in the minors. He came back to the Pittsburgh Penguins, but is now out of hockey.

Derek Sanderson, living in Chicago, is 33 years old.

5. He grew up in Willimantic, Conn., graduated from UConn, and rode into

the sports world looking for balloons to puncture. And he found many, this terrific phrasemaker whose worst enemy was himself.

He wrote sports in New Haven, Detroit, Houston and San Francisco and had arguments everywhere with bosses, cameramen, athletes and other writers.

But his talent was undeniable. He wrote outstanding biographies of George Blanda and Frank Leahy. In the book on the Notre Dame coach, he wrote: "The great surge of excitement had passed and the dark dog of melancholy was sitting on his soul."

Too much eating and drinking and self-imposed pressure brought the same dark dog of melancholy to this man's doorstep. Wells Twombly was 41 years old when he died on May 30, 1977.

9

1980

A sad day when he 'knew his place'

January 1, 1980—This is a story that's 40 years old, but on a day given over to nursing hangovers and watching bowl games, perhaps it deserves to be retold.

Forty years ago today, the Boston College football team played Clemson in the Cotton Bowl without one of its star halfbacks. The runner not only didn't play, he wasn't within 2000 miles of the stadium.

When the Eagles embarked from South Station on Dec. 26 to begin practicing in Dallas, the player was left home.

He was left behind not because he'd flunked out of school, or had been suspended for a training infraction, or because he'd been hurt and wouldn't be able to play on Jan. 1, 1940.

The reason he stayed home, however, in the context of that era, was as credible as the ones listed above.

Lou Montgomery didn't go to Dallas simply because he was black.

The other BC players felt bad. Montgomery was a popular member of the team, a small but extremely fast runner, and everybody wanted him to be with them on Jan. 1.

But nobody protested. Nobody carried picket signs and sang freedom songs and took over the dean's office. Nobody said, "Hell, no, we won't go."

There is no record of BC coach Frank Leahy proclaiming that unless Montgomery was welcome, the Eagles wouldn't show up.

Only about 5000 fans attended the game, but the small crowd wasn't the result of a boycott. This was in the early days of the Cotton Bowl, and the game just wasn't an attraction to Texans, who only a couple of days before had jammed the huge stadium to watch Waco play Lubbock for the state schoolboy championship.

Montgomery's was not an isolated situation. Blacks (Negroes was the operative word then) did not play against southern college teams. It was not the law of the land, it simply wasn't done. When Florida, Auburn and Wake Forest came to Boston to engage BC in football combat, Montgomery did not play for the Eagles.

A gentlemen's agreement, it was called.

"It sounds bad when compared to what it's like today," said Charlie O'Rourke, the star tailback on that team. "But everybody accepted the situation then. We all thought, 'Too bad, but there's nothing anybody can do about it.' That's just the way it was."

Even Montgomery accepted the indignity, at least publicly. He volunteered not to make the trip, to take any possible heat off his school.

He was quoted as saying, "Don't kid yourself, Boston College doesn't need a climax runner to win this football game. The Eagles can't miss."

He was widely praised for knowing his place.

In a biography of Leahy, Boston Record sportswriter Murray Kramer is reported to have written this about Montgomery after talking to him a couple of days before the game:

"This is a grand guy. He's taking adversity with a grin. This could easily be the story of a man who is upset because he doesn't play in his team's biggest game. There isn't a man on the team that doesn't hate the fact that Lou can't be there."

Montgomery, who came from Brockton, sent a good-luck telegram to the team on the morning of the game. Photos appeared the next day in Boston papers showing him sitting by the radio listening to the accounts of the clash, won by Clemson, 6-3.

Jerry Nason covered BC football for the Globe then. He said that though everybody felt sorry for Montgomery, no one was outraged or professed a sense of injustice.

"I was a guy who didn't mind stirring things up," he said yesterday, "and, looking back, I wonder why I didn't get up on a soapbox over that. Today I'd be storming. But in 1940, that's the way things were."

Charles Toole, a freshman in 1940, now lives in Ontario, Calif., and many years later talked with Montgomery about the indignity.

"I was surprised when he told me how much it had hurt him and the mixed emotions he had about not being allowed to play," said Toole yesterday. "He never let on when it happened."

Montgomery told Toole that his main feeling had been not to hurt the team. He knew that if he insisted on suiting up, the Cotton Bowl officials would tell BC to forget the game.

"It wasn't a question of not wanting to rock the boat," Toole said, "because in 1940 nobody knew there was a boat to rock."

Until a couple of years ago, Montgomery worked for Western Airlines in San Francisco, but neither Toole nor John Yauckoes, a tackle on the 1940 team who keeps in touch with his former teammates, has been able to locate him recently.

Today, Montgomery, once decreed a football untouchable, would be just another face in the huddle. At least 17 blacks will suit up for Alabama this afternoon in the Sugar Bowl at New Orleans. BC beat Tennessee in 1941 with Montgomery again barred from playing.

And at the Cotton Bowl in Dallas, 18 of the top 22 players on the host Southwest Conference team, the University of Houston, are black.

Forty years after the injustice, only Lou Montgomery can properly appreciate the irony in those numbers.

Is winning everything? Not to Beth Heiden

February 18, 1980—Winning. How important is it? Is it, to use the late Vince Lombardi's most famous quote, not merely everything, but the only thing? Or is winning simply one of two by-products of the ingredient that really matters, namely playing the game—the other by-product being, of course, losing.

I bring up the subject this morning only because of a couple of over-the-weekend happenings.

Up on Commonwealth Avenue, the Boston University hockey team, a group accustomed to success over the years, but one that has fallen upon hard times this season, is having trouble dealing with defeat.

A player has been banished from the team by the coach for an indifferent attitude in practice. Another player attempting to intercede was told to take a hike.

The pressure of non-winning was taking its toll on a team with a winning tradition.

At the other end of the spectrum was young Beth Heiden's quote after finishing a disappointing—at least to the media, which had touted her as a possible medalist—seventh in two speed skating events in the winter Olympics at Lake Placid.

Said Beth when asked if she herself was disappointed: "Hey, it's only two minutes out of my life."

Her reaction might well have been a defense mechanism to hide the disappointment she might have felt within herself.

But where within the range of those two examples—the BU self-induced pressure to succeed and Ms. Heiden's shrugging off her also-ran performance—does winning fall? How important is it to grab the gold ring? How devastating is it to miss and wind up holding a handful of air?

For every aphorism that takes the Lombardi position, there is another that adheres to a flower-child philosophy.

"Show me a good loser," says the cynic, "and I'll show you a loser."

Back comes the answer, "And if I should lose, let me stand by the road, and cheer as the winners go by."

"If it doesn't matter who wins or loses," asks the Lombardi clientele, "why bother to keep score?"

"It's not whether you win or lose," counters the Flower Child A.C., "but how you play the game."

Back in the dark ages, when Joe DiMaggio played for the Yankees, Tommy Harmon was running wild for the University of Michigan and anybody taking a one-handed shot in basketball was offered a seat at the end of the bench—in other words, when I was a kid—it never occurred to anybody in our sporting circles that playing and winning weren't synonymous.

We played a sport because it was fun, but quickly discovered (or did our coaches program it into us?) that it was more fun to win than to lose and no fun at all unless a score was kept.

I don't ever recall playing anything, even Crazy Eights, and not caring whether I won or lost. The game may have been the thing, but not the only thing. And that attitude has stayed with me, long after my reflexes took a bus out of town.

The sports I play now are mainly for exercise, but winning still is important. I can't just aimlessly whack a tennis ball around without a goal more important than staying in shape. I don't play golf because it's a pleasant way to walk five miles. I play for the challenge of the competition, the excitement of the match. I play for the chance to beat somebody, to win, if you will.

Eons after I'd passed the maximum age limit, Little League hove into view, and with it, the philosophy that winning wasn't as important as letting everybody play.

And I've always had mixed emotions about that, because, while letting everyone play is an admirable objective, if I were one of the sub-teen regulars who had built up a lead, I would not appreciate seeing that lead go down the drain because of a "let everyone play" rule.

There has always been a little more Lombardi in me than I'd admit.

I recall some newspaper stories, a few years ago, about a game called earthball, or something like that, in which there were no sides, and which involved no score. The joy of playing the game was supposed to be enough. There would be neither winners nor losers, and therefore no animosity or post-game bitterness.

The newspaper ran photos of smiling people playing earthball. They seemed to be having a good time. But if someone had tried to recruit me, I'd have had to decline, possibly citing a need to catch up on my latest work, a translation of Howard Cosell into the modern Greek.

To play earthball, or any other game, I need, at the very least, a scoreboard, an accounting.

But the danger then becomes an over-emphasis on winning, which brings situations such as the one that bubbled up with the BU hockey team. It brings the tangled web that hangs over the sports scene at Cambridge Rindge & Latin. It creates Woody Hayes and Bobby Knight and other assorted bully coaches.

So where, on a scale of 1 to 100, should winning lie? When I'm sitting at a typewriter trying to be objective, I say somewhere in the middle.

But when I'm bending over a 3-foot putt that means victory or defeat in a 50-cent Nassau match, the lever is much closer to 100.

Such a situation is, no offense to Ms. Heiden, more than two minutes in my life. Which is probably why I don't make too many of those 3-footers.

A wedge of cheese, a jug of wine and wow; amazing!

February 24, 1980—At 6:30 p.m., Don Gillis told me the Soviets were ahead of the Americans, 3-2, at the end of two periods. That was enough.

I didn't want to know anymore. I didn't want to know the end of the story until Jim McKay, Al Michaels and Ken Dryden brought it to me on delayed tape.

I realize this is a highly unprofessional approach. I'm in the news business more than I am in the entertainment business. Don't give me any of the television hype. Don't give me the CBS golf classic, taped months in advance with the result kept secret so there can be phony suspense.

Don't give me the "Superstars" competition, with the winners hushed up so that there will be a suitable audience on a cold Sunday in winter.

Whatever happens, happens, has always been my approach to the business of sports. Don't show me Holy Cross against Providence in basketball at 11 o'clock and pretend it's a live show. If I know the score before the delayed tape comes on, that's okay with me.

But this was different. I didn't want to know. I turned the news off. I didn't watch Frank Reynolds or John Chancellor or Walter Cronkite. I killed time with "M*A*S*H" and "Wild Kingdom" and Donald Duck—programs I knew would not tell me that Alexander Maltsev had scored 12 goals in the third period to beat a plucky but outmanned United States team.

I played the game I never thought I'd play. I played television's game. I waited until 8:30, when the nightly Olympics program hove into view.

Dah-dum-de-dah. There it was, the flame, the balloons, the Roman numeral XIII sliding into view and then McKay, the guy next door for two weeks every four years.

I searched McKay's face as he said that if there was one American out there ("hey, Jim, it's me") who wanted to be surprised, it was worth not giving the final score. I looked for a tell-tale smile, a furrow in the forehead that might give away the secret.

But McKay was as inscrutable as Charlie Chan in a roomful of murder suspects. Maybe the butler did it, but McKay wasn't telling.

The first two periods ended as Gillis said they had, 3-2, Soviets. The Americans seemed tentative, Dryden said, not skating their positions, trying to do too many things at once. The Soviets seemed as awesome as remembered, swooping, buzzing, flying.

The United States had few chances, the Russians many. The goal that tied the game for the Americans one second before the end of the first period was the worst kind of fluke.

"What's going on here?" I thought. The Soviets don't make mistakes like that. Are they bored? Are they tired? Would goalie Vladimir Tretiak be shot at dawn?

For Tretiak, the punishment was even worse. He was benched, even though he'd always been brilliant against the Americans, and Vladimir Myshkin took his place.

Was that good for the United States? Myshkin, after all, had shut out the NHL All-Stars, 6-0, in that series at Madison Square Garden last year.

ABC messed around with the slalom in between periods, and though I'm sure the slalom is regarded with great respect in Austria, Sweden, Switzerland and Stowe, Vt., I find it exciting only when compared to speed skating, which I rate a cut below mowing the lawn on the entertainment scale.

What it amounts to, I guess, is that I am programmed to have athletes compete against athletes, not against a clock.

Finally, the third period, the crucial 20 minutes began. Let me mention here that I was watching this alone, just me and a bottle of wine and some cheese in the television room.

Let me also say I am in the Guiness Book of Records for pessimism. If something bad hasn't just happened, I am sure it is about to, and so, as the Russians swarmed around U.S. goalie Jim Craig like bees around a honeycomb, I was certain Camelot was about to go up in flames.

Just about the time I was thinking "He's playing great, but this can't last," a Soviet was called for hooking.

It was, as Dryden noted, a chintzy penalty. Replays showed the Russian's stick had barely brushed the U.S. player. Had it been called against the Americans, much hissing and booing would have poured from the stands.

But it was a big chance for the U.S., and when Mark Johnson tied the score at 8:29, I came out of my chair.

"Awright," I yelled and looked around for a hand to slap. There was nobody, so I poured another glass of wine, just in time to celebrate, when Mike Eruzione put the Americans ahead, 4-3, with exactly 10 minutes remaining.

Ten minutes. A coffee break. A walk to the corner. Forever.

Those 10 minutes seemed an eternity at home. The screen kept switching to the computerized clock—7:15, 7:11, 7:10. Forever.

Though both teams had five skaters and a goalie, it was a 10-minute power play for the Soviets. They had the puck most of the time, and usually it was somewhere in the vicinity of Craig.

But toward the end, the strangest thing happened. The Soviets, kings of the ice, panicked, and the Americans, not old enough, perhaps, to know panic, took control.

In the last couple of minutes, the Russians had no good chances. American skaters had the puck more often than not. The Soviets never pulled their goalie for a sixth skater, never had the opportunity for one last desperate onslaught.

Then it was over and the American players were hugging each other and I was a one man applause meter. I sat there by myself and applauded and yelled: "Way to go" at the television set. Only Bernie Carbo had extracted a comparable show of sports emotion from me.

In actuality the game had been over for three hours, yet I wanted to run into the street and yell to the neighborhood, "Hey, did you watch it? Wasn't it great?" as though it all had just happened.

After a while, I turned to another channel, which was showing a Vancouver-Philadelphia NHL game. The players seemed to be skating in molasses, moving in slow motion.

The announcer was shouting about what great action it was. Yeah, action. I watched for three minutes, turned the set off, went to bed and started worrying about the Finns.

New arena? Don't fret

April 13, 1980—The Ghosts of Stadiums Past called an emergency meeting the other day to discuss the Celtics' proposal for a new arena at Suffolk Downs.

"We've let this thing go too far without taking action," said The Ghost of South Station Arena. "It's the biggest threat to our organization since they built that joint in Foxboro."

"No doubt about it," agreed The Ghost of the Stadium Over the Turnpike. "It took us a long time to recover from that. Foxboro almost put me out of business."

"Put you out of business?" screamed The Ghost of The Neponset Dump Stadium. "What about me? I was the laughing stock of the neighborhood. People made jokes about not being able to get tickets on the 50-yard line to watch the wrecked cars rust."

"That's nothin'. How'd you like drunks sleeping in your men's room all night?" South Station wanted to know. "How'd you like somebody knocking down your walls? Don't tell me about hard times."

The Ghost of Fens Stadium, chairman of the group, gaveled for order.

"We're wasting time chewing on old bones," he said. "The question before us is how to shoot down this latest proposal. I'd appreciate some intelligent discussion on the matter."

The Ghost of Watertown Armory Stadium giggled.

"What does intelligence have to do with anything?" he asked. "This one will self-destruct just like all the rest."

"Don't underestimate this Mangurian person," yelled The Ghost of The Harvard Stadium Takeover Plan. "Everybody thought he was throwing money into a bonfire when he bought the Celtics, but look what happened."

The Ghost of Dorchester Stadium Past, feeble and wrinkled and attended by a nurse, banged on his wheelchair and demanded to be heard.

"I got shot down in 1939, 1947 and 1960," he cackled. "I've been around longer than any of you people and I say there's nothing to worry about. This arena will never be built."

The other ghosts began shouting at the old guy, telling him he was out of touch with reality, that times had changed.

The Ghost of The Broadway MBTA Stadium got up on a chair and yelled:

"Let Old Folks speak. Let him speak."

A hush fell over the hall as the old man was rolled to the front of the group and spoke his piece.

"They want a tax break from the mayor. That's the mistake. Getting help from a politician is impossible, a contradiction in terms.

"Maurice Tobin was behind me and I went in the soup. James M. Curley backed me—promised me 86,000 seats—and I sank a little further. John Collins was in my corner and I disappeared forever.

"You get politicians into this thing and it is a guaranteed failure. Who among you has ever had a shovelful of dirt removed by a politician? Thrown at you, maybe, but never moved."

The old man fell back into his wheelchair, exhausted, as the hall erupted in tumultuous applause.

"I second everything the old man said," cried The Ghost of Schoolboy Stadiums Past. "The politicians promised they'd put me in Cleveland Circle. Then it was Revere, then Neponset. Then they were going to remodel White Stadium. I'm still waiting."

The Ghost of East Boston Stadium snickered.

"When I was on the drawing board I was going to seat 75,000. I'd be a stadium other cities would envy. I settled for 7500 and a million airplanes 10 feet over my head."

The Ghost of Fens Stadium Past pounded again with his gavel and asked for order.

"We can't take anything for granted," he said. "This latest proposal should be treated as something that might work. Mangurian has a barrel of money. Suppose he goes ahead without political help?"

"In that case, I propose an all-out scare blitz," said The Ghost of Somerville Arena. "We send out pamphlets describing the terrible jams in the tunnel. We mention the noise and pollution from Logan Airport. We inform people that the proposed site is over a marsh and pilings will have to be driven at least 800 feet into the ground. Toss in a story or two about possible toxic gasses."

The Ghost of The Stadium in the B & M Railroad Yards raised his hand.

"Emphasize the hominess and accessibility of The Boston Garden," he said, "plus all the extra parking in the tow-away zones. Play on the heartstrings. Do an Up Close and Personal on The Jacobs Brothers, Boston's leading absentee sportsmen."

"Suppose none of that works," said The Ghost of Ft. Point Channel Stadium Past. "Suppose it looks as though Mangurian's actually going to pull it off. What then?"

The Ghost of Quincy Arena Past smiled.

"Then we hit him with our high hard one," he said. "We sit him down with the governor."

Grueling marathon . . . and his feet never touched ground

April 20, 1980—I traveled the 26-mile, 385-yard Boston Marathon course the other day, and would like to file the following report: Heartbreak Hill was a snap but Wellesley was murder and Kenmore Square a migraine headache.

Whaddya mean, was I tired when I finished? Why should I be tired? My car did all the work. I drove the distance.

However, I was a mental and emotional wreck by the time I reached the Prudential Building. Bill Rodgers may push himself to the brink of physical exhaustion, but he doesn't have to stop for red lights or squeeze into one lane because of road construction or deal with one-way streets.

No, all he has to do is put one foot after another. He gets a police escort. He has people cheering and hosing him down and handing him freshly squeezed orange juice and when he finishes he's rewarded with a helping of—oh, yummy—strawberry yogurt. Rodgers does not have the mental pressures that come from tooling down Rtes. 135 and 16 in a 1974 Audi with almost 93,000 miles on it. What Tarzan told Jane is so true. It's a jungle out there.

I'd put in plenty of training for the ordeal, driving Rte. 3A at rush hour from Wollaston Beach to Hingham, risking life and limb on Rte. 1 from Suffolk Downs to Danvers, weaving my way through Waltham on Rte. 20.

Still, nothing really prepares one for the Marathon distance, so it was with apprehension that I approached the starting line in Hopkinton Center one afternoon last week, at 2:55 p.m. on the car clock, odometer reading 92,933.4 miles.

I'd gone only a mile at the posted speed limit of 40, when a police car appeared in the rear-view mirror.

Why is it a patrol car puts the fear of J. Edgar Hoover into a motorist? I broke into a mild sweat, wondering if he'd seen me make the U-turn in the middle of Hopkinton.

But the cruiser turned down a side street, leaving the law-breaker free to continue his race against time.

Two miles down 135 I caught up to Mass. license 440EAZ, driver hunched over wheel, car going 27 mph. I wouldn't make Boylston Street before sunset at this pace.

The two of us snailed our way over the Ashland town line and then, a break—440EAZ turned right, into Romeo's Supermarket.

In Ashland, I drove under a banner stretched over the road, reading: "Boston, 22.6 miles, Good luck to Marathoners, Timex Clock Company, Clocktown, U.S.A."

I looked at the Timex watch on my wrist. It was stopped at half past 11.

At 92,938.6 miles and 3:05 p.m., with the sun out and brooding clouds behind me, I crossed the line into Framingham. Past St. Tascisius church (bingo Sundays and Thursdays), past the tumble-down, abandoned, art deco railroad station in Framingham Centre, refuge of a thousand pigeons, I rumbled smack into a traffic jam.

Red light. Move two cars. Red light. Move three cars. Red light. Junction of Rtes. 135 and 126, Concord, 15 miles to the left in case you're a Redcoat.

The jam finally broke and I came abreast of the immortal Happy Swallow saloon. Should I make a pit stop? Who, after all, would know?

Summoning up a previously untapped source of mental discipline, I rolled on past, getting up to 50 mph by the time the outskirts of Natick were breached.

In the middle of Natick, another slowdown, a four-corners offense featuring a city bus, a truck, an unconcerned traffic cop and overmatched me.

At 3:23, I crossed into Wellesley, where legend has it, hordes of pretty college girls toss garlands in your path. All I saw was—honest—sportscaster Bob Lobell in a jogging suit.

In the center of Wellesley, a double-parked, souped-up Buick with oversized tires incurred my wrath, which I keep in the glove compartment for just such situations.

I swung left onto Rte. 16, to be stopped by a policeman when a butterfingered kid coming out of school dropped his notebook in the middle of the street. Motorized marathoners have no rights.

At the Newton Lower Falls line, 16.4 miles from the start, I fell in behind an old Chevy that touted a cleaner environment on its bumper stickers, a philosophy that did not extend to the beat-up, smoke-belching Chevy.

Over the turnpike I went, to reach at last a Marathon landmark—the fire station at Rte. 16 and Commonwealth Avenue.

I shifted into second and began the climb up Heartbreak Hill. Had I paced myself, or would the Audi get shin splints on this murderous stretch of macadam? Would the tires develop blisters?

A surge of excitement passed through me as I shifted into third, and then fourth, going 52 mph, yet avoiding a small dog seemingly intent on committing canine suicide.

New Hampshire license plate 482221, piloted by one of those casual, sling-the-right-arm-over-the-seat drivers, slowed my progress just before Boston College. At Lake Street, panicking badly, I ran a red light.

But now I was onto Beacon Street, and through Coolidge Corner, and the crowds were getting bigger. The people made believe they were shopping or just walking around, but I could tell they noticed.

Fred Lynn was at bat with the bases loaded as I drove into Kenmore Square, with the odometer at 93,959.3. Lynn walked as I stopped for a red light in front of the Hotel Eliot, home of running guru Tommy Leonard. Talk about your symbolism.

Hereford Street, the last little stretch before the finish line, was off-limits, being one-way coming at me. I drove past Hereford, therefore—try saying that three times fast—turned onto Gloucester and reached the Pru with 93,960.1 on the odometer, 26.7 miles from Hopkinton.

The time was 1 hour, 11 minutes. I'd beaten Rodgers by 58 minutes, 27 seconds.

It would have been even more except for that damn kid with the notebook.

Hey, listen, this is an emergency

April 27, 1980—Hello, Acme Repair Co.? Bill Fitch here. Fitch. F-i-t-c-h. That's right. Coach of the Boston Celtics basketball team.

Listen, I know it's the weekend and you don't make housecalls, but I need some help in a hurry. By 1 o'clock this afternoon, as a matter of fact. It's an emergency.

Let me give you the picture and maybe you can suggest some things over the phone. In a nutshell, it's this way.

My pretty green machine is making funny noises and acting strange. Out of sync, if you know what I mean. It'll be purring along nice and smooth and for no apparent reason start sputtering and missing terribly. Sometimes it comes to a dead stop altogether.

Sounds like the Big Carmine Machine on Yawkey Way and also the Red, White and Blue Machine in Foxborough? Hey, I don't know about those, but this hasn't happened before to the pretty green machine, not as long as I've had it.

No, it's not new. Been around a long time, as a matter of fact, but it's been remodeled completely. Sleek lines, some flashy stuff but not overly ostentatious. You must have seen it around town. Got a big bird on the hood. Uh-huh, that's the one.

What's driving me crazy is that the machine ran so great all year. Shifted gears without making a lot of noise, know what I mean? Always able to come up with that little extra on the hills, and terrific on the straightaway. Averaged almost 114 every time I took it out for a spin. Now it barely gets up to 90.

I gotta admit it's not economical to operate. I'd hate to tell you how much we had to pay to get that bird I was talking about. Bought it at an auction and I thought the bidding would never stop. But the green machine wouldn't have been the same without the bird. Everybody agrees with that.

Sorry, I got carried away there. I always do when the bird comes up. If you got any questions, just jump in.

Traffic? Oh, it's always handled great in traffic. Always under control, never overheated. And it accelerated beautifully. Just touch the gas and this little baby was flying.

When did I first notice it was acting funny? I'd say about 10 days ago. It just began wheezing and coughing and not responding. I'd turn the wheel left and the machine would go right. I'd ask for more power and the poor baby would stall. Friday, would you believe it, I had trouble getting out of the driveway.

One of the great things about the machine was the way it could stop on a dime, spin around and go the other way. Now this seems to take forever.

The machine had always cornered so well. But in the last 10 days it keeps bumping into posts, 6-foot, 11-inch posts. It swerves into the wrong lanes and even goes off the road.

Sluggish? A good word. Let me give you an example. This limousine from Pennsylvania—a well-built piece of work, by the way—has gone past my green machine three times in the last 10 days. Whoosh, like that.

I don't mind admitting the whole business is making me sick. I know I'm getting an ulcer and haven't been able to take solid nourishment since the trouble started.

Have I seen a doctor? Oh, Acme Repair Co., the question is dipped in irony. Have I seen a doctor? The doctor is driving that infernal limousine. That's what's making me sick.

But listen, you're the one who can make me better. Just tell me by 1 o'clock this afternoon what I can do to fix my pretty green machine and the world is yours.

No, a major overhaul isn't necessary. The motor is sound and the transmission was rebuilt this fall. Some minor adjustments ought to do it, but which ones?

Uh-huh. Open the throttle wide at the start and keep it open? I'll try that. Stay in overdrive as much as possible, even in traffic? I dunno. I've tried that and got nothing but dents and crinkled fenders.

Keep the pressure gauge at a consistent level? Okay. What else? You think the machine will work better in the open country? No doubt about it, there's more room to operate in the open spaces than there is in the city, where tall buildings have been jumping in my path.

But frankly, it's been in the wide-open spaces that the pretty green machine has been missing the most. You think I should change the oil? Use the Maravich longer-lasting brand? Hey, I'll try anything.

What about the doctor who drives that limousine from Pennsylvania? Uh-huh. Sure I got another Carr in the garage. Use it for small errands, to get bread and milk from the corner, stuff like that.

You think if I use this Carr from start to finish to run the doctor off the road, the pretty green machine will have clear sailing. I'll think it over, but my feeling is: It's gonna take more than that.

Hey, Acme Repair Co., thanks for listening. If things work out, I'll get back to you by Wednesday. If they don't, well, it was a nice ride while it lasted.

I won't miss the players . . . I'll miss the game

May 6, 1980—The major league baseball people begin three days of meetings today in New York—three days that ought to tell us which way the wind is blowing.

Strike on May 23? No strike on May 23? Compromise and common sense? Self-righteous standpatism and pigheadedness? We ought to know which has the upper hand after the next three days.

The dreary sameness and non-progress of the talks since March have brought the expected "who cares?" backlash from fans who conceivably have problems that somewhat supersede the worry over a ballplayer's right to a single hotel room on the road, or an owner's desire to turn the clock back to 1912.

The business of baseball is not quite so essential as, say, picking up the trash every week, and so the backlash expresses itself in such remarks as:

"We can get along without greedy owners and greedy ballplayers. They might find out we won't miss 'em as much as they think. They might find out they need us more than we need them."

I can't argue with all that. One wearies of owners raising prices and telling us how expensive it is to run a ball team, while at the same time stuffing big TV money in the bank and signing mediocrities to contracts that would make an oil sheik blush.

One also tires of athletic millionaires suggesting they are just average working men trying to throw off the shackles of oppression and obtain what should be clear are their unalienable rights.

No, I wouldn't miss management and would even be able to steel myself for a summer without the players. But one thing I'll find it difficult to get along without. One item I'll miss.

I'll miss the game itself. I'll miss major league baseball, a game Bill Veeck has called an island of sanity in a world gone crazy.

And I don't say this because I sometimes write about baseball, and so might be considered, in an oblique way, dependent upon it for part of my living.

I dare say there are other things to write about during the long, hot summer. I suspect there are other, vastly more interesting people in the real world who would fit nicely as the subject of a column. There is more to the summer than the people who inhabit Fenway Park.

But not feel a loss over a summer without major league baseball? Not feel somehow deprived of what should be rightfully mine?

Uh-huh. You might as well tell me the ocean has been transferred to Des Moines for a year, or that the White Mountains have been optioned to Death Valley.

I'll tell you what I'd miss if a strike were called. I'd miss just plain being at Fenway on a perfect June night, when a full moon is hanging like a wheel of cheese, about five feet from the Prudential Building.

I'd miss coming up the runway and into the stands on a sultry July evening, into this marvelous green cocoon of a ballpark made even more green by the stark whiteness of the lights.

Little pleasures, perhaps, but little pleasures help lessen the sting of the big displeasures.

I'd miss the excitement and anticipation around the park on a Friday night with the Yankees the opposition—the traffic, the lines, the sidewalk people talking baseball, the pre-game buzz under the stands that's a prelude to the game's full-throated roar.

I'd miss a lazy Sunday afternoon, with the busloads in from Springfield and Providence and Portland, the Holy Name Societies and the CYO leagues and the sandlot champs and the fraternal clubs on their once-a-year pilgrimage to the shrine.

Oh, and the confrontations. The slugger, up with the bases loaded and the bullpen cart bringing in the relief ace. The batter knocked on his tail by a high inside fastball, then climbing out of the dust to smash the next pitch against the wall. The runner trying to score the tying run from first on the drive to the gap in right center, racing the relay home as the catcher sets himself up for the inevitable collision. The manager, nose to nose with the umpire.

And the second-guessing:

They shoulda bunted. He left the pitcher in too long. He doesn't rest the regulars enough. Why didn't he pinch hit? He plays favorites. He can't hit lefties. He's got pitchforks for hands. He chokes in the late innings.

No game surpasses baseball for second-guessing.

I'd miss the singular grace of baseball, as exemplified by the shortstop-second baseman double play with the runner, spikes high, sliding in from first; the roar as a runner decides to go for three bases on a ball up the alley; the race between the outfielder and the baseball on a long fly.

Front offices come and go and so do ballplayers, and if each side feels so strongly about its respective position that there can no compromising, good luck to both of them.

I've always taken baseball for granted, assumed it was forever. Naive me.

Sure, I'd find something else to write about, but I'd miss baseball. You bet I would.

10

1981

A baseball tale of old

January 4, 1981—The kid was helping his grandfather put away the Christmas ornaments in the attic when he came across the old glove, the tape-wrapped baseball and the dog-eared newspaper photo of Dom DiMaggio.

What were these, the boy wanted to know, and this is what his grandfather answered:

You're too young, I suppose, to remember baseball. Died out back there around the turn of the century, just about the time Celebrity Bowling became the national pastime.

Well, you missed something. Nice game, baseball was. Quiet, and a lot of the time there wasn't a whole lot going on. Still, there was something about the sport that tugged at you.

You didn't have to be 8 feet tall or 10 feet wide to play baseball, or run the 100-yard dash in six seconds or tear telephone books in half with one hand tied behind your back.

It was a game for an average person, and didn't cost much to play, either. Just a vacant lot and a ball and a bat and some kids looking for something to do on a hot summer's day.

You may find this hard to believe, but once upon a time there were plenty of vacant lots and a million kids looking for something to do on a hot summer's day. This was before it became more fun on a hot summer's day to burn down a vacant building or hold up a grocery store or knock down an old woman and steal her purse.

Baseball first began to fade when kids stopped playing unless they had uniforms, expensive gloves, real live umpires, lined fields, grandstands, score-keepers and mama driving them to the game in station wagons.

Boys pretty much gave up baseball once they reached driving age. The closest the average 16-year old came to baseball was when he'd drive over to a playground—where a generation before there'd have been a ball game going on—and drink a six-pack or two among the weeds.

Still, enough players came out of the organized kids' leagues to keep professional baseball going. Even though not many people played anymore, millions continued to be baseball watchers.

The World Series was still very big and professional baseball players remained among the best-known and admired athletes in America.

In those days, baseball was called "family entertainment," though the family's enjoyment of the game had a good chance of being spoiled by the behavior of a permissive minority whose idea of great sport was to start a fistfight, pour beer on everybody and shout four-letter words in the ear of an eight-year-old.

Then came the revolution. I won't bore you with the details, but something called the reserve clause, which had always been the foundation of professional baseball, was ruled illegal, not to mention immoral and fattening to the owners' pocketbooks.

Baseball players, handed the key to the mint, backed the wagon to the door and began loading up. Reserve shortstops got multi-year, six-figure contracts. Ordinary outfielders were treated like princes. Two-eighty hitters became millionaires overnight. Madness prevailed.

Players demanded clauses in their contracts that would allow them to play only on alternate Tuesdays, or only against righthanded pitchers, or only if less than one-tenth of an inch of rain had fallen in the previous week. The inmates were in charge and had posted a new set of rules on the jailhouse door. The escalation never stopped. A contract which seemed a king's ransom when it was agreed to became, only a few years later, a pauper's salary.

"More, more," the players cried, and the echo came back: "How would you like it, in bags, or in the bank?"

All anyone read or heard about was money. Off-season discussions were not about baseball, but about baseball money. Every statistic had a dollar sign in front of it.

A front office announcement that ticket prices would *not* be increased was made as though a presidential citation should be conferred for holding the line.

Because players received so much money, fans expected them to perform better. But of course they didn't. The fans had little patience with failure, but baseball was essentially a game of failure (even .300 hitters failed seven times out of ten). And so there was growing discontent throughout the land.

Then one day, the baseball public, up to its eyebrows in inflation and its own problems, opened a window and yelled: "I'm mad as hell and I'm not going to take it anymore."

Baseball laughed, because how many times had this happened in the past without a letup at the turnstiles? America needed baseball, didn't it, as an escape valve?

But, lo and behold, the public did stop going to games. The winds whistled through the empty stadia, where athletes still were going through the motions to fulfill cable television commitments.

At home, however, nobody watched baseball on TV, preferring instead such activities as tug-of-wars in Hawaii and motorcycle jumps off the Golden Gate Bridge.

Pretty soon the advertising dollar dropped away to nothing. Teams began to fail for lack of capital—the Minnesota Twins were first, followed by the Boston Red Sox and the Chicago White Sox.

Other owners, seeing the red ink on the wall, got out of the business. Soon only the New York Yankees and the Los Angeles Dodgers were left, playing 162 games to determine who would have home field advantage in the World Series.

All that remains now is an Oldtimers' Game held every July 4 in Cooperstown,

N.Y. Nobody pays any attention to it except old fogies like me, who remember baseball when the grass was real.

Baseball was a terrific game, son. You'd have liked it, liked it a lot, before the vultures picked it to pieces.

Ah, spring, and ideas turn to . . .

April 5, 1981—Spring was peeking around the corner, winking at him, so the middle-aged man decided to walk to the library. On the way home, he cut through French's Common, where some kids were practicing baseball.

"Nice," the middle-aged man thought, stopping to watch. "You don't see much of this anymore, kids without uniforms just messing around on a scruffy ballfield."

A righthander was throwing batting practice, and in between pitches, a gray-haired man would hit ground balls to his infielders.

It wasn't much of a batting practice, because the pitcher wasn't throwing the ball over the plate. Inside, outside, high, low—anywhere but where the batter could hit it. The pitcher would receive the ball from the catcher, go through all the major league preliminaries and then throw another bad one.

The kids in the outfield were bored stiff. They stood there, arms folded, as the pitcher and catcher threw the ball to one another. The outfielders' practice consisted of shifting from one foot to the other.

The middle-aged man wanted to yell to the kid, "Hey, stop trying to be Nolan Ryan and just throw the ball up there. Let him hit it."

More than that, the middle-aged man wanted to go out there and do it himself. He wanted to be like Rabbit Angstrom, the former high school basketball star in John Updike's novel, who would stop off on the way home from work and go head to head with the young punks in 3-on-3 games to show he could still play.

The middle-aged man wanted to take the ball and glove from the pitcher and tell him, "Here's the way to do it. Nice and easy. No big windup. You're supposed to be giving these guys batting practice, not strike them out."

He wanted to take the bat from the lefthanded hitter's hands and stand in there himself, show the kid the way Ted used to stand, hands close to the body, slightly open stance, eyes concentrating on the pitcher.

"Don't commit yourself too soon," the middle-aged man wanted to say to the batter. "Don't stride until the ball leaves the pitcher's hands. Stay back as long as you can. Don't drop the left shoulder. That makes you uppercut the ball."

But the middle-aged man didn't say or do anything. He just watched as the pitcher and catcher continued to throw the ball to each other and the batter continued to foul off the one out of eight pitches he swung at and the outfielders continued to fidget with their feet.

Right field on French's Common stops abruptly, perhaps 200 feet from home plate, because a building is there. City Hall, as a matter of fact, and the windows that face the field were screened to protect them from fly balls hit in that direction.

The kids must laugh at how short right field is, the middle-aged man thought. But then he remembered playing some baseball in Corinth, N.Y., which is north of Saratoga Springs, and it wasn't until 25 years later, on a nostalgic return to that area, that he saw the field again and realized how tiny it really was. Awesome is in the eye of the beholder.

Pretty soon, the softball leagues would be starting up on the fields behind the high school, and soon guys in their late 30s would be young again, at least until they pulled a hamstring muscle sliding into third base.

The middle-aged man thought about how few ballplayers out of all those who play the game make the majors. Do fans really appreciate that? But then, do ballplayers really appreciate where they are and how many—people with really good jobs—would change places with them in a minute?

The sun was getting low now, and there was a chill in the air, so the middle-aged man figured he'd better get on home. He walked past the left fielder, who stood, arms folded, staring into space. A penny for his thoughts would have been no bargain.

The middle-aged man walked past a pickup basketball game on a typical outdoor court—uneven asphalt, netless baskets and bent rims.

He walked past a tennis court, also without a net, which made the sport easier to play. The sun glistened off shards of broken beer bottle glass at midcourt, another contribution from the do-your-own-thing generation.

The middle-aged man had ambivalent feelings every April. The return of spring made him feel good, made the juices flow again after a freezing, messy, dreary winter.

But the kids playing ball on a vacant lot was an arrow straight to the heart of his youth, a time forever gone but remembered with fondness. He knew that living in the past put no bread on the table, but early in the spring, he couldn't resist the temptation.

The middle-aged man looked back to the field. The pitcher had thrown a ball in the dirt. The catcher was chasing it to the backstop, and in left field, a boy shifted from his left foot to his right.

The champ? There was only one then

April 13, 1981—The big ark of a radio was 90 percent wood, with a tiny dial and RCA's magic eye, a mysterious green blinker that was supposed to help the listener hone in to the proper station.

The radio sat next to the wicker rocker and overstuffed armchair, and out of this marvelous machine came wondrous programs—Little Orphan Annie ("Who's your little chatterbox?"), Tom Mix ("Ralston Cereal can't be beat") and The Lone Ranger ("Who was that masked man?").

But for a boy growing up in the late '30s, one treat was better than anything else, better even than Jack Armstrong, the All-American Boy ("Wave the flag for Hudson High, boys").

The best was being allowed to stay up late to listen to the heavyweight championship fights. The absolute best was to huddle next to the radio and hear the gravel-voiced Clem McCarthy rasp: "The Brown Bomber is stalking Schmeling. He hits the German with a hard left and a right to the stomach, and Schmeling is down. Schmeling is down. It's over. It's all over. Joe Louis has retained his championship by knocking out Max Schmeling in 2 minutes, 4 seconds of the first round."

Joe Louis—just to write the name is to step into a time machine. Does any name more effectively evoke the feel, the smell, the touch, the memory of how it was in the '30s and '40s in the United States of America?

"Counting for the knockdowns at the bell . . ."

"The Brown Bomber will begin workouts next week at his Pompton Lakes, N.J., training camp."

"The referee, Arthur Donovan, scores it 12 rounds for Louis, two for . . ."

"He can run but he can't hide."

"He's a credit to his race."

"Hey, champ. Howya doin', champ?"

Joe Louis was the champ, all right. Every kid in America knew that. He was no Bob Arum Top Rank creation or Don King Enterprises bozo. He was no public-relations ragamuffin, put together with thumbtacks and Elmer's Glue in a 25th-floor office.

He was *the* champion. Period. He fought anybody who would get into the ring with him. Some were bums who couldn't outbox your Aunt Alice, and some were legitimate opponents, and he dispatched them all.

The worn and outdated phrase, "He was a credit to his race," indicates how long ago that really was. Kids didn't understand that the words were really an insult to his race. The kids didn't know that the ones saying Louis was a credit to his race thought they were being terribly liberal and accommodating by giving a "Negro" a pat on the back.

And the kids didn't care. All they knew was that Louis had thunder in his fists and lightning in his step, and when he knocked out Schmeling at Yankee Stadium, it was as though Hitler had gone down for the count.

I was in the sixth grade when that happened but in the hospital recovering from an appendectomy. The sixth-grade teacher, spotting a marvelous opportunity to have her pupils show their writing ability, had each of them compose "cheer Ray up" letters.

All but one were along the line of "Hi, how are you? Get well soon." The renegade letter began, "Well, the German got his block knocked off."

In 40-odd years, I've never read a better analysis of a fight.

We never saw Louis, of course, except in Paramount film clips on Saturday afternoons at the Park Theater. But we knew from the papers and the radio that he was a panther stalking his prey, that he never took a step backward, that he was gentle outside the ring but a killer inside.

Louis had 71 fights but only one in Boston. On Dec. 16, 1940, he scored a TKO over Bum of the Month Club member Al McCoy at the Garden when McCoy failed to answer the bell for the sixth round. The reason he failed to answer the bell was that his left eye had been so badly damaged by Louis' punches, doctors were afraid any further punishment might result in the loss of that eye.

Louis raised thousands of War Bond dollars for the United States by fighting charity bouts while in the service. The government showed its appreciation by yanking Louis around when the war was over and hounding him for income-tax money he didn't have.

Louis should have retired an undefeated champion, but he needed the money so came back and was outpointed by Ezzard Charles. And on Oct. 26, 1951, Rocky Marciano knocked him out in the eighth round. The fight ended with the 37-year-old Louis sprawled awkwardly in the ropes, glazed eyes searching in vain for the Madison Square Garden clock.

But, of course, the kids who huddled around the radios were kids no longer by then. The "new" kids could sit in their very own house and watch pictures that moved. They could be Mousketeers and sing along with Buffalo Bob and wear a coonskin hat just like Davey Crockett, and what did they know or care about any old Brown Bomber?

Then Muhammad Ali came along and told the world that he floated like a butterfly and stung like a bee and that he was the greatest.

Maybe it was true. Maybe Ali *was* the greatest. But Joe Louis, dead at 66, was the best.

Surviving month's fast

June 14, 1981—Ring the bells. Beat the drums. Break out the champagne. I did it. I spent a month in Scotland and Ireland, out of touch with the American sports scene, and I survived.

It was my personal Outward Bound program, my climb over the rugged mountains of sports indifference, my swim through shark-infested waters where never is heard a Cosellian word.

When I left, the Celtics and Rockets were 2-2 in the NBA championship finals. The Stanley Cup champion Islanders were in the finals again, this time against the North Stars.

Pleasant Colony was tuning up for the Preakness. Baseball players and owners were on their annual journey to a picket line. It was a busy, exciting time.

And I walked away from it all, kicked it cold turkey. I read my final Globe sports page, tipped my cap goodby, flung a flight bag over my shoulder and headed for Dublin, where Molly Malone rolled her wheelbarrow and Moses Malone was unknown.

I knew the transition would be difficult. For longer than I care to remember I've been sitting in America's sandbox, thinking, writing, talking and reading about the country's sports and those who play them. They've never been further away than tomorrow morning's newspaper.

Could I last a month without knowing if Red Auerbach had lit his 14th championship cigar? Could I survive ignorant of baseball's fate? Who had been hired, fired, injured? Who had Billy Martin punched?

The first few days, like giving up cigarettes or taking up jogging, were the toughest. Not an hour went by that my mind didn't wander back to the Garden or Fenway from the task at hand, which more often than not was avoiding a sheep in the road.

There were moments when I had to fight the urge to make an emergency transatlantic call to Al Rudnick, proprietor of the Globe's Scoreboard page, for a quick agate type transfusion.

Were there temptations? Certainly. The International Herald Tribune, with American sports information, is sold in principal European cities. Also, sports-minded American tourists are not uncommon. Ask one and I would have been told the outcome of what I had left behind.

But I vowed there would be no cheating. A promise made would be a promise kept.

However, I'm only human. I needed, every so often, a newspaper fix, and got it through a Scottish or Irish journal. So it was that in Oban, Scotland, I was relieved to learn, through headlines as high as the World Trade Center, that "Wife of Yorkshire Ripper Will Stick by Convicted Hubby."

In The Scotsman, I read that railroad officials deplored the hoodlumism and drunkenness on trains heading to and from the Scotland-England soccer football match at Wembley Stadium. A little touch of the MBTA there.

I took in some non-American sports. In Dublin, I saw a cricket team practicing, an endeavor that makes the America's Cup races seem a maelstrom of action.

I also watched the televised highlights of the Dublin-Wicklow Gaelic football match, a game in which players lay about quite heavily on one another's shoulders and heads. The rules allow a player to dribble the ball ("hop it," the expression is), and also to kick it niftily to himself as he runs along.

Film clips of a golf tournament brought a contemptuous response from an Irishman sitting next to me.

"The bloody game is a bore," he suggested as a player bent over to putt. "That fellow with the stick would have a hard time putting the ball into the hole if another man with a stick was coming at him." There is no disputing that.

I played golf at LaHinch, on the coast of Clare, a links without a tree or a pond or a creek, or at least as far as I was concerned, a fairway.

In Sligo Town, I went to the races, held in a cold, driving rain. The mile track, over scraggly and uneven grass, went uphill and downhill and out of sight. In the infield, sheep grazed. There is no starting gate. Instead the horses seem to mill about and at a signal from somebody, simply begin the race.

There was no fancy clubhouse. The refreshment area consisted of a large shed that dispensed Jameson's whiskey and Guiness stout, and another smaller area that sold fish and chips. The liquid far outsold the solid, which seemed only right.

Though there were tote windows, most bets are made with one of 20 bookmakers. These legalized gentlemen sit on high stools, next to a board on which they've chalked the names and odds of the competing horses.

Because one bookmaker's odds differ from another's, it is important to not only choose your horse wisely, but also your bookie. I wagered a pound on a 10-1 shot whose name escapes me, handing the note to a bookmaker named Austin Quinlivan. Mr. Quinlivan flung the money into a well-worn satchel and called out my bet to an assistant, who duly noted it.

The horse ran exactly like most of those I bet on in the United States, that is, at a leisurely pace ill-suited to the endeavor. But somehow, losing to a bookmaker seemed more personal and less painful than losing to a tote machine.

On the plane home, I broke my fast. In Sports Illustrated I discovered the Celtics were champions and so were the Islanders. Jean Ratelle had retired. Pleasant Colony had won the Preakness but lost the Belmont, Gene Mauch had replaced Jim Fregosi and Fernando Valenzuela had returned to earth.

Not a line about Cork vs. Tipperary. You can never find what you're looking for in a magazine these days.

A bird's-eye view

June 16, 1981—Wally the Wonder Pigeon wasn't particularly happy when I cornered him yesterday at Fenway Park, looking for an interview. "You never come around to talk when those overpaid stiffs are playing baseball," he pouted. "I could be in a kamikaze dive off a light tower and you'd never notice. It's always Yaz this and Rice that and why don't the Red Sox learn to bunt? Pigeons get no respect, here or anywhere else. A fact of life; you could look it up."

I told him all I wanted was a pigeon's view of the baseball strike. Though several stories had appeared detailing the effect of the strike on concessionaires and businesses in the vicinity of Yawkey Way, nothing had been written on the plight of the Fenway Park pigeons.

"I'll give you 15 minutes, but please don't ask me to explain the infield fly rule or I'll get a headache," said Wally, waddling to a box seat and sitting down, or whatever it is pigeons do when they aren't standing up or flying.

Wally said the strike was the most potentially dangerous thing to happen to pigeons at Fenway Park since the great massacre of 1940.

Ted Williams, annoyed because pigeons on the roof were laughing themselves silly every afternoon watching him stumble around in left field, hauled out a rifle one morning and gunned down an estimated 40 of the birds.

Pigeons dropped from the sky like April raindrops, and feathers littered the outfield like fallout from Mt. St. Helens.

"My great-grandfather was hit," said Wally. "He fell, badly wounded, into the left-field net and eventually sailed off to the great pigeon coop in the sky."

Wally gestured toward center field. Great granddad's buried out there, just behind the flagpole.

Wally said that though Williams apologized for the outburst, he's never been forgiven. "He may be in the baseball Hall of Fame, but to us, he'll be remembered only as a ruthless pigeon killer."

He said the Williams outburst left much more ill feeling than the Willie Horton incident a few seasons ago. Horton lofted a high pop foul which struck a pigeon in mid-flight and killed him instantly.

"My Uncle Bruce," said Wally, his eyes misting over with the memory. "Died before he hit the ground. Never knew what hit him. He looked so peaceful lying next to home plate with Lee MacPhail's autograph across his chest.

"But listen, that was an accident. Pigeons can step off a curb and get struck by a car. Humans, too. Happened right here in Boston to Casey Stengel. I never blamed Horton for Uncle Bruce's demise."

Wally said it would be some time before the full effect of the strike was felt by the Fenway pigeon colony.

"We need an average crowd of 18,000 to feed every pigeon who operates here," he explained. "That many people will spill enough popcorn and drop enough pizza crusts to keep us going."

He said the Fenway Flock started an emergency fund after the 13-day players' strike in 1972 and at the moment have a 30-day reserve supply of popcorn stashed way under the grandstand eaves. If the strike lasts longer than that, they'll apply for federal aid.

The Wonder Pigeon said that until the current strike, times had been good since 1967, with sellout crowds spilling record amounts of popcorn almost every night for the last several years. However, the '50s and early '60s were another story.

"Crowds seldom reached 10,000," said Wally. "As a result, a pigeon in those days had to battle to get a square meal. Some of our less aggressive members would go days without a kernel. Of course, a lot of us didn't have much of an appetite anyway. Who could be hungry after a day spent watching baseballs bounce off Don Buddin's glove?"

Wally added that many of his confreres had taken advantage of the strike to go on vacation at such resorts as Boston Common, City Hall, Boston Garden, the Old North Church and even as far north as Suffolk Downs.

Others, he said, would fly to Pawtucket to pick up any crumbs left lying around McCoy Stadium, or to Frazier Field in Lynn, where they'd have to battle the gulls for any available largess.

Wally said, however, that he'd stay at Fenway, continue to work out in the rafters and hope the strike would be of short duration.

"I'll tell you this," Wally the Wonder Pigeon said. "If I could get together with Ray Grebey and Marvin Miller, I might not be able to end the deadlock, but you can bet I'd leave my mark on them."

Sure, Ma, but it'll never replace TV

June 28, 1981—It is a typical Saturday afternoon in suburbia, USA. Father is playing golf. Mother is baking a cake. Teenage son is glued to the television set. Mother speaks:

Tommy, you're getting on my nerves. It's too nice a day to stay in the house. Why don't you go outside?

And do what?

Do what other kids do. Steal a hubcap. Kick a pigeon. Play some baseball.

Some what?

Baseball.

What's that?

Baseball. You know, where you hit a ball with a bat.

A bat?

That's right. That piece of wood down cellar by the oil burner, the one with the knob at one end.

You mean the stick that has someone's autograph burned into it—Ronnie Johnson or something like that?

Jackson. Reggie Jackson.

Yeah. Well, it's not there any more. Dad used it to tie up his tomato plants.

Then go ask Billy if he wants to play catch.

Catch?

Uh-huh. Get your glove and you and Billy can throw the baseball to each other.

Get my what?

Your glove.

You talking about that old piece of leather the cat had her kittens in last week?

Oh my goodness. Don't you remember baseball at all, dear?

On the late show, I saw an old Gary Cooper movie that had goofy looking men in knickers sliding into square sacks.

Those were Yankees and they were sliding into bases.

It didn't look like much fun to me. Why were they getting themselves all dirty?

They were sliding so they wouldn't be thrown out.

Out of what?

No, they weren't being thrown out of anything. That's just a baseball expression. If you aren't out, you're safe.

My feelings exactly. That's why I'm in here watching television. It's a jungle outside.

I don't think you're catching on. Let me give you a basic description of baseball, so that if it ever makes a comeback, you'll be ready for it.

OK, but make it short. There's a celebrity water polo match coming on that I want to watch.

Well, to begin with, the pitcher throws the ball and tries to make the batter swing and miss. If he swings and misses three times, he's out.

Unless he slides.

No, sliding comes only when a batter is running the bases.

Is running the bases anything like walking the dog?

What the expression means is running to a base. There are four bases—first second, third and home.

Wouldn't it be logical to call it fourth instead of home?

No. If you did, how would you ever have a home run?

Don't ask me, it's your game.

Now pay attention. If the pitcher throws the ball and the batter hits it, the batter quickly drops his bat and runs toward first base. Meanwhile, the fielders try to catch the ball.

The fielders?

The ones wearing gloves.

Do they own kittens?

It doesn't matter.

It does to the kitten.

Don't change the subject. If the ball that the batter hit is a fly . . .

The ball changes into a fly?

No, a fly is something in the air.

Do you think I'm dumb? Everybody knows that.

Let me put it this way. If the ball is hit in the air, the batter is retired if a fielder catches the ball on the fly.

Ouch. You'd think it would be the fielder who'd have to retire.

Never mind the smart remarks. If the ball is hit on the ground, however, the fielder must throw out the batter.

How far does he have to throw him?

No, it's the ball that's thrown, not the batter. The ball must be thrown with enough speed and accuracy to reach first base before the batter does. If it isn't, the batter is safe, and then is entitled to try to steal second base.

Now I get it. The first player to steal all four bases and take them home is the winner. That's what you mean by a home run.

Uh, not quite. The winner of the game is the one who scores the most runs in nine innings.

Innings?

That's right. Each team bats for nine innings, with three outs to an inning. If your team can come up with clutch hitting and play airtight ball in the field and get sharp relief pitching, you have a good chance of winning the game.

I've got an idea.

Want to go play some baseball?

No, let's buy some peanuts and Crackerjacks and watch a Randolph Scott double feature.

He's the last of a dying breed

July 26, 1981—Two small boys playing in an old abandoned tenement house stumbled upon the old man and notified the authorities.

"He says he's The Last Baseball Fan in America and won't come out until the strike is settled," one of the boys told the desk sergeant.

"I thought we'd flushed out the last of those lamebrains in that West Virginia cave," the sergeant sighed. "OK, we'll send a patrol. He's harmless, but he gives the country a bad name."

When the police arrived, they threw a cordon around the dilapidated tenement and issued an ultimatum.

"We know you're in there, Last Baseball Fan in America," the captain said over the bullhorn. "You've got 15 minutes to surrender or we're comin' after you."

"You'll never take me alive," cackled The Last Baseball Fan In America. "As sure as three strikes is out, I'll fight until I drop. As sure as Lou Gehrig was The Iron Horse, I'll battle you butchers to the end."

The police captain turned to his lieutenant. "Three strikes? Iron Horse? The guy is nutty as a fruitcake. Here, you talk to him."

The lieutenant took the bullhorn.

"You haven't got a chance, silly old man," he said. "Baseball is dead and is never coming back."

For an answer, The Last Baseball Fan in America played Robert Merrill's recording of The Star-Spangled Banner and emptied a box of popcorn out a third-story window onto the officer's head.

The lieutenant brushed some stray kernels from his sleeve and tried again.

"Hey, Last Baseball Fan in America, what makes you think the game isn't dead?"

"Comr. Bowie Kuhn says the National Pastime will survive these perilous times." The Last Baseball Fan in America shouted, "Bowie Kuhn says the Toronto Blue Jays will live to play again. I believe in Bowie."

The police lieutenant shook his head.

"Bowie Kuhn runs a flower shop in Teaneck," he shouted back. "He hasn't been baseball commissioner since the major leagues went out of business in 1981. Now come down out of there before we have to get rough."

The front door opened, and a baseball came flying out, missing the lieutenant's head by inches and bouncing off a nearby squad car.

"The Jugs gun had that one timed at 92 miles per hour, sir," said an aide. "Look, the baseball is signed by someone named Ford Frick."

"That was my brushback pitch," yelled The Last Baseball Fan in America. "Don't crowd me or I'll stick the next one in your ear."

The police lieutenant and captain huddled to discuss strategy.

"We'll give him one final chance," the captain said. "Then we bring out the tear gas and rush him. Let me talk to him again."

The captain took the bullhorn and told The Last Baseball Fan in America he was out of touch with reality.

"You're living in the past," the captain shouted. "Nobody plays or talks about baseball anymore."

"I do," yelled back The Last Baseball Fan in America. "Take two and hit to right. Hey, ump, you're missin' a good game. Get the ball over, you stiff. Hit the cut-off man. Hey, get your cold drinks right here, cold drinks. The Bambino, the Splendid Splinter, the Boomer, the Say Hey Kid, the Philly Phanatic. Yaz sir, that's my baby."

"Make any sense out of that gibberish?" the captain wanted to know.

"Ragtime," replied the lieutenant.

Suddenly, The Last Baseball Fan in America, wearing a San Diego Padre warmup jacket, appeared in a second-story window. "Time for the seventh-inning stretch," he said. "Hey, coppers, do me a favor. Tell Miller and Grebey they will sleep with the fishes if they don't settle the strike in the next couple of days."

"Miller? Grebey? Stop the nonsense," the captain yelled back. "You got 10 seconds to give up; otherwise, we're coming in. One . . . two . . . OK, boys, get ready to charge. Five . . . six . . . Prepare the tear gas. Nine . . . 10 . . . On with the masks."

When the police broke down the barricades on the stairway and got to The Last Baseball Fan in America, they found him, tears streaming from his eyes and gasping for breath, slumped over a scrapbook of the 1975 World Series.

"Ya got me, coppers," he said. "Tell the world I went out fast and clean, like a Jim Rice home run. Tell 'em I died with my spikes and wristbands on. Tell 'em the game is never over 'til the last man is out.

"And most of all," said The Last Baseball Fan in America as he coughed and sputtered his last breath, "tell 'em they should never have pinch hit for Willoughby."

Baseball makes a comeback

But this skeptic may stay away

August 1, 1981—

Oh, somewhere men are laughing,
And children are having fun,
But will there be joy in Mudville
Now that the strike is done?

Early yesterday, the news wire rattled out terms of the baseball strike settlement. Big deal. Plenty of dollar signs, followed by several ciphers and dozens of whereases and wherefores. Dreary paragraphs about pools and compensation and central funds. Perfunctory quotes from players, owners, officials, negotiators.

After 49 days, the baseball strike, one of the dullest disputes in the history of the civilized world, was over, settled where much of the clandestine activity in America takes place—in a hotel room at 3 in the morning.

The All-Star game will be played Aug. 9 in Cleveland, with the season picking up again the next day.

"Who cares?" the once and former fan said yesterday, combing his hair in the mirror.

"Whaddaya mean, who cares?" his mirror image answered. "I care. America cares. The National Pastime is back."

"Baseball has lost me," said the fan. "The greediness of those people has turned me off. I didn't care if they ever settled the strike."

"Yeah, so you say," replied the mirror, "but you gotta admit you missed the box scores in the paper every day."

"At first I did," said Joe Fan. "But after a while, I got used to it. There were plenty of other things to read about in the summer besides major league baseball."

"Like what?"

"Tennis. Golf. Arm-wrestling championships. Five-car smash-ups in automobile races."

"Sure," laughed the mirror.

"Honest," replied the fan. "In a way, I'll even miss the baseball strike."

"How's that?"

"You know, the thrill of negotiation and the agony of no comment," replied the fan. "No more Marvin Miller on the 11 o'clock news, smiling like a Cheshire cat. The George Steinbrenner-Rusty Staub debate was as good as a twilight doubleheader."

"Be serious," said the mirror.

"OK, I'll be serious," replied the fan. "The players and owners did what I never thought possible. They took a great game and twisted it into little pieces. They took a lifetime of illusions and dumped them into the river."

"Ahhh, the strike wasn't that bad."

"Yes, it was. Baseball's a business. I knew that. But I kidded myself that somehow baseball was different, that it cared about me. Now I know how wrong I was."

"But the strike's over," insisted the mirror.

"Not for me it isn't," replied the fan. "They yanked me around for two months, and I'm supposed to jump up and down and wave the American flag because two people shook hands? No way." The face in the mirror grimaced.

"You're overreacting," it said. "Ken Singleton of the Orioles says that when the players get back in condition, fans will see some of the best baseball that's ever been played."

"Terrific. The middle of August, and he's talking about players getting in shape. Somebody ought to ask him what happened to June and July."

"OK, so it's a short season," the mirror said. "But it should be exciting. All-Star game next weekend, and then the second season begins."

"The All-Star game is a fraud," said the fan. "Pitchers will be lobbing the ball over the plate so they won't hurt their arms. Guys will be going at half-speed to avoid a hamstring pull. If Cleveland had any sense, it would farm the game out to Ashtabula."

"C'mon," scoffed the mirror. "In a month, you'll forget the strike ever happened."

"Nope, I've had it with the game," the fan said. "I'm boycotting major league baseball. You'll never see me at the park again, and I'm not going to watch it on television either."

"What'll you watch?"

"I dunno. 'McHale's Navy' reruns. Old Barbara Stanwyck movies. 'Candlepins for Cash.' Anything but Red Sox baseball."

"Do a lot of people feel the way you do?"

"Millions," said the fan. "Forty-six percent of the fans say good riddance to baseball, and I'm one of them."

"You really think fans are that angry?" the mirror asked.

"Damn right I do."

"Then you probably won't want those tickets to the Yankees and Red Sox on Sept. 18," the face in the mirror said.

"Day game or night game?" the once and former fan wanted to know.

Sanderson's salvation— He only swings in golf

August 8, 1981—The $36,000 Rolls Royce is up on blocks in Niagara Falls, Ont. The eight-bedroom, 60-acre ranch with the 10 horses is gone. So is the financial interest in the three Boston nightclubs. The $2.65 million contract went up in smoke long ago.

Derek Sanderson let the good times roll, and they did. They rolled over him—smothered him, almost killed him, and left him a battered hulk of a human being.

Bottles filled with drink and with pills turned his mind to mush and all but wrecked a body that once was such a treat to watch on the rinks of the National Hockey League.

The miracle is that Sanderson escaped the physical and emotional quicksand he'd thrown himself into and that his spirit has survived the battering he gave it.

The former Bruin, rookie of the year in the NHL in 1967-68, is making a comeback—not in hockey, but in life. He's working at the Andover Country Club as an assistant to pro Spike Boda. His goal is to get his PGA card and become a golf professional at a club.

He is still a charmer, this Peck's bad boy of hockey, and eager to talk about his slide to oblivion, hoping that his story might help others avoid the canyon of misery he fell into because he was unable to handle the change from hockey player to millionaire.

The drinking and pill-popping began when he was still a Bruin. He disliked flying so much, he said, that he gulped Valium to quiet his nerves before a flight.

"The pills made me irritable and belligerent, so I started drinking. I'd have a glass of whiskey, a Coke, some 7-Up, chew some gum, have a cigarette, and then do it all over again. Then I'd throw myself on the plane."

But the real trouble came after he left the Bruins and signed the big contract with the Philadelphia Blazers of the newly formed World Hockey Assn.

"I was a good player and helped others look better, but I wasn't worth $2½ million. I wasn't a franchise. Bobby Orr was a franchise. Phil Esposito was. Taking the Philadelphia offer was a mistake. I underestimated the value of friendship and the security of being in Boston."

He went to Philly, but all his friends were in Boston.

"I was depressed one rainy day, so I bought the Rolls. Paid cash. Up till then, I'd never really thought about how much money I had or what it could do."

Sanderson caught on quickly. He became an expert at spending money. He went through it in Guinness Book of World Records fashion. He carried $4000 in cash and says he spent as much as $40,000 a month. He'd take a trip to Hawaii, but didn't want to go alone, so he would bring an entourage with him for a month and pay all the bills.

The Blazers went gurgling down the drain, and so did Sanderson. He began eating pills like candy—sleeping pills, antidepressants, Valium—washing them down with whiskey.

"I'd get sicker than a dog, so to make myself feel better, I'd wake up and drink myself out of the sickness."

Sanderson became a one-man traveling show. He came back to the Bruins in 1973, went to the Rangers for a year, to St. Louis for two more, to Vancouver, to Kansas City, to Pittsburgh, to Tulsa and back to Kansas City.

In 1977, he signed with Vancouver but was farmed out early in the season. About that time, his engagement also fell apart.

"I went back to New York and partied every night," he said. "I never knew where I'd wake up, or if I would."

He went home to his Ft. Erie, Ont. ranch for Christmas, drank himself into a stupor, and one morning burned himself badly trying to boil some grease. He recovered from the burns in the hospital, where doctors tried unsuccessfuly to convince him he had a drinking problem.

A man named Rudy Krulik visited Sanderson in the hospital. He'd played Junior B hockey when Sanderson was a stickboy with Niagara Falls, and as Sanderson put it, "had always been a religious nut."

"How'd you know I was here?," Sanderson asked Krulik. "Nobody knows I'm here."

"You wouldn't believe me if I told you," replied Krulik. "God is looking after you."

Sanderson laughed at Krulik, told him he wasn't interested in that nonsense and to leave him alone.

Krulik showed up again when Sanderson, who had ballooned to 230 pounds, was trying to make a comeback and was working himself back into shape in Windsor, Ont.

"I'd decided to sleep late instead of practicing," said Sanderson, "and there was Rudy knocking on the door. He saved my skin, because I'd have been canned if I hadn't shown up for practice."

Krulik told Sanderson that God had given him talent, fame and fortune, but that he thought he'd done it all himself, so God was taking everything away to test him, teach him a lesson.

"It was phenomenal the way he showed up at just that time," Sanderson said. "I began to think there was something in what he was saying."

There were still lessons to be learned. Sanderson fell on hard times in Chicago and said Orr saved him.

"Bobby told me he couldn't let me destroy myself, that he couldn't let me go off the deep end. He grabbed me and put me in a hospital and paid the bills, about $6000 worth," Sanderson said.

He was in and out of a detoxification hospital in St. Catharine's, and one day a worker there said to him, "Your problem is that you think you're better than you are. You think you're a big shot, but your big-shot days are over. You're a drunk, that's all you are. You're not a hockey player. You're nobody special. That's all over. You've got to face the fact that alcohol has beaten you."

"He said I shouldn't be embarrassed to pray every day," said Sanderson. "Pray to what?" I asked him, and he told me, 'To the ceiling, to anything. Just admit you can't do it alone.'"

Last winter, Sanderson helped coach the Niagara Falls Juniors and loved it. He'd like to get back into hockey, but is aware of the realities.

"People are apprehensive. You can't blame 'em. They say, 'I hope you make it, but I'm not going to hand it to you.' They're dealing with a recovered drinker and they think, 'What if he loses it in the middle of a season? What if he lets us down?'

"This is my humbling period. I gotta pay my dues. It's like I'm a rookie all over again."

Sanderson says he hasn't fallen in more than a year.

"I felt so good on my first anniversary," laughed the man who thought he owned the world only a decade ago, "I almost went out and had a drink to celebrate."

Take that, Bowie, and that

October 21, 1981—

> *News item: Baseball commissioner Bowie Kuhn has turned down Yankee owner George Steinbrenner's request to have acting legend Jimmy Cagney throw out the first ball for the opening game of the World Series at Yankee Stadium.*

NEW YORK—You'll get yours, Bowie, you dirty rat. You've turned down Cagney and you're in big trouble. You'd better have somebody start your limousine for you. You'd better not walk down a lonely street at night. Watch your wallet, commissioner.

The guys at the bighouse were really upset and began banging their dinner pans with spoons when they heard the news. I wouldn't be surprised if a couple of the tougher guys aren't planning a breakout right now, so if I were you I'd change the locks on your house. Not that it will do much good.

You made the Red Sox give back Rollie Fingers a few years ago, Bowie, and got away with it, although there were several gentlemen along the waterfront who were anxious to fit you with a cement overcoat.

You pushed a split season on America and we sat still for that, Bowie, but now you have gone too far. You say that there is a standing rule that no politicians or actors will throw out the first ball at a World Series.

But we are not talking about a politician or an actor here. Steinbrenner is not asking you to allow John Travolta to disco his way into a box seat. He doesn't want to bring in Nixon and Spiro Agnew for a game of pitch and catch.

This is Cagney. We are talking legend here. We are talking America. We are talking "White Heat" and "Public Enemy No. 1" and "The West Point Story."

This is Yankee Doodle Dandy you have given the back of your hand to. This is a real-life nephew of our Uncle Sam you have kicked in the teeth. You have told somebody born on the Fourth of July that he is a nobody on Oct. 20. You have ordered the Yankee Doodle Boy to get on his pony and call it macaroni, and stay the hell out of Yankee Stadium.

I don't understand. The Captain and Tenille have sung the national anthem at Dodger Stadium so often they're eligible for a Series share. Frank Sinatra and Don Rickles spend so much time in the Dodgers' clubhouse they know the bunt and steal signals better than Davey Lopes.

Robert Merrill, who is an opera star, sings the anthem at every Yankee game, though some insist the one who does that is not a live human being, but several straw dummies in Robert Merrill suits hanging in a closet underneath the Stadium. Some say the Yankees use a different Merrill dummy every game, depending on the weather.

Regardless, Robert Merrill is, or at least was, an actor. And what about Steve Garvey? When he becomes president, will you tell him he can't throw out the first ball because he's a politician? He'll knock you into the left-field bleachers, Bowie.

Opening Day is big in baseball, commissioner, and politicians have been throwing out the first bull—excuse me, the first ball—since President William Howard Taft and his 325 pounds were hoisted into a box seat with a derrick in 1910. Why should the ceremony be different at World Series time? Yet, you've rubbed out Jimmy Cagney. The mob ain't gonna understand that, no way.

You've picked Joe DiMaggio for the honor instead. Now, it goes without saying that Joe DiMaggio is a big hero in Yankee Stadium, but you certainly must be aware that he's an actor. Not a very good one, true, but he's on my television set almost as much as Brooke Shields, doing commercials.

It seems to me that, everything considered, Yankee Doodle Dandy would be as appropriate a first-ball thrower as Mr. Coffee.

Steinbrenner isn't asking you to let Richard Widmark push an old lady down the stairs. He doesn't want Jack Palance to punch out a blind orphan in an alley. He hasn't applied for some starlet from a casting couch to cutsie-pie a baseball to Rick Cerone.

All Steinbrenner wants is to give an 80-year-old song-and-dance man one final moment under the bright lights.

So I'd be careful the next few weeks answering the doorbell, commissioner. It might be a hit man with a ripe grapefruit to push into your face.

Or it could be a Cagney imitator—there are millions of them in this country—ready to serenade you with the following singing telegram:

"Give my regards to Bowie.
Remember me to Mr. Square.
Tell all the gang at Yankee Stadium,
I wish that I was there.
Tell them of how I'm yearning,
To wind up with the op'ning pitch.
Give my regards to Bowie Kuhn.
That no-good son of a . . ."

Hey, Rip, look what's been up

November 15, 1981—Hello, Mr. Van Winkle, good to hear from you again. Been away a long while, sir, and it's nice to have you back. You sound refreshed. Hope you had a good nap. Pardon? You want me to catch you up on what's been going on in sports? Boy, that's a tall order, but I'll try to fill you in on where we are right now.

Hockey's in full swing. Pretty exciting, and high scoring, too. The North Stars beat the Jets the other night, 15-2. Uh, Minnesota and Winnipeg. I *am* talking about the National Hockey League. That's right, 15 goals in one game. What'd you say? Winnipeg must have pulled its goalie on the opening faceoff? Ha, ha, you haven't lose your sense of humor, Mr. Winkle. Oh, you weren't trying to be funny.

I really don't know why the scoring is so high. The 21 teams in the league certainly try on defense. At least they say they do. I see. You think the fact that there are 21 teams in the league might have something to do with the high scoring? Gosh, I never thought of that.

Pro football is very big now, Mr. Van Winkle. The National Football League has teams from San Diego to Seattle, from Foxborough to Tampa and none is much better than the rest. Comr. Rozelle cals it parity. You call it what? Mr. Van Winkle, I can't put that in the paper.

Foxborough? It's a little town in Massachusetts. The Patriots play there. What are the Patriots like? Uh, I really don't think it's the right time to go into that in detail, Mr. Van Winkle, with you just coming out of a long nap and all. Some day when you have a little more time, and we're sitting down with a nice bottle of strong whisky, maybe.

Anyway, every Sunday they have a bunch of games on television—uh, that's kind of like radio with pictures—and it's really neat to watch players maiming one another.

Certainly they get hurt, Mr. Van Winkle. I mean, these are 285-pound people bashing each other. No, nobody gets arrested. It's all legal. Upset? Well, fans do get upset when they see somebody lying in a heap, but they forget it in a hurry. After all, it's not like anybody is killed. A few permanent limps, maybe, but that could happen walking off a curb. A couple of operations and the knee is as good as new. Well, almost as good as new.

Oh, certainly they still play football in college. Some colleges, they don't do much else. You're glad some things haven't changed? Mr. Van Winkle, you're a caution.

College basketball has caught on in a big way. You know there's no more center jump after every basket. Yes, I realize that was a radical rules change but I think it's caught on. That must mean what? Well, yeah, teams do score more than 30 points a game. As a matter of fact, in the pros, they go over 100 most nights. Not both teams, Mr. Van Winkle. Each team. Individual players often score 30 points or more. Wilt Chamberlain once scored 100 points.

Not in a season, Mr. Van Winkle. In a single game. He's seven feet one inch tall. No, no, no. He wasn't put together in a laboratory. No, batteries weren't extra. Oil can? C'mon, Mr. Van Winkle, you're putting me on.

Baseball? Yep, still alive, but there've been some changes. Too bad you missed the strike. It was really exciting. No, no, not the one Grover Alexander threw to fan Tony Lazzeri. This one was a labor strike. Oh, huh, like steel-workers or anybody on an assembly line. management against labor. The players couldn't agree to what the owners were offering them and refused to play without a contract.

Minors? No, the players couldn't be sent to the minors. the judge said it was illegal. No, not Judge Landis. He's been gone a long time. A man named Bowie Kuhn is commissioner now. Yeah, like the racetrack, but he gets jumpy when his name is in the same paragraph with a racetrack.

Yeah, they finally settled the strike. You'd have had to be an MIT professor to figure out the terms. I think if a player was born when the moon was full and the sun was over the yardarm he is classified as a Type A player, except in February, which has 28.

They picked up the season after the strike but it wasn't much. Had a World Series, too. You want my opinion, it was awful. Some guy broke his hand in an elevator is about all I could get out of it.

Nah, no big trades. They don't have trades anymore. they have the free agent draft. Free agents. If a guy gets sick of playing for one team, he becomes a free agent and can sign with the highest bidder. It's boosted the average salary quite a bit, Mr. Van Winkle. Take a guess how high?

Fifteen thousand dollars a year? Oh, Mr. Van Winkle, you joke. Uh, no. $15,000 wasn't too high a guess. Try $150,000. That's right, but anybody who's been in the league for more than five minutes makes more than that.

Here's something you might find interesting, Mr. Van Winkle. Are you sitting down? The Yankees just signed an outfielder for five years at a million plus per year. You're making funny noises, Mr. Van Winkle. Last year the Yankees signed an outfielder for 10 years for $23 million and he had one hit in 22 bats in the World Series.

Did you hear me, Mr. Van Winkle? Damn, he's gone back to sleep. I never got to tell him what John McEnroe says to tennis referees.

Abuse? No, they need our pity

November 23, 1981—We've all had our little jokes about the Patriots. We've amused ourselves with Murphy's Law and how this sad sack of a football team will somehow always find a way to lose. We've analyzed the Patriots' chances in the upcoming Stupor Bowl against the equally sad sack Colts, and we've come to the conclusion that their chances of getting the No. 1 draft choice for 1982 are pretty good.

We've held a mock funeral for the Patriots. We've had them wailing from the inside of Willie Nelson's guitar and we've had them twisting in the chill autumn wind. To keep from crying over the weekly misfortunes of this train wreck in shoulder pads, we've laughed and snickered and hummed another chorus of "Send in the Clowns."

We've bounced one-liners off the Patriots like rain off a tin roof. If John Hancock were alive today, the Patriots would put him on waivers, yuck, yuck, yuck. Millions for defense and not one cent for tribute, but with the Patriots, it's the other way around, yuck, yuck, yuck. The Patriots' idea of good field position is flat on their backs, yuck, yuck, yuck.

I've been as guilty as anyone else. No, guilty is not the right word. Guilt has nothing to do with it. The Patriots deserved the needling, the wisecracks, the criticism. Before the season, they had come at us like a politician's promise, assuring us of streets paved with gold, of multicolored rainbows, of pie in the sky.

The promises, we quickly found out, were in the eye of the beholder. The streets turned out to be paved with quicksand, the rainbows hid storm clouds, and what we thought was pie in the sky was egg on the face.

Somehow we felt cheated, as though we'd come downstairs on Christmas morning hoping for a new bicycle under the tree and found instead a pair of sweatsocks with a hole in them. In frustration, disappointment and much puzzlement, we lashed out with increasing venom as defeat followed gut-wrenching defeat and the best 2-6 team in football became the best 2-7 team in football and then the best 2-8 team and so forth.

We need take back nothing written or said about the ability of this team to turn good fortune into bad or its habit of grabbing opportunity by the neck and twisting it until opportunity choked to death.

But enough is enough. I refuse to aim my typewriter into the barrel this morning and shoot the helpless fish. I will not kick the poor besotted creature further into the gutter. This morning I feel nothing but compassion for what happened to the Patriots yesterday afternoon in Rich Stadium, Orchard Park, N.Y.

They had not played a great game. They never do anymore. But they had played a gutty game and had stayed close to the Bills in that ice palace of a ballpark, and then, finally, something strange had happened. The Bills had done what the Patriots usually do. The Bills had slipped on the banana peel. The Bills had taken the custard pie in the face.

Pats' quarterback Matt Cavanaugh had sent a prayer aloft, attached to a 65-yard pass. Buffalo defensive back Mario Clark fell down—what a switch!—leaving Stanley Morgan free to catch the ball. One play later, the Patriots scored to take the lead.

There were less than two minutes left, and when the Patriots intercepted a Joe Ferguson pass following the kickoff, surely victory was assured. Not even the Patriots could find a way to lose this day.

And they didn't. That's the point. Nobody fumbled, or threw an interception. Nobody missed a block or a tackle or jumped offside or held or clipped or fell asleep in the huddle. The Patriots played Ferguson's everybody-run-down-for-a-pass desperation heave into the end zone the way it should have been dealt with.

Five, six, no, seven Patriot defenders were in the end zone when Ferguson's pass arrived. Each one, conscious of the way fate had conspired against his team for so many weeks, was going to make certain the fickle creature did not get a hand on the football. Each defender strained, each defender reached high. Frank Lewis of Buffalo never had a shot at making the catch.

Mike Hawkins batted the ball, not up in the air but down, so that it wouldn't be floating around for anybody to grab. Hawkins, however, knocked the ball straight into the arms of Buffalo's Roland Hooks. Hooks did not have to dive or do anything more difficult than open his arms.

Touchdown, Buffalo. The thrill of victory.

Touchdown, Buffalo. The agony of defeat.

When someone falls into a mud puddle, it can be good for a laugh. When somebody falls into a mud puddle every week, it is reasonable to interrupt the giggling and wonder why that somebody doesn't figure out a way to walk around the mud puddle.

But when that somebody is hit by a truck just as it appears he's finally avoided the mud puddle, it is not a proper time for laughter.

So I stifle the wisecracks this morning. I leave the joke book on the shelf. I think of how it must be to lose when losing seems impossible, and I have only compassion for a coach and a team obviously working with an albatross around their necks.

11

1982

Of promises broken

January 2, 1982—"Have a seat, young man, and read a National Geographic or something. Be with you when I'm finished filling out this questionnaire for the Bureau of Broken Resolutions.

"Let's see now, where was I? Oh, yeah. 'In column A, list resolutions unkept in 1981. Give approximate date and reason.' OK, they asked for it:

"1. Resolution: Not to criticize Haywood and Buddy. When broken: Spring training. Reason: Carlton Fisk.

"2. Resolution: Not to make fun of Bowie Kuhn. When broken: Start of baseball strike. Reason: General bumbling.

"3. Resolution: To avoid writing stories that focus on money. When broken: The signing of Magic Johnson and Dave Winfield. Reason: The obscenity of $25 million contracts.

"4. Resolution: Not to make fun of the New England Patriots. When broken: After overtime loss to Steelers. Reason: It hurt too much to cry.

"5. Resolution: To write column on Celtics without mentioning name of Larry Bird. When broken: First game of season. Reason: Unrealistic resolution.

"6. Resolution: Never to divulge my breakfast to Ernie Roberts. When broken: Pro-press golf tournament in April. Reason: He promised to pick up check.

"7. Resolution: To keep George Steinbrenner's name out of my column. When broken: The same day as his hand. Reason: I'm a pushover for fairy tales.

"8. Resolution: Not to write disparagingly of New York City. When broken: Morning of first game of World Series. Reason: $8.25 for juice, toast and coffee.

"9. Resolution: Not to pick Patriots to win division championship. When broken: Jan. 2, 1981. Reason: I'm a fool.

"10. Resolution. Never to end a sentence with a preposition. When broken: Jan. 2, 1981. Reason: None I can think of.

"Now, then, what next? 'In column B, list resolutions kept.' OK. Resolutions kept: I never wrote about indoor soccer, the Jacobs Brothers, the Indianapolis 500, Phyllis George and Jimmy the Greek, all-star balloting, people who take their shirts off at football games in December, artificial turf vs. natural grass, hockey violence, the Garden State Bowl, hair dryers in the clubhouse, lawn bowling and the infield fly rule.

"There we are. Done at last. Now, young man, sorry to keep you waiting, but today was the deadline for filing. What did you say your name was?"

"Eighty-two, sir. Nineteen Eighty-Two."

"Of course. Eighty-Two. I take it you're applying for the vacancy that opened up yesterday."

"That's right, sir."

"Have you had any experience in this line of work, Eighty-Two?"

"No, sir."

"Then what makes you think you can handle the assignment?"

"I learn fast. I'm not easily discouraged and I'm willing to work long hours."

"Commendable, Eighty-Two, but it takes more than eagerness to make it around here. Did you notice the stooped and wrinkled old man who left the office just as you came in?"

"The wretched creature with the scythe over his shoulder? Yes, sir."

"His name is Nineteen Eighty-One. He came into this office a year ago, all fresh and ready to go. You can see what 365 days on the job did to him."

"Poor devil."

"Exactly. So what makes you think you can hold up better than he did? What makes you feel you won't walk out a beaten old man?"

"You're going to have to trust me on this one, sir. I have some great ideas and a game plan that will knock the world for a loop. I can be a terrific year if you'll just give me a chance."

"I've heard all that before. Let me warn you, it's a jungle out there, kid. You'll have to deal with money madness, self-satisfied athletes, short-sighted owners, rapacious agents, cable television, watered-down leagues, the shrinking entertainment dollar, NFL parity, the Colorado Rockies, incompetent officials, boxing without Muhammad Ali, the tantrums of John McEnroe, inflated parking prices, aborted arena plans and terrible hot dogs. And even if you can handle all that, there's still Billy Sullivan."

"I can do it, sir, I know I can."

"Kid, I like the cut of your jib, not to mention the gleam in your eye and the shine on your shoes. OK, the job is yours, but don't forget, it's seven days a week, with a half-hour for lunch. You get Abner Doubleday's birthday off."

"Thanks, sir, I know you won't regret it."

"Don't thank me, just get started. You're 24 hours late already. And, kid . . ."

"Sir?"

"Watch out for Howard Cosell."

Tony C, as in courage, comebacks, coronary

January 12, 1982—Tony Conigliaro, fighting for his life at Mass. General after suffering a serious heart attack last Saturday, was the No. 1 maker of headlines during his short career with the Red Sox. Not even Carl Yastrzemski had as much flair for the dramatic as this former St. Mary's of Lynn All-Scholastic.

Whether it was for hitting a game-winning home run or dating glamorous Hollywood actress Mamie Van Doren or writhing at home plate in agony or making a courageous comeback or calling a press conference at 3 in the morning to announce his retirement, Tony C. had no peer as a sports newsmaker in Boston.

From the time the teenaged Conigliaro put on such a batting show at Scottsdale, Ariz., in the spring of 1964 that the Red Sox promoted him from Class D to the starting lineup on Opening Day, to his final futile days of trying to see a baseball well enough to hit it in 1975, he was one of a kind.

Conigliaro's latest adversity has brought back a bunch of memories for a Red Sox baseball writer—me—who was new to the beat during Tony's years on the team. Some of those years were thrilling, some poignant and a couple still bring a lump to the throat.

The days and years and games run into one another, but I especially remember two particularly dramatic home runs. On a warm June night in 1967, with the White Sox ahead, 1-0, in the bottom of the 11th, Conigliaro hit a two-out, 3-and-2 pitch over the Fenway screen. Sometimes I have trouble remembering my middle name, but almost 15 years later I *know* without looking it up that a righthanded Chicago pitcher named John Buzhardt gave up the homer.

In 1969, in a grueling night game that seemed as though it might last forever, Conigliaro slammed a home run to deep left-center field in Chicago off Joel Horlen to beat the White Sox again, this time by 7-6.

Conigliaro had the perfect Fenway Park stroke. Many a left fielder watched helplessly as a lazy Conigliaro fly ball—a poke that would have been an easy out in every other American league park—barely made the net. But he could hit prodigious homers, too. If he had been a major leaguer until he was 36, and thus had played for 17 seasons, there is little doubt he would have hit at least 500 home runs.

He was a fearless hitter, and never backed away from a fast ball. Once, when sidearmer Fred Lasher of Detroit hit Conigliaro on the leg with a pitch, Tony dropped his bat, raced to the mound and attempted to nail the pitcher with a karate kick.

But the very characteristic that made him a great hitter was the one that shortened his career on that hot August night when a Jack Hamilton fastball crashed into the side of Conigliaro's face. A smoke bomb thrown on the field had held up the game for several minutes and I've always felt the delay might have taken away some of Conigliaro's concentration.

He was out the rest of that season and all of 1968, and then made two dramatic comebacks. He tried pitching in the Instructional League early in 1969, but that didn't work out, so he went to spring training determined to make it again as a hitter. For a while, his swings were so bad that it was painful to watch him in the batting cage.

But gradually, the stroke returned and with it the confidence, and I remember him saying one day after getting a couple of line drive hits in an exhibition game at Sarasota that he no longer doubted his ability to hit big league pitching again.

In his first regular-season game back, on April 9 in Baltimore, Conigliaro hit a 10th-inning homer with a man on base that put the Red Sox ahead. He returned to Fenway Park a few days later and got the most prolonged ovation this side of Bobby Orr.

In 1970 Conigliaro hit 36 homers, an amazing total for someone who had been considered all done two seasons previously. He was traded to California that winter and in 1971 his vision began to deteriorate again. And one night, after he'd struck out several times in an extra-inning game, he called a press conference to announce his retirement.

Four seasons later he came back one more time with the Red Sox. After another tumultuous ovation on Opening Day in Fenway, he singled to right in his first at-bat after being away almost four years.

However, although he had a few key hits early in the season, he had been away too long. He went to the minors in Pawtucket in an attempt to recapture the graceful swing, but this time he couldn't do it.

Conigliaro, Hollywood handsome, with soft Italian eyes and a quick smile, was often controversial and might not always have been the easiest player to manage. But nobody could ever accuse him of giving less than his best on the field.

Tony C. was a headline maker who had more talent in his line of work than most of us are given in ours, but he was seldom at the head of the line when good luck was being handed out.

He could use what fate owes him right now.

Tricks of the trade

September 13, 1981—People are always asking a sports columnist where he gets his ideas. Personally, I've been inundated with the question, getting two letters to that effect in 1973 and one last year.

All three began with the greeting "Dear Stupid," which tempted me to write back that I purchased all my thoughts, perceptions and observations at the Great Notions Boutique on Newbury Street, a quaint little shop that scoffs at off-the-rack merchandise and custom makes its own ideas out of thin air.

Actually, unbeknownst to the public, the whole business of writing columns is a trick, much in the manner of the magician sawing the lady in half. Just as every joke is merely a variation of one from a master list ("Take my wife, please"), so it is with sports columns. There is a basic stockpile of ideas and every column is a spinoff from one in the pile.

I won't burden you with the whole list this morning, but just so you'll have an inkling of how the system works, here are some serviceable ideas that can always be rolled out of the garage whenever a columnist needs a ride into tomorrow.

• A favorite is the "Violence in Sports" column. A writer occasionally will defend such activity as being an unavoidable part of the action, but the more popular stance is to speak out against it in violent terms, as it were.

He is sickened by football knee injuries and hockey fights. He frets over fans who run out onto the field, or who punch each other out, or who call athletes vile names and, in some instances, actually grapple with them. He likes to call violence in the grandstand "a microcosm of life."

• Another surefire winner is the "Things Ain't What They Used to Be" piece. This is a catch-all in which the columnist deplores six-figure contracts, expansion, athletes' attitudes and lifestyles, artificial turf, slam-dunks, rising ticket prices, agents, humans in animal suits and hairdryers in the clubhouse.

He looks back with fondness to the center jump, day games, train rides, the St. Louis Browns, Vince Lombardi, Joe D, The Splendid Splinter, the reserve clause, the six-team National Hockey League and the Fort Wayne Zollner Pistons.

The beauty of this is that the columnist needn't be a school chum of Ty Cobb to long for the way we were said to be. There are enough books that specialize in wallowing through our yesterdays to make even a 22-year-old wax sentimental over the good old days he never saw.

• A columnist also can't go wrong by knocking all-star games. If it's baseball, he rips the way the players are selected; he calls the process a sham, a fraud and a disgrace to the national pastime. If it's the NBA, he labels it playground basketball and a one-on-one circus that is obviously a sham, a fraud and a disgrace to James Naismith's grand old game.

The columnist criticizes pro football and hockey all-star games for lack of hitting. Football and hockey all-stars don't go all out because nobody wants to be hurt. What you have as a result, the columnist writes, is a game that is a sham, a fraud and, of course, a disgrace.

• A column that features plenty of capitalized initials is always useful, as it shows the reader how in tune the columnist is to relevant, off-the-field sports activity.

Eight hundred words on the dispute between the NCAA and the CFA can be very impressive. Toss a few ACLUs or NLRBs into a column and you are half way home. Any piece involving cable television is by definition heavy with capitalized initials and, therefore, "important."

• A do-nothing commissioner column about Bowie Kuhn is always a day-saver. The terrific part of a Kuhn column is that he is like one of those carnival games: Knock him down with some well-aimed invective and he bounces right back up, ready for more punishment.

Mention must be made of Kuhn's attending World Series games without an overcoat, and, of course, his nonrole in the recent strike settlement. If there is room, toss in his refusal to let Willie Mays work at Atlantic City because it would be against the best interests of baseball, while at the same time condoning the racehorse ownership of the Pirates' John Galbraith and the Yankees' George Steinbrenner.

Steinbrenner columns, incidentally, are currently hot, along with those on Al Davis and John McEnroe. Operative words and phrases that are musts when writing about these individuals include "self-centered," "ruthless," "stop at nothing," and "win at all costs."

• Each local professional team has its sure-fire column idea. When all else fails and the brain has turned to mush, the writer has only to update a "Patriots Can't Win the Big Ones" piece, or a "Haywood and Buddy are Cheap" diatribe. Eighty lines of "Celtics Pride" can't miss and neither can a discourse on the "Hardworking Lunch Pail Bruins."

These few ideas represent only the tip of the columnist's iceberg. Lack of space prohibits further illustrations, but there are many other trade secrets, many other tricks.

If you've read this far, you've just been exposed to another one.